C000285209

THE ROYAL
MILITARY CANAL

200844141

To
WILLIAM PITT
1759–1806
promoter of the Royal Military Canal
and
MAJOR-GENERAL JOHN BROWN
1756–1816
projector of the Royal Military Canal
who conducted its execution with an
extraordinary zeal, ability and integrity

THE ROYAL MILITARY CANAL

An Historical Account of the Waterway and Military Road from Shorncliffe in Kent to Cliff End in Sussex

P. A. L. VINE

Author of *London's Lost Route to the Sea*

AMBERLEY

Other works by P. A. L. Vine

London's Lost Route to the Sea (1965)
London's Lost Route to Basingstoke (1968)
The Royal Military Canal (1972)
Magdala (1973)
Ethiopia (1974)
Introduction to *Our Canal Population: George Smith* (1974)
Pleasure Boating in the Victorian Era (1983)
West Sussex Waterways (1985)
Kent & East Sussex Waterways (1989)
Hampshire Waterways (1990)
London to Portsmouth Waterway (1994)
London's Lost Route to Basingstoke (1994, new ed.)
London's Lost Route to Midhurst (1995)
London's Lost Route to the Sea (1996, 5th ed.)
The Wey & Arun Junction Canal (1999)
The Arun Navigation (2000)
London's Lost Route to Portsmouth (2005)

Front Cover: Hythe from the Canal Bridge, 1829.

Frontispiece:
1. William Pitt.
William Pitt as colonel of the Cinque Ports Volunteers. Pitt was
Lord Warden of the Cinque Ports 1792-1806 and prime minister
1783–1801, 1804–1806.

WEST SUSSEX LIBRARY SERVICE

20   0844141

V I N   5/10

S
386

This edition first published 2010

Amberley Publishing Plc
Cirencester Road, Chalford,
Stroud, Gloucestershire, GL6 8PE

www.amberley-books.com

Copyright © P. A. L Vine, 2010

The right of P. A. L Vine to be identified as the Author
of this work has been asserted in accordance with the
Copyrights, Designs and Patents Act 1988.

All rights reserved. No part of this book may be reprinted
or reproduced or utilised in any form or by any electronic,
mechanical or other means, now known or hereafter invented,
including photocopying and recording, or in any information
storage or retrieval system, without the permission in writing
from the Publishers.

British Library Cataloguing in Publication Data.
A catalogue record for this book is available from the British Library.

ISBN 978 1 84868 450 8

Typesetting and Origination by Amberley Publishing.
Printed in Great Britain.

Contents

List of Illustrations

Illustrations in Text

Maps and Plans

Chronological Table

1644	River Rother linked with Rye
1723	Act for new harbour at Rye
1769	Channel of the Rother turned into the new harbour at Winchelsea
1788	New harbour at Winchelsea abandoned
1802	Peace of Amiens
	Lt-Col John Brown appointed Commandant Royal Staff Corps
1803	War resumed against France
1804	Napoleon Bonaparte crowned emperor of the French William Pitt sanctions building of Royal Military Canal and Martello Tower fortifications
1805	August — Serious threat of invasion
	October — Battle of Trafalgar
1806	The Commander-in-Chief sails from Hythe to Iden
1807	Royal Military Canal Act passed
1808	Opening of Iden lock
1808-10	Building and completion of Hythe Barracks
1809	Royal Military Canal completed
1810	Royal Military Canal opened to public navigation
	Passage boat service introduced
1812	Highest toll receipts on Royal Military Canal
1813	Colonel John Brown promoted Major-General
1815	The Royal Staff Corps supports the Duke of Wellington at Waterloo
1816	Death of Major-General Brown
1827	Death of HRH Frederick, Duke of York
1833	Royal Waggon Train disbanded
	Section of military road between Appledore and Hythe closed
1837	Second Royal Military Canal Act
1838	Royal Military Canal transferred to the Board of Ordnance
	Royal Staff Corps disbanded
1842	Military barge horses withdrawn from service
1846-8	Highest annual revenue from tollgates on the Royal Military Road
1847	Greatest tonnage carried on the Royal Military Canal
1851	Opening of Rye swing railway bridge over the Rother
1853	School of Musketry formed at Hythe
1855	Royal Military Canal transferred to the War Department
1860	Hythe Venetian Fête first held

1867	Third Royal Military Canal Act
1872	Fourth Royal Military Canal Act
1877	Royal Military Canal leased to Hythe Corporation and the Lords of Romney Marsh
c. 1880	Barge traffic to Hythe ceased
1903	The swing bridge over the River Rother at Rye replaced by a fixed span
1909	Barge traffic on the Royal Military Canal ceased
c. 1928	Barge traffic to Newenden and Bodiam ceased
1968	Small Arms School moves from Hythe to Warminster
1974	Royal Staff Corps barracks at Hythe demolished
1990	Hythe Marina Bill defeated in the House of Commons

Preface

From the high ground by Shorncliffe Camp the sentries survey the gradual curve of the flat shore of St Mary's Bay studded with its ruined martello towers and the broad enfiladed channel of the Royal Military Canal. Here the onlooker can conjecture as Pitt did, what might have happened if Napoleon's finest legions had descended on the Kent and Sussex coast and fought Sir John Moore's Light Brigade. Indeed the name of Romney Marsh might well have taken its place in history with those of Waterloo and Dunkirk.

The renewal of war with France in 1803 and the return to office of William Pitt, saw Britain face to face with the greatest menace to her safety since the Spanish Armada. Napoleon, now convinced that the conquest of England was an essential preliminary to the successful conclusion of his schemes for world domination, had built flat-bottomed boats, had the Grande Armée encamped at Boulogne and waited for the English fleet to be dispersed before attempting his planned invasion. Pitt's plans for meeting this particular danger were based on attacking the French Navy at every opportunity and blockading their ports. At the same time the threat of invasion led to the creation of a local defence force, the building of a network of defences along the south coast, including martello towers and a military canal and road. It is the story of how these latter works were built and their later commercial use which is the subject of this book.

Opinions have differed as to the influence of the victory at Trafalgar in October 1805 on the course of the struggle of Europe against Napoleon. It did but reaffirm the strength of British naval power which was clear before; it did not materially increase that supremacy. Napoleon had known before that the British fleet was his greatest enemy, and that conviction was deepened. Had the battle not been fought at all the issue of the struggle would probably not have been seriously altered. And if Napoleon had won? He is reported to have said, 'If we are masters of the Straits for twelve hours England is no more.' But if he really believed this he was certainly in error. The nation was more closely identified with the Government in Britain than it was among the countries occupied by the French, and, there can be no doubt that a fierce national resistance would have followed under conditions favourable to the defence. If the Grande Armée had disembarked on the shores of England in strength it would almost certainly have won victories, but Napoleon would have found himself committed to a struggle that would have anticipated the exhausting war in Spain, and might have proved as fatal as his march on Moscow. The role played by the military canal in the defence of Kent and Sussex might well have constituted a turning point in the battle for London.

No detailed study of the canal has been previously published although an interesting monograph was written by Lt-Col C. H. Lemmon in 1963 and S. P. G. Ward's study of 'Defence Works in Britain (1803-5)' provides a useful summary of the steps taken to protect our shores against invasion. I have received considerable assistance from Charles Hadfield, Vincent Rendel, H. Catt, Miss B. Catt, R. Sharp, Gerald Walter, A. G. Stirk and A. S. T. Saint in ascertaining the whereabouts of documents relating to the history of the military canal and the Rother Navigation and from Lt-Col F. T. Stear and Major John Hancock for piecing together the history of the Royal Staff Corps and the biographies of their officers.

I am also grateful to the archivists of the East Sussex County Record Office at Lewes, of the Kent County Council at Maidstone, of the Borough of Hythe, to the Kent River Authority, and to the librarians of the British Museum, the Guildhall, the House of Lords, the Institution of Civil Engineers, the National Library of Scotland, the Patent Office, the Public Record Office and the Royal Engineers Corps for their help in finding original material; to Miss B. Catt of Iden lock, and R. Sharp of Hythe for the loan of illustrations, the National Army Museum at Camberley for permission to reproduce plate o and to the British Museum for permission to reproduce plates oo, oo, oo and oo.

My thanks are also due to Pauline McColl for a souvenir ashtray, to Michael Cardew for details of martello towers, and to Frank Harber and my daughter Deirdre Ann for assisting with some of the illustrations; also to Rosalind, who spent many hours in gloomy places, as well as in sunshine and shadow deciphering a variety of correspondence and ledger entries; to her I am equally indebted for locating suitable illustrations, the typing of the manuscript and the compilation of the index.

P. A. L. V.
Pulborough
April 1971

Preface to Second Edition

Some months after this work was first published in 1972 and while I was working in Ethiopia, Professor Richard Glover completed his book on how England was defended against invasion during the period 1803 — 1814.* This gives a much broader picture of the subject of which the canal was only a part. Two chapters are of particular interest. The first deals with the great Boulogne flotilla of 1803 — 5, and the second with other fortifications built along the English coast. Of equal interest to the historian is Wheeler and Broadley's story of the Great Terror which, although published in 1908, describes Napoleon's earlier invasion projects.*

There has been much care lavished on the military canal and road over the past thirty years. Both the Kent and East Sussex County Councils have assisted a variety of countryside orientated associations to improve public access to the waterway and to promote its historic importance. The sadness engendered by what many people felt was the wanton destruction of Hythe's barracks has been partially dispelled by the failure of the Hythe Marina Bill in 1990 which would have caused the character of some 1,100 yards of the eastern terminus at Seabrook to have been changed beyond recognition. Since then Shepway District Council has undertaken a £3 million restoration programme to improve the waterway from Shorncliffe to West Hythe.

The Romney Marsh Countryside Project set up in 1996 has, with the support of the Heritage Lottery Fund, done much to help visitors discover and enjoy the surrounding villages. The White Cliffs Countryside Project manages those stretches of the canal which are sites of special scientific and nature conservation interest.

It is however disappointing to report that little has happened since 1972 to give encouragement to those who would like to see the Royal Military Canal restored to full navigation. In view of the success of the canal associations like the Kennet & Avon Canal Trust, the Surrey & Hampshire Canal Society, and more recently the Wey & Arun Junction Canal Trust, in restoring derelict waterways for pleasure boating, the difficulties posed in reopening the Royal Military Canal would not seem insurmountable. It might benefit tourism if, for instance, a pleasure barge service was introduced from Rye which could provide voyages along the Brede to Winchelsea, the River Rother to Bodiam Castle, and the Royal Military Canal to Appledore and Hythe. However the fact that no active local restoration Society has been formed appears to recognise the realities of the situation. The efforts made by the Kent & East Sussex Branch of the Inland Waterways Association in the 1970s to reopen the waterway met with little support and some opposition. The main problems remain the limited headroom for boats beneath most of the road bridges, the cost of restoring Iden Lock and ensuring correct water levels in both summer and winter. Furthermore one also has to take into account the attitude of those members of the various angling associations who fish the canal and who are not overly anxious to see boating developed. Lastly there is the Environment Agency's inclination not to encourage boating because it may interfere with the utility of the canal as a primary drainage channel.

P. A. L. V.
Pulborough
December 2009

Acknowledgements

It is sad to report that few of those who helped me previously have survived. Rosalind now lives in New Zealand and it is she to whom I remain indebted for the 300 or so pages which resulted from her research into the canal's history at the Public Record Office. More recently, Hugh Compton together with other members of the Railway & Canal Historical Society have made useful contributions to the original work. Alan Joyce, John Keeffe and Denise Rayner of the Hythe Civic Society have also been particularly helpful, as has Leigh Lindsey and her colleagues at Hythe Library. Catherine Bingham (Rye Arts Festival) gave me encouragement. Andrew Pearce (The Environment Agency), Mike Austerberry and Janet Baker (Kent County Council). Alistair Stewart, Martin Commons, Kate Hayes (Shepway District Council), Joanna McKenna (The National Trust), Ann Mervin (The Ramblers' Association), Owen Leyshon (Romney Marsh Countryside Project), Tim Lawrence of Prospect House Hythe, Callum Wanliss (House of Lords Library), and Huw Williams (Oxford & Cambridge Club Librarian) have each patiently and promptly lent me original documents and answered my many enquiries. Martin Easdown and Linda Sage kindly allowed me to reproduce an early photograph of the Town Bridge in Hythe.

Once again I gladly pay tribute to Susan White and the courteous staff at Pulborough Library who have, in addition to tracking down obscure reference works, mastered the latest technology and the art of enlarging miniscule archive material. More importantly for the sake of my publisher I thank Kay for a lot of hard work on summer days. Edwina too has played her part. I was particularly pleased that Alan Sutton found time to drive down to Pulborough twice not only to ensure the book was completed on time but to give me sound advice and the pleasure of his enterprising company.

P. A. L. V.
Pulborough
December 2009

*see bibliography

chapter 1

The Defence of Kent and Sussex against Napoleon (1803–1804)

The Peace of Amiens (1802)—resumption of war with France (May 1803)—Napoleon prepares to invade Britain—assembly of craft in Channel ports—plans to defend the South Coast—intended flooding of Romney Marsh—martello tower project—Pitt's return to power—invasion scare of August 1804—coastal defence conference at Rochester (October 1804)—decision to build martello towers.

The safeguarding of our shores against an enemy landing was the sole purpose of defence in time of war until the advent of the aeroplane. In the days of sail, accidents of wind might at any time prevent the navy from intercepting an enemy crossing the English Channel. However, since the Spanish fleet had sailed round our coast in 1588, no greater threat of invasion had arisen until the war with the French Republic in 1793. By 1802 there had been numerous scares, several periods during the struggle when a landing on the coast of England might have been attempted, and indeed in very minor fashion one had been achieved in 1797.* In March 1802 the Peace of Amiens had been signed, leaving France supreme in Western Europe and England mistress of the oceans. The peace, however, was to be no more than a brief respite, for Napoleon was bent on ruling Europe and the failure of the French to meet the conditions agreed over the future of Malta resulted in war being resumed on 18 May 1803.

---

* In February 1797 a small party of Frenchmen landed at Ilfracombe and burnt a farmhouse before embarking. The expedition then landed near Fishguard where it surrendered to the local militia.

At the commencement of the war, France's influence extended over the ports from Brest to the Texel — a relative position unknown in any former contest, and which exposed the frontier of Great Britain to invasion from Land's End to the northern extremity of Scotland. The danger arising from this situation was soon considerably increased by the seizure of the north of Germany, and the consequent control of the ports and naval resources of the Ems, the Weser and the Elbe. The likelihood of invasion began to be taken more seriously.

In July it became known that Napoleon had inspected troops and barges at Boulogne. That same month Pitt became Colonel of the Cinque Port Volunteers, raised three infantry battalions and commanded the brigade himself. The threat to the country inspired much ribald and patriotic verse and cartoons. Charles Dibdin told how:

'The French are all coming, so they declare
Of their floats and balloons all the papers advise us
They're to swim through the ocean and ride on the air
In some foggy evening to land and surprise us.'

Bunbury has well described the preparations that were being made on the opposite side of the Channel for the embarkation of an invading army: 'In the meantime Bonaparte had proclaimed his determination to conquer London and to this task applied himself with characteristic energy. Throughout the summer and autumn of 1803 every river and port from Ushant to the Texel was ringing with the clink of hammers and the din of multitudes employed in building the greatest flotilla that ever darkened the sea. Napoleon hoped at first that he should be able to make his attack at some time in the winter of 1803–4, and such were the exertions used that nearly one thousand of his vessels were collected at Boulogne before December. Various establishments on a gigantic scale were found to be indispensable at and near Boulogne. Great basins, too, were to be excavated there, and at Etaples, Ambleteuse and Wimereux for the reception of the vessels. Forts also were to be constructed, and with great difficulty in the sea, for the protection of the outer roadsteads.'[1]

It was Bonaparte's intention to cross either on a foggy night or in the sudden calm after a gale. While the British frigates, driven from the Channel by the storm, were lying becalmed, the great flotilla would slip out of its ports and paddle swiftly to England. Fifteen hundred barges packed with soldiers were to start from Boulogne, Wissant, Ambleteuse and Etaples, 300 from Dunkirk, Calais and Gravelines, 300 from Nieuport and Ostend and 300 more with a Dutch army from Flushing. The boats designed were to be of three kinds: large sailing vessels called prams, more than 100 ft

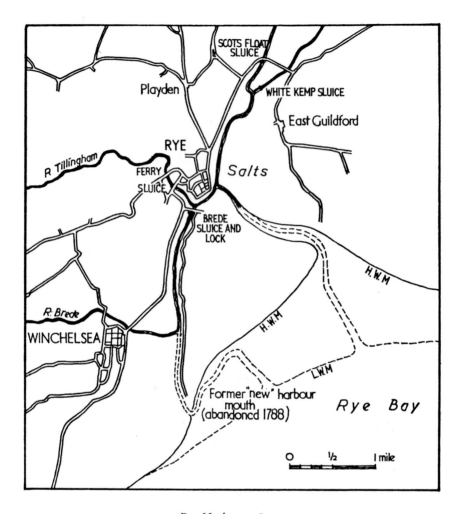

Rye Harbour, 1800.

long, armed with 24-pounders and each carrying 150 men; escourting *chaloupes*, *cannonierès* with howitzers; gunboats for transporting horses, ammunition and artillery; and — by far the most numerous — 60 ft pinnaces armed with small howitzers and each capable of accommodating 55 soldiers. All were equipped with specially designed landing bridges. If attacked the flotilla was to defend itself; with the issue nothing less than the conquest of Britain, It would matter little if 10,000 or even 20,000 troops were sunk on the way. Together with artillery, supplies and 6,000 horses, Napoleon planned to transport nearly 120,000 veterans.[2]

Assembling such a fleet posed many problems as during the months ahead they were moved from the harbours along the north coast of France, at Paris, on the Rhine and in Holland, by river and canal, by voyages along the coast from fort to fort and creek to creek to Boulogne and its adjacent ports. The most determined efforts on the part of our naval officers failed to prevent these craft from slowly gathering. But there Napoleon's success ended. These craft could not be sent to sea. The fine schemes for combining troops and transports remained mere schemes. The ports cleared for the transports silted up almost as soon as they were made. When the vessels were anchored in the harbours, they could only get out a few at a time. When they lay outside, they were harassed by English attacks, and injured by gales. However, our sea-going ships could not push their attacks home on a shallow coast, and an attempt in October to sink the vessels assembled around Boulogne by a species of floating mines called 'catamarans', much favoured by Mr Pitt, proved a failure. The best the invasion craft could do was to escape destruction. They could not go to sea; a new strategy had to be planned.

The defence of the realm was in the hands of the Commander-in-Chief, HRH Frederick, Duke of York, a well-known but variously regarded prince. By some he is remembered more for his notoriety than his achievements. Sir John Fortescue, on the other hand, wrote that the steady improvement in the administration of the British Army in the Napoleonic period belonged chiefly to the Duke of York.[3] He wrote clear and able appreciations, he displayed great skill in showing ministers what needed to be done and in getting them to do it. He restored discipline, reduced chaos to order and made the British Army the most efficient in the world. And at the Horse Guards he surrounded himself with a very competent staff which included Robert Brownrigg the Quartermaster-General.

Under the Duke and responsible for the co-ordinated defence of Britain was General Sir David Dundas, GOC The Southern District. He had started in the army as a private and was to become Commander-in-Chief from 1809–11 as well as field marshal. In 1803 he was known as a keen student of tactics, the writer of the authorised training manuals of the day for both cavalry and infantry, and a historian of the Seven Years' War in which he had served through five campaigns under Ferdinand of Brunswick. According to Bunbury he was 'a tall spare man cribbed and austere, dry in his looks and demeanour, who introduced unity where all previously had been uncertain and dependent on individual caprice'. Under him was Sir James Pulteney, who commanded the Sussex district and Sir John Moore that of Kent. It was the task of these soldiers to decide with the aid of their staff what was needed to make the coasts secure, and for the commander-in-chief to obtain the government's authority to carry out the work.

Although the military preparations in Britain were greater than at the commencement of any former war, they were 'wholly inadequate to provide for the security of so extended a line of coast' wrote the commander-in-

2. HRH Frederick Duke of York.
The Duke of York was Commander-in-Chief of the British Army 1798-1809 and 1811-1827. He was appointed one of the Royal Military Canal commissioners. In August 1806 he and his brother, the Duke of Cambridge inspected the canal from Hythe to Iden. The Royal Staff Corps was formed in 1800 at his express wish.

3. Sir John Moore.
Sir John Moore (1761-1809) lieutenant-general, introduced improved systems of drill and manoeuvre at Shorncliffe camp 1804, historic retreat to Corunna 1809.

chief to Lord Hobart, the Secretary of State for the War Department, on 25 August 1803.[4] Of the 130,000 men available for the defence of the country half were set aside to protect London and the south coast. In October 1802 Moore had moved to Chatham, and had begun planning the formation of the training camp at Shorncliffe, which not only created the light infantry division of the Peninsular War, but was the introduction of a new form of discipline, different altogether from that of the time. Early in 1803 he wrote to Brownrigg of his proposals; In May, Brownrigg warned him of the necessity for immediate steps to be taken to defend the kingdom, and; at the end of the month Moore took command of the brigade at Sandgate with responsibility for defending the coast from Deal to Dungeness.

The Dungeness peninsula was indeed an object of peculiar anxiety to those planning the defence of the coastline. The bay provided a safe anchorage for large ships within an easy distance of the shore, and good facilities for the landing of troops on its low shelving beach, which long rendered this spot notorious for smuggling. Few localities could be found so favourable for the rapid disembarkation of troops. It formed the only flat shore nearest to Boulogne and it was virtually undefended in the belief that as the greater part of Romney Marsh lay below the level of high water spring tides, and a large portion below the level of an ordinary high tide, it could be quickly flooded. At least it was the presumed view that no enemy could cross the maze of ditches and sewers that criss-crossed Romney Marsh and which could, it was assumed, be made an impassable morass by the simple process of letting in the sea. The Duke of York advised Lord Hobart that to give further security to this line of coast he had directed measures to be prepared to ensure the inundating in a certain degree the districts named Romney Marsh and Pevensey Level. This was to be achieved by opening the three sluices in the Dymchurch Wall, a fourth at Scots Float on the Rother and a fifth at East Guldeford near Rye.[5] As the Pett Level had only one sluice, plans were made to breach the dykes along the river Brede, and the Rother. At least there was on paper a reasonable plan of defence but no one apparently was prepared to approve it.

On 1 July 1803 Moore wrote to Dundas that he had been with Col Twiss round Dungeness and that the works there were so faulty that 'it is hardly possible immediately to adopt measures to make them defensible,' Dundas confirmed the intention of flooding the marsh and 'driving the county,' which Moore thought only practicable if ten days' notice of the enemy's intention was given in advance. And so wrote the Duke of York on 25 August to Lord Hobart:

I strongly recommend to the consideration of the Master-General [Lord Chatham], the principle of permanent defences in the shape of towers proposed by Colonel Twiss in a very able report on the coast from Eastware Bay in Kent [where the cliff end nears Folkestone], to Selsea Island on the coast of Sussex — being the most important line of defence to the coast of France. The advantage proposed by the towers is to keep possession of the coast defences to the annoyance of an enemy during the whole operation of his landing — and the probable prevention of his disembarking stores until he can bring his artillery against them. These works [martello towers]* from their construction require but a feeble garrison for the defence nor viewing the permanency of the work are they to be considered expensive.

Lord Hobart requested the master-general to put the scheme before the Committee of Engineers, but the latter looked with disfavour on projects for permanent fortifications initiated by departments other than his own, and it was not until February 1804 that Hobart received a reply in which Chatham informed him that 'as it is entirely novel in principle and connected with an infinite variety of details, I should be unwilling to occupy the time of the Committee on this point unless your Lordship continued to feel a desire to receive a report on the subject, and that the idea was generally approved by His Majesty's Confidential Servants.'[6]

Meanwhile, the towers had become a political matter. Windham had urged them in a speech in the House of Commons on 9 December 1803.[7] The Admiralty had suggested them to the Home Secretary, Charles Yorke, at about the same time.[8] Pitt, though out of office, was, as Lord Warden of the Cinque Ports, known to be in their favour. The Duke of York had attempted in March 1804 to have them constructed as fieldworks, tactfully suggesting that the Ordnance should produce approved plans and engineers should supervise their building.[9] But the Ordnance Committee made no move until summoned before the Cabinet on 18 April. Their report, signed by Morse, D'Aubant and Twiss, was submitted on the 26th. 'Towers,' they concluded,

as sea-batteries appear to have little or no advantage over any other battery of the same number of guns. It is admitted that upon first landing of an enemy a tower is not to be taken by assault; but a few shells thrown by small mortars brought on shore might in a short time destroy the carriages of the guns on the platform or top of the tower

---

* Martello towers were named after a tower defended by the French at Mortella Point in the Bay of Fioprenzo on the island of Corsica. The fact that General Dundas was present at the time of the attack on 9 February 1794 may well have influenced him in supporting their construction along the south coast.

and thereby render its effect as a sea-battery useless. Therefore, after a full investigation of this subject, we do not recommend the erection of towers as sea batteries or to obstruct the landing of an enemy.

During the late summer of 1803 the country sensed the danger and the leading figures of the day urged every man to defend the liberty of its people from the barbarous yoke of military despotism. The Mayor of Folkestone issued an order commanding every inhabitant, who possessed a defensive or offensive weapon 'to bring all they possess, whether sword or gun or spade or shovel' to resist the invader.[10] Offers of help from corporate bodies were general. The Basingstoke Canal Company offered to make available to government, ten of the company's barges, free of charge, to transport stores from London to any part of the canal 'in the event of invasion or the appearance of the enemy on the coast.'[11] Pickfords, the canal and road carriers, proffered 400 horses, 50 waggons and 28 boats. Meanwhile the commander-in-chief put in hand various emergency measures. Bread waggons were provided to improve the bread supply, three extra troops were added to the Waggon Train and 30,000 sacks of flour were stored on the banks of the Upper Thames as a reserve for the London market.

Wheeler & Broadley, in their excellent account of Napoleon's planned attempt to invade England, include an order issued by the commander of a regiment of the Royal Edinburgh volunteers which gives sound advice to the troops on how to conduct themselves when confronted by the enemy when attempting a beach landing. When this directive was issued in October 1803, neither the martello towers nor the canal had been built, but this sound advice would have been well taken (see Appendix F).

Moore's mother and sister stayed with him at Sandgate until some movements of the French made him decide that they had better return to their home at Richmond. On 2 October 1803 he wrote to his mother,

I am glad you arrived safe, and found everything so comfortable. The day you left this spot we had an alarm, which I am glad you escaped. The signal officer at Folkestone mistook a signal, which was, that the enemy's boats were out of Calais; and hoisted one which signified that the enemy's ships and transports from Ostend were steering west; which, as the wind was, would have brought them to us in a few hours. All was bustle, and an express with the above information, and that the brigade was under arms, found me at Dungeness Point. My horse suffered; I galloped him the whole way back. The Volunteers, Sea Fencibles, and all, were turned out, and very cheerful — not at all dismayed at the prospect of meeting the French; and as for the brigade, they were in high spirits. By the time

I reached camp, the mistake was discovered. Government are, however, much more apprehensive of the invasion than they were some time ago; I am glad, therefore, you are at home. Three more regiments are coming to me on Tuesday. Sir David Dundas is this instant come to me; I must therefore conclude.[12]

As winter advanced the sea became too boisterous for an invasion and the army went into winter quarters. Moore wrote to his mother, 'I consider invasion over for this winter and therefore probably over for ever, but with the winds I now witness, a naval expedition cannot be undertaken; therefore send me your receipt for minced pies; yours to taste are the best I meet with.'

But as winter turned into the spring of 1804 complacency about the adequacy of the defences of Romney Marsh dwindled as the number of troops encamped on the cliffs of Boulogne increased. Inquiries into the time required to flood the land indicated that if no action was taken until the enemy had landed at Dungeness, the marsh was likely to remain passable for from 36 to 48 hours. To admit the water before the enemy was ashore posed a difficult problem since the sea water would sterilise some 28,000 acres of rich pastures for several years, for which the farmers would require compensation.

The problem was referred to the Secretary at War, Lord Camden, who would have to authorise all money payments. The War Office, however, did not appear to comprehend the importance of the matter for after a fortnight's delay they suggested that General Dundas should seek the advice of his chief engineer, Brigadier-General William Twiss. But clearly the latest intelligence regarding the enemy's preparations as well as the payment of compensation, were matters which were very much the concern of the minister.

So there the matter also rested through the summer of 1804, with Dundas having no authority to evict farmers and incur compensation claims in time to secure the marsh against a beach landing; and yet the more the matter was considered so did the coastline between Hythe and Winchelsea seem the more promising a place for a beach landing. Its distance from the enemy's coasts and ports was short. Ambleteuse lay only 28 miles from Hythe and 37 miles from Rye Harbour. 'Between these two points stretched a thinly populated flat coastline to Dungeness, which offered an easy landing at most states of the wind or tide. The beach was sandy and from whichever quarter the wind might blow, Dungeness point usually offered a sheltered tide where small boats could safely be brought to shore.'[13]

On 18 May 1804 a decree of the Senate gave Napoleon the title of

'Emperor of the French'. Pitt emerged from the retirement into which he had entered as the result of his difference with King George III over the Irish Union, and formed his last administration on 7 May. He soon built up a new and powerful coalition — the third coalition — against France. First he won over the power of Sweden, then Russia and then Austria, but in the meantime Britain herself had to be defended.

Napoleon had collected his army and a large fleet of flat-bottomed boats at Boulogne. The manoeuvre of embarkation was constantly practised so that when conditions were favourable the soldiers might be taken across the Channel in the shortest possible time. On 14 August Lord Hawkesbury wrote to his father, the Earl of Liverpool, 'From the intelligence which has lately reached us we are inclined to believe that the attempt of invasion will soon be made. Their preparations are very great; and they have stopped building, which looks as if they considered them complete. They have about 3,000 vessels of different descriptions and 180,000 men between Ostend and Cherbourg.'[14] The following day was the emperor's official birthday, and at the camp at Boulogne he distributed honours before 60,000 men. Lord Hawkesbury then believed this was but a rehearsal for the real thing. Madame Junot described the scene toward the end of the ceremony when

> we soon discerned a flotilla, consisting of between a thousand and twelve hundred boats, advancing in the direction of Boulogne from the different neighbouring ports and from Holland. The emperor had made the choice of the 15th of August as the day for uniting the flotilla with the other boats stationed in the port of Boulogne, in the sight of the English vessels which were cruising in the straits; while, at the same time, he distributed to his troops rewards destined to stimulate their courage, and excite their impatience to undertake the invasion of England.
>
> But the satisfaction of Napoleon was not of long duration. An emphatic oath uttered by M. Decrès warned the emperor that some accident had occurred. It was soon ascertained that the officer who commanded the first division of the flotilla had run foul of some works newly erected along the coast. The shock swamped some of the boats, and several of the men jumped overboard. The cries of the people at the seaside, who hastened to their assistance, excited much alarm. The accident was exceedingly mortifying, happening as it did, in the full gaze of our enemies, whose telescopes were pointed towards us, and it threw the emperor into a violent rage. He descended from the throne, and proceeded with Berthier to a sort of terrace which was formed along the water's edge. He paced to and fro very rapidly, and we could occasionally hear him utter some energetic expression indicative of his vexation. In the evening, a grand

dinner took place in honour of the inauguration. About six o'clock, just as dinner was served for the soldiers, under tents, a heavy fall of rain came on. This augmented the emperor's ill-humour, and formed a gloomy termination to a day which had commenced so brilliantly.[15]

A skirmish which took place under the eyes of the emperor at the end of the month between a British frigate and three sloops with 90 of his brigs and gunboats showed that no flotilla of small vessels would be sufficient to protect his transports, and the emperor's hope that the crossing might be effected under some favourable conditions of the weather without a previous battle against the British Navy; the more he studied the problem the clearer it became that success could not possibly attend such a scheme, and that the Channel must be held by a French naval force before the fleet of transports could, with any prospect of success, be launched upon the waters. There were three French squadrons; one at Toulon, the second at Rochefort and the third at Brest. Napoleon projected a scheme for decoying away the English fleet from its watch over the Channel by an attack upon the West Indian islands. His aim here was twofold; if our West Indian possessions really fell into his hands, that would be a great and most valuable prize; if the British fleet left the Channel in order to protect the West Indian islands, that might give to Napoleon the period of safety which he required for the crossing of the Channel.

In early September 1804 Pitt; accompanied by both Moore and Twiss, met the lords and bailiff of Romney Marsh at Newhall near Dymchurch to consider how best to inundate the marsh. The meeting agreed that on the appearance of the enemy on the coast the sluices should be opened to admit the sea so as to fill the dykes, and which might, it was said, be done on one tide and in case of actual invasion a further tide would, it was believed, flood the whole level.[16] However readers of the *Kentish Gazette* must have been disturbed a week later to learn that the Government had ordered that after the appearance of the enemy's gun boats off the Sussex Coast, Romney Marsh and Pevensey Levels were to be flooded.

The martello tower scheme still hung fire. In June 1804 Twiss had been instructed to find, in conjunction with Dundas and his officers, suitable positions and to make arrangements for the construction of such towers,[17]

Having been provided with little indication of the plan of the official tower, with no materials to construct them, and feeling as he said 'old age creeps fast upon me' — he was 59 and suffered from rheumatism — Twiss found his task uncongenial. He was not assisted by Chatham, who, having delayed the project for more than six months, now demanded to know why its author should not have made better progress.[18] Twiss also raised the question of who should man the towers but here Dundas showed impatience, and over a dinner at Walmer with Pitt, exclaimed: 'Give us the towers and we'll find the men!' On 12 September, after consultation with Pitt and Colonel Hope, who appear to have chosen certain of the sites themselves, and having apparently discarded the committee's scheme and fallen back on the more extensive proposals of the QMG's, he had recommended the construction of 88 towers at an estimated cost of £221,000.[19] In October Dundas was still reporting on its limitations.[20] It was impossible, he wrote, to fortify the whole coast with formidable batteries and lines but the towers would be some impediment to retard possible descent by hindering the enemy's attempt to anchor and by preventing the formation or progress of large bodies. Garrisoned by few men they could occasion delay. The plan of water defence would effectually cut off the enemy from advancing but the towers would impede descent. However, the immediate execution of water defence could delay the execution of a considerable number of these towers.

It was at this point that the Privy Council summoned a conference to consider and decide upon the whole system of coast defence. The conference was held at Rochester on Sunday, 21 October, at which Pitt, Camden and Chatham attended, together with all the military officers responsible in any way for defences; the Duke of York, Sir David Dundas, Brownrigg, Morse, the Inspector-General of Fortifications and Twiss, the CRE in the Southern District. The outcome of the meeting was to decide the controversy in favour of the towers and to fix their number at 81, though on 3 December this was altered once more to 86. As to design, it was decided there were to be two kinds of tower, a large one mounting eleven guns and a small one mounting an 18-pounder and two carronades. Of the larger variety two only were to be built; one at the Seahouses near Eastbourne and one at the east end of Dymchurch Wall. The remainder were to be of the smaller variety. The entrance was to be 10 ft above ground level. The ground floor was to contain the magazine and storerooms, the middle floor accommodation for an officer and 24 men, communication with each being provided by a stone staircase in the thickness of the exterior wall. The platform above was supported on brick arches springing from a central pier, and the foundations were strengthened by means of inverted arches.

The procrastination of fifteen months over whether to build these towers at a time when Napoleon was assembling his invasion fleet is proof of the government's failure to initiate a proper scheme of defence. On Pitt's return to power decisive measures were at once taken, and as will be seen in the next chapter a new and competent scheme of defence was sanctioned within a week of its submission.

chapter 2

The Planning of the Royal Military Canal – 1804

Lt-Col John Brown—early life in the West Indies and service in the Irish Engineers—enters the quartermaster general's department—becomes Commandant of the Royal Staff Corps (1802)—reports on coastal defence (September 1804)—proposes a canal from Shorncliffe to the Rother—plan approved by General Dundas and the commander-in-chief—the prime minister sanctions the scheme—Indicates the economic as well as the military benefits—wins the approval of the lords of Romney Marsh—John Rennie appointed consultant engineer—makes two reports—Brown's views on martello towers.

'The landing on this part of the coat is extensive, and everywhere excellent,' wrote Lt-Col John Brown following his survey of the south Kent coast in a report dated 19 September 1804. 'And as the present batteries are placed at a considerable distance from each other and could make little or no resistance after the enemy had gained the beach,' Brown suggested that to contain the enemy a canal should be built from Shorncliffe Battery passing in front of Hythe under Lympne Heights to West Hythe as a second line of defence.

This canal or cut should be sixty feet wide at top, forty at bottom and nine feet deep, which would always ensure seven to eight feet of water and being everywhere within musket shot of the Heights, under such circumstances it might be deemed impregnable. This would only form part of a greater plan which might be advantageously extended on the same side along the rear of Romney Marsh by Appledore to join the Rother above Boons Bridge.'[1]

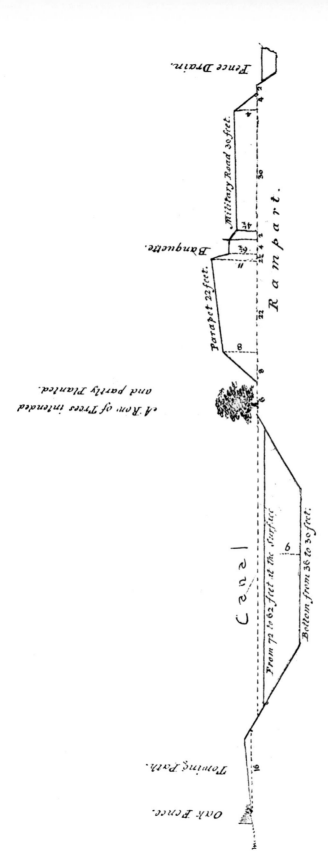

1804

Profile of The Royal Military Canal

John Brown, the originator of the Royal Military Canal project* was a Scotsman born in 1756. He appears to have gone out to Tobago as a young man, but writing to his brother in 1780 he revealed that he had been prevented from going to St Lucia to join the army because he had little money left 'without selling my negroes' that he had been employed 'doing some small job in the surveying way just to raise a little money to leave this damned country at the first opportunity,' that he had been sick on this 'very unhealthy island, a great number of people dead' and concluded by saying that surveyors there were not 'absolutely' necessary and were very ill paid indeed.[2] However, seven months later he reported that he had decided not to leave the island, the surveying business was a little better — he had been appointed Chief Surveyor of Tobago "which entitles me to "Esquire"' — and that he was determined to make as much money as possible or perish in the attempt.[3] However, he left Tobago in 1782 to become a cornet in the 27th Enniskillen Regiment of Foot, and served in St Lucia, Antigua, Grenada and Barbados on the staff of the assistant adjutant-general. Until 1784 he was employed as an engineer; then he joined his regiment in England and in February 1785 was made a burgess and freeman of Elgin his home town. In 1787 he was promoted subaltern and served in Ireland; then in October 1789 he transferred into the Royal Irish Engineers as captain-lieutenant, being employed chiefly on defence works in the south of Ireland under Major-General Vallernay. He became a captain in November 1793, major in May 1795 and in October of that year took part in the possession of the Little Pan goldmine, which had been found the previous month at the foot of Croughan, near Kinshelly in Wicklow.

The appearance of the French fleet in Bantry Bay in 1796 caused Brown to be sent there to erect batteries at Whiddy Point, Ardnagashel Point, Chapel Island, Eagle Point and Horse Island. Writing from Bantry in May 1797 to his friend James Willoughby Gordon, the future quartermaster-general, Brown told him about the defence works in progress, the fact that there was no bedding, barrack furniture or 'firing' for the guards, that he was interested in Bonaparte's campaigns and thought that he could amuse the young officer 'for two or three days sailing about the harbour. I am the commander of a very fine cutter sent by the admiral to assist. I have not yet, however, had time to pleasure in her and by myself should have but little amusement in it'.[4] Brown was then engaged on defending Cork Harbour. However, in October of that year he wrote to the master-general,

---

*In a letter to General Dundas dated 31 October 1804, Rennie wrote that it was 'Lt-Col Brown to whose judgement and able advice the nation is indebted for this important work.'

justifying his actions against criticisms by Vallernay of the inadequacy of the defence works, which apparently had collapsed after very heavy rain.* In 1798 the master-general of Ordnance, Ireland, reported that Brown had laid out a great deal of money in fortifying Fort Camden at the entrance to Cork Harbour; in the autumn of 1799 he took part in the Helder expedition; the fact that he was not acquainted with foreign languages except a little French being judged of no importance. His sketch of Cork Harbour dated 17 August 1800 shows transports about to sail for Egypt with the Coldstream and 3rd guards.[5] On 1 April 1801 he was reduced to the rank of major when the Corps of Engineers of Ireland was disbanded on the Act of Union. However, 'in consequence of your long and meritorious services and in consideration of the arrangement made in regard to the incorporation of the Irish Engineers with the British' he was appointed on 1 May surveyor of Ordnance lands in Ireland, an appointment for which he was paid until the end of 1802.

Brown, however, was not to remain much longer in Ireland. On 14 June 1801 he left Cobh and arrived in London on the 18th. The following month Maj-Gen Brownrigg made him an assistant quartermaster-general at the Horse Guards. In May 1802 he was appointed Lt-Col Commandant of the Royal Staff Corps whose headquarters were at Chatham while retaining his post at the Horse Guards. On 5 July he took rooms on the first floor of 15 Leinster Place. On 5 November his piles had for the first time 'bled a little and continued a few days'.

For the next two years he was actively engaged on surveying Britain's roads and defences. In March 1803 he was given special responsibility for the direction of the topographical department — Brownrigg wrote to the commander-in-chief 'The ability and topographical science of Lt-Col Brown now in the department have already been so highly approved of by Your Royal Highness that I am induced to request that this important branch may be confided to his direction'.[6] Later that year he was asked to comment on Col Twiss's report on building martello towers in Ireland; then as it was thought that the eastern side of London was the most accessible to an enemy advancing from the Thames estuary or Essex coast, he accompanied the commander-in-chief and John Rennie on 1 August on a survey of the Lea Valley, which subsequently led to dams being built with

---

* Sir John Moore examined the defences at Cork in January 1798 'where large sums have at different times been expended on its defence but with so little judgement that it still is in a precarious state, and upon the whole the works in Cork Harbour are a disgrace to the country. The batteries erected at Bantry since the French were there would throw some impediments in the way of an enemy, but nothing but a considerable corps of troops would possibly prevent his landing.'

Statement of the Service of Lieut. Col. John Brown

RANK	In what Corps	Number of Years	Where employed, specifying the period of each Service:- the Names of any Siege, Battle or considerable Action, where personally present:- the periods on half pay:- Regimental leave, or other leave of Absence:- Modern Foreign Languages acquainted with:
Cornet, or Ensign 1st July 1782	27 Engineers Killed reg.ts	5½	In the West Indies viz.t St Lucia Antigua Grenada & Barbadoes employed on the Staff as Assistant Adjutant General to the Forces & Assistant, Surveyor & Draftsman to the Army & as Engineer. Situations which I held near two years prior to the date of my first Commission viz.t from 1780 to 1784. After the peace I return.d to Europe. Joined my Reg.t & served with it in England Scotland and Ireland — in the end of 1784 I had two months Leave
Lieutenant 26th Dec.r 1787	do	1	Doing Duty with the 27th Reg.t at Limerick Dublin &c.
Captain 1st October 1789	Roy.l E. Engineers	6	Employed chiefly in the South of Ireland (under the Command of General Vallancey) in reconnoitring the Country & Construction works for the Defence of Cork Harbour &c.a — In the end of 1790 I obtained three months leave.
Major 19th May 1795	do	5	In 1795 I was attached as an Engineer to the Commander in Chief (Lieut.t General Cunningham) and in that Capacity I was employed in all parts of Ireland in reconnoitring and taking up Military positions. — I was also employed on the Staff as A.D.C. — from 1796 to 1800 I was Commanding Engineer in the Southern District & charged with the Direction of the works on Cork Harbour Bantry Bay &c. &c.
Lieutenant Colonel 1st Jan.y 1800		9¾	In 1799 I served at the Helder as assistant Q.r M. General. The Royal Irish Engineers being reduced at the Union 1801 I was soon after appointed and as Q.r Mas.r Gen.l to the Forces in South Britain and on the 6th May 1802 Commandant of the R.l S.r Corps which I now hold and for the last four years I have been chiefly employed on the Coast of Kent & Sussex.

It will appear by the mem... statement that altho' it has not fallen to my lot to have been employed on ... d services, still they have been varied, ... and for those interruptions for twenty seven years & a half, ... months leave excepted — I am not acquainted w.t Foreign Languages except a little French. —

John Brown Lt Colonel

which to flood the valley; in the summer of 1804 he surveyed a military road from Rochester to Guildford and Farnham to facilitate the passage of artillery and carriages. On Brown's advice the idea of making a continued road some 70 miles long was abandoned and 4 miles of military road were made along the chalk ridge to link up existing roads.[7]

Here then in Brown's report on coastal defence was the kernel of the idea for the military canal. The plan had many advantages. The canal would render unnecessary the doubtful and destructive measure of flooding the countryside. Its length of 19 miles would cover 30 miles of coastline. It would be all on one level with only an entrance lock at Iden. On the interior side a great military road could be constructed.

Dundas who commanded the Southern District, commented that this project would most effectually bar the entry into the country out of Romney Marsh.

> Such a ditch or canal would not be totally unproductive and be of use for commercial or husbandry purposes. Floating defences would be movable and manageable, and contribute much to its strength and the quick movement of troops. Without pursuing this idea further at present, it seems essential that something of this sort should be adopted, perhaps on a lesser scale ... and I am persuaded will prove the readiest in execution and the most effectual in defence and the least expensive plan that can be resorted to, to place this part of the coast in a state of perfect security.

Brown's report, together with Dundas's comments were forwarded to the commander-in-chief on 18 September 1804.[8] On 27 September the commander-in-chief, Frederick, Duke of York sent both reports to Lord Camden, the Secretary of State for War and added in his covering letter:

> In regard to the proposal of cutting a canal betwixt Hithe and the river Rother, for the purpose of military defence, by separating an enemy landed upon the coast of Romney Marsh from the interior of the country, I am to press this measure most earnestly upon the consideration of His Majesty's Government. Your Lordship is aware of the great embarrassment attending the water defences of this important line of coast — a considerable doubt being entertained should the inundation be delayed till an enemy is on the point of sailing, whether a sufficient effect can be produced by the influx of the sea, previous to the moment when we are to apprehend that some of the principal sluices may fall into his possession, and whether to avoid a greater evil this may not necessitate a previous destruction of property to a large amount — and which ultimately should the enemy's demonstration be confined to a threatening appearance upon his own coast may prove to have been unnecessary. As a considerable security would under all circumstances be given by the proposed line of water defence — the first advantage to be proposed from this measure, is the necessity being done away of inundating, previous to the moment that the enemy's attempt is deemed certain. Consequently, should his force not prove very considerable, this measure of ruinous consequence may possible be altogether avoided.

The Duke of York then went on to say that should an armed flotilla be stationed in the port of Rye for the defence of Pevensey Bay, the same gun vessels might be able to move up and down the canal as movable batteries to defend the whole of Romney, Marsh.

On the previous day (26 September) however, the commander-in-chief himself had met and obtained Pitt's authority to start work, and explained the position in a second and rather abrupt letter to Lord Camden:

> I this day officially communicate to Your Lordship a report received from General Sir David Dundas, proposing measures of great importance and considerable expense, upon the coast of Kent. Before copies could be made of these different papers in order to be transmitted to Your Lordship, I had an opportunity of communicating with Mr Pitt, who gave a full consideration to the subject. By his desire, the different measures proposed were immediately authorised,* for the purpose of avoiding the delay which must otherwise have attended the receiving Your Lordship's official sanction, but which you will be pleased to remark it is necessary should be sent. For Your Lordship's more perfect understanding of the whole subject I herewith enclose copy of my instructions to Sir David Dundas.

These were dated 26 September and began:

> The quartermaster has brought under my consideration, the report presented to you by Lt-Col Brown, Assistant Quartermaster General, upon points which have been investigated under your authority. I have further perused with the utmost attention, your remarks upon the different suggestions contained in this report, upon the whole matter of which I have also communicated with His Majesty's Government.
>
> The great work proposed of cutting a canal betwixt the Rother and the beach in Hithe Bay for the purpose of separating an enemy landed upon the cost of Romney Marsh from the interior of the country is approved by H. M. Government, and I am now to sanction its being immediately undertaken under your authority, and further, to desire that this canal in its whole length from the Rother to Hithe may be the greatest dimensions proposed, namely sixty feet top breadth and forty feet at bottom, nine feet

---

* The decision to build the canal so promptly may have been influenced by the report by the French General, Charles Dumouriez, who had defected from the French Republican Army and had come to live in England. Dumouriez, who twenty years earlier had been planning the invasion of England, now acted for the British Government and spent more than six months writing a paper on the defence of the country. He was in regular contact with both the Duke of York and Lord Camden, as well as with Pitt. His paper, which highlighted the ease with which an enemy might land on the shores of the Dungeness peninsula, was completed in May 1804. (J. Holland Rose, *Dumouriez and the Defence of England against Napoleon*, 1909, p. 291 et seq.)

deep, and should it appear to you that any particular advantage would arise to the defence, or convenience to the inhabitants of the country the proposed continuation of the same line of the water defence from Hithe to Shorncliffe may be done upon the same scale; otherwise upon that proposed by Lt-Col Brown for this part, namely thirty and twenty feet top and bottom breadth and seven feet deep.

The military road proposed to pass in the rear of this canal will of course, only commence from beyond Hithe where the present great road along the coast goes in front of its line.

This lengthy despatch went on to confirm that the general direction of the work should be given to Rennie and that Dundas should provide working parties unless it was found to be more expedient to call in navigators. Brown and Major Nicolay were to construct the field works. A plan was enclosed and a postscript mentioned that since writing, General Dundas had seen Rennie and found that the preliminary parts of the business could be settled in London.

On 3 October 1804 Brown produced a further report for the benefit of the prime minister and the commander-in-chief on the proposed inundations of that part of Romney Marsh towards Rye and particularly of Pett Level, which drew attention to the fact that the subject of inundation had not been sufficiently considered, and that it was not accurately known what effects would be produced by admitting the tide at different periods. 'Spring tides admitted at Scots Float and White Kemp would cover a considerable part of the meadows towards Appeldore. Retained by these sluices it would form on spring tide only a sufficient barrier. On neap tides, however, only a few ditches would be filled, in no way formidable to an enemy who will not be destitute of the means of passing them.' In other words only the western part of the marsh would be flooded under the most favourable conditions.

On the same day the prime minister formally replied to the Duke of York's letter of 27 September with which Brown's report and Dundas's recommendation had been forwarded, stating that it would be for His Royal Highness to determine which parts of it could be best executed under the Board of Ordnance and that His Majesty's ministers left that choice and the rest of the execution of the plan with perfect confidence to His Royal Highness's judgement.

And I give the sanction of the authority of Government upon the measure of cutting the canal between Hythe and the river Rother with as much anxiety for its execution as Your Royal Highness urges the undertaking, as besides the military advantages which are pointed out, this measure affords the fairest prospect of being the most essential benefit to the country in its neighbourhood, from the circumstance of the junction which it appears probable may be made with Rye Harbour. I have therefore, great satisfaction in conveying to Your Royal Highness the approbation of His Majesty's ministers to this proposal which I shall take the first opportunity of laying before His Majesty, but in the meanwhile, I lose no time in giving Your Royal Highness this information, and I trust every exertion will be made to complete the work.

Not until three weeks later was an almost exactly similar letter sent by Lord Camden to the Duke of York.

Dundas had made a further report on the projected water defence from Sandgate to Rye on 15 October 1804 which he sent to the Duke of York:

Romney Marsh may be considered as a quadrant of a circle of which Dungeness is the centre and equidistant from Rye and Hythe along the coast, the circumference is bounded by the heights of Lympne, Aldington, Appledore, Isle of Oxney and Playden and the water of the river Rother. The country behind is wooded and intricate and except in fine weather difficult of passage for a large corps.

Every effort on the certainty of an enemy attack should be made to clear and excavate the marsh, destroying whatever could be useful to the enemy. To such a state he would be quickly reduced to the last extremity and to an endeavour to reimbark if the means remained to him. One arch of all the bridges must be easily removed.

It is supposed that this kind of work can only be carried on in the dry and good season, and the quantity of tools, planks, wheelbarrows, ropes, pumps etc. required is a great expensive article. Every precaution will be necessary to preserve the health of those employed in this aguish country and when the labour is of so moist and watery a nature.

The whole requires the arrangement, inspection and direction of an able and experienced engineer, and on the conduct and distribution of work, where so great a proportion is bodily labour, will defend much of the expense.

The troops at Hythe and Playden Heights are well placed in support of the flanks of this line. Those at Brabourne, Ashford and Reading Street are well situated for the centre of the line and would arrive at Aldington, Horton [near Ruckinge] and Appledore besides the accumulating force of the surrounding country.

The commander-in-chief being only too well aware of the delay likely to attend the work if it was carried out by the engineers on the instruction of the Board of Ordnance, decided to treat the canal as a field-work and not as a fortification, and gave the responsibility to the quartermaster-general. The fact that the government had sanctioned the plan for the canal within a week of Brown having completed his report was not only due to the enthusiasm of General Dundas and the C-in-C for the scheme but to the energetic direction of the prime minister, who being fully aware of the need for the coast to be better defended, appreciated that the plan would 'kill several birds with one stone'.

The acquisition of land for the works was itself a major problem. The urgency of the matter precluded normal practice so Pitt in his capacity as Lord Warden convened a meeting, attended by Dundas, Moore, Rennie and Brown at Dymchurch on 24 October in order to try and win the agreement of the landowners and the lords of Romney Marsh. Sir John Honeywood was asked to take the chair after which the prime minister explained in the clearest manner and with a 'perspicacity peculiar to himself', how this great work would affect the interests of the marsh, and how the canal would

> intercept the floods from the hills in heavy rains — that by its means many thousand acres of land now inundated in wet seasons would be preserved — that in dry seasons, not only the whole water which arises from the hills would be turned into the marsh for the use of cattle and other stock, but that the canal would act as a reservoir to supply the marsh with water when other sources failed; that by its means the produce of the country would be conveyed, at a cheap rate to the sea coast; that materials for the making of roads could be afforded in great abundance, and at a moderate expense, and that in general it would be the means of improving the country to a degree they could scarcely imagine.

The *Kentish Gazette* related that the prime minister took considerable pains to reconcile the measure to those present and as the alternative was the inundation of Romney Marsh in case of invasion which they so much dreaded, Pitt soon convinced them of its advantages. Indeed, he was so convincing that those present 'unanimously agreed to give the ground for the work and to leave the valuation and damages to a jury', but as the names of these persons were not taken and could not therefore be distinguished from those proprietors (of which there were a great many), who did not attend the meeting, little advantage was derived from the resolution.[9] The *Kentish Gazette* concluded its report by stating that 'these resolutions were passed, the meeting adjourned and Mr Pitt returned to Walmer Castle'.[10]

John Rennie, the builder of London Bridge and Waterloo Bridge, and who had just completed the London & West India Docks, was now retained as consulting engineer and asked to advise on the best means of keeping the

works free of water while under construction. On 29 October he reported
to General Dundas that he had examined the line between Shorncliffe and
the river Rother near Boons Bridge in nearly thirty different places, and
that to a depth of 5 or 6 ft, it was generally mould and clay and below it
was generally peat and sand.[11] That part in particular, which lay between
Shorncliffe and Bonnington was very sandy, 'in some places quite pure, like
that on the seashore;' in others, it was mainly silt. Rennie commented that
if the canal was dug to a depth of 9 ft the expense of pumping the water
would be very great, and the time of executing the work, much prolonged.

> Brown has been an eye witness to the nature of the ground in many
> places, and I believe means to propose that the canal shall be dug only to
> the depth of 7 feet below the general surface of the marshes, instead of
> nine feet as originally intended; but that it shall be widened ten feet; so
> that nearly the same quantity of earth will be excavated in the one case,
> as in the other — Of the propriety of this alteration in a military point
> of view, I am unable to judge; but, if an opinion is permitted, I would say
> that the ten feet additional width will render it more defensible than 2
> feet of additional depth;

Rennie went on to say that in other respects, however, 'I have no hesitation
in giving a decided opinion'. Ordinary spring tides rose about 4½ ft above
the level of the marshes which would be much above the surface of the
proposed canal, but that as neap tides would not rise to within 3 ft of the
surface, natural drainage into the sea would be achieved by means of a
trunk laid under the beach near Shorncliffe and by means of the additional
guts (sluices), to be laid through Dymchurch Wall; similar trunks were to
be made, to discharge part of the water into Rye Harbour. Rennie pointed
out, however, that at the west end, no very effectual drainage could be
looked for, until the beginning of next summer because the Rother was
'subject to great floods in winter and which continue often till late in
the spring, so that its water would most probably outride the sluice and
prevent the drainage from being effected to any considerable degree'. He
therefore advised that a steam engine should be purchased

> without loss of time, and erected in a proper situation so as to supply
> the probable deficiency of drainage towards the Rother. The Kennet &
> Avon Canal Company have the principal iron material, of a steam-engine
> of Boulton & Watts' construction which is intended to erect on their
> canal — but as they will not have occasion for this engine until about the
> beginning of next summer, they have in consequence of an application I
> made to them, agreed to give it to Government, on condition that another

engine of Boulton & Watts' construction of equal power and value be furnished to them at Hungerford where the engine now lies, by the month of May next — of which no doubt need be entertained. If this meets the Commander-in-Chief's approbation no time should be lost in ordering it to be sent to the work. A beam has been purchased for them, and which is now in London and a boiler has been ordered of Messrs Boulton Watt & Co. and is nearly ready; all these should be forthwith brought to London, and sent for the earliest conveyance to Romney Marsh.

The pumps belonging to the Kennet & Avon Canal Company being prepared to raise water to a different height to what is wanted at the proposed canal, need not be taken, as they will answer for the canal company engine — new pumps should be ordered of Messrs Boulton & Watt, suitable to the circumstances of the canal — and they can be sent there by the time the engine lever is ready.

Rennie also mentioned that it was his intention to have made some observations respecting a proposed alteration in the contract with Bough & Co.

in consequence of the water which has been discovered and likely to obstruct and occasion some delay in the execution of the works. But, as these gentlemen seem inclined to undertake the keeping of the work, clear from water, on condition they are furnished with a steam-engine and the trunks through the beach at Shorncliffe and Dymchurch Wall, I have thought it better to delay my opinion in this part of the business. In the meantime, I have taken the liberty to purchase 5,000 feet of 3 inch memel deals at Dover at 7½d per foot, and carriage at the rate of 30/– per waggon load to Shorncliffe for the making of a trunk through the beach and have set Mr Bough to work with it, that no time may be lost in procuring a partial drainage, in order that the work may proceed. Mr Hollingsworth has in his possession twenty-two cast iron pipes — 2 feet diameter and nine feet long each, which he offers in London at £12 per ton — this, I think a very reasonable price, and should be purchased, as they will be immediately wanted for culverts underneath the canal.

Two days later Rennie wrote a further report on the best means of supplying the canal with water and the kind of bridges to be used.[12] Brown had recommended that the canal should be cut through the low reach or valley of Romney Marsh, lying close by the foot of the hills, where the normal surface of the water would be level with the general surface of this part of the marsh. 'No situation,' said Rennie, 'could therefore have been better calculated, for the supply of water than this is; but . . .' and here the engineer went on to point out that there was likely to be too little in the autumn and too much in winter and spring. Additional quantities were also to be introduced into the canal, which did not then enter Romney Marsh at all, namely the Seabrook Mill stream near Shorncliffe, two streams at Hythe and another small stream to the eastward of Hythe. 'If the canal should prove watertight, these streams I hope will be able to keep it full in very dry seasons,' continued Rennie, but if it soaked away 'it may still be unequal to the filling of the canal 3 ft above the level of the marsh and thereby defeating as I understand, one principal object of this canal — namely of producing an inundation in front of the works, whenever it shall be required.' Rennie also drew attention to the marsh owners' objections to the canal on the grounds that the canal passing along the foot of the hills, would intercept all the springs and rainwater which ran into the marsh, and that the canal would get overcharged in winter. 'I have been thus particular in stating the objections to this excellent scheme, in order that I might have an opportunity of pointing out, how perfectly some can be overcome and how unfounded are others.'

Rennie explained that the huge sluice, 200 ft long with doors pointing to sea and land, to be constructed at Shorncliffe would be able not only to regulate the water level of the canal but be capable of raising it 3 ft to flood the marshes 'in one day of a spring tide'.

Rennie recommended that a navigation lock capable of admitting such vessels from Rye Harbour or from the Rother above, 'as shall be judged proper to assist in defending the rampart — or for vessels to convey produce on the canal,' should join the tideway 'either below Scots Float Sluice or that sluice must be altered, to render it more suitable to such craft; it being very inconvenient and ill adapted to the present vessels which navigate the Rother.'

> The next objection which has been made to this project is that it will not only cut across all the roads leading into the marsh but that it will leave farms across and under them very inconvenient in the occupation.
>
> To the above objections, I answer, that bridges are intended to be made at the principal roads, and that a military road is to be made on the upper side and a towing path road on the lower side — there will be ready and convenient passages or communications from one side of the canal to the other, and as most of the land is in grazing farms, driving their flocks a few hundred yards further, can make no material difference to them; this occupation of land however will only be a temporary inconvenience to the landowners, as in time exchanges will be made and farms rendered much more compact and easier in their occupation than now.
>
> A material question however, arises here, namely: what kind of bridges across the canal will be the most suitable, whether standing bridges or

draw or swivel bridges; and of what material. Standing bridges of wood, would be a cheap mode of construction, as well as a speedy one; but then they must be destroyed on the approach of an enemy — and as this would require some time, so much would be lost for the driving of cattle, stock etc. from the marsh — swivel or draw bridges of wood would also come reasonable, and they would have the advantage of being kept fit for cattle and stocks to pass over till the last moment, when they could be turned off and the passage stopt — Swivel bridges I would prefer to drawbridges, because they are less exposed to the enemy on the whole, much less expensive than drawbridges; wooden bridges of all kinds are liable to decay, the abutments might be built of brick and the upper parts of cast iron if swivel but this would greatly increase the expense as well as the time of execution and as these works can always be repaired (being above water, I would advise wooden abutments & wooden swivels.

Rennie estimated that 250 loads of oak timber and about 200 loads of best memel timber would be required for the trunk at Shorncliffe and recommended that they be contracted for immediately. Six curved iron pipes were likewise wanted to complete the culverts 'for which the twenty-two pipes, mentioned in my former report will be used; and as little time should be lost with these; they had better be got from some iron founder in London.'

Rennie concluded his lengthy report by mentioning that as the bridge in the street of Hythe would be much more used, than any of the others — it should be made of more durable materials, that he would after the designs were made, submit comparative estimates, and that 'as soon as I am honoured with His Royal Highness, the Commander-in-Chief's directions respecting these matters, I shall make out the requisite designs, and enumerate such materials as may be wanted next in succession.'

The commander-in-chief wrote on 31 October that the canal's progress might be expected to be rapid and

when completed, may be fairly considered as an almost insurmountable barrier against an enemy's penetrating into the country. From the difficulty of approach across the marsh, the time that will be afforded for assembly from every quarter and the numbers that may thus oppose him; it ought to operate as a great discouragement from making any effort by this the shortest line of passage.

However, General Dundas was quick to point out that the canal was too far removed from the coast to prevent actual descent, and 'an effectual opposition to such in the moment of attempt is a thing most desirable.' Although the government had approved the building of martello towers, it was not until 27 December 1804, that Lord Camden had given the Board of Ordnance definite instructions to start work. And so nearly eighteen months had gone by since the question had been originally canvassed and no land had been taken, no contractor had been chosen, nor a single brick laid. Altogether eight single and five multiple martello towers were planned to be built near to high-water mark between Beachy Head and Dover by the end of 1805 at a cost of £221,000. Thirty-eight of these were to be constructed between Shorncliffe and Cliff End.

John Brown had been very much against this project. He had attended the conference on coastal defence called by the Privy Council in October 1804 at Rochester (see p. 27). He and Rennie had been 'occasionally called in' to prove that little dependence could be placed on the scheme to flood the marshes. At this meeting Brown's own report on the canal was only briefly touched upon with few but favourable remarks as it had already been partly adopted; but to his intense disapproval

> the expensive and diabolical system of Tower Defence was finally resolved on to an unprecedented extent, contrary to the opinions of the best and most experienced officers in our service; but it was carried by the influence of the Ordnance people — only whose opinions were by no means supported by reasoning. Mr Pitt, from whom one would have expected a decided opinion, gave into that of others and without requiring, what indeed he would not have obtained, a satisfactory and well-digested plan of defence, all that was advanced was Tower, Tower, Tower; some large and some small was all the variation proposed by the engineers, and when General Morse was asked if he thought even the number of towers proposed would be sufficient, he thought not, but proposed to place cannon between them in open batteries. The tower system appeared in some parts of the coast to be too scanty, in others too profuse. Brigadier-General Twiss, having proposed two towers for the protection of each of the sluices on Dymchurch Wall, being asked if one would not be sufficient for this purpose, said it was highly important to defend the sluices, because at all events they would admit saltwater enough to destroy the fresh, so that, should the enemy land, they would have nothing to drink. This from Brig-Gen Twiss, and the open batteries between the towers from General Morse, are a sufficient specimen of the importance of their remarks.[13]

It will, therefore, be seen that the canal was to form part of a triple defence scheme to resist invasion: firstly on the beaches were to be the martello towers, secondly Romney Marsh was to be partially flooded and thirdly the canal would form a second line of defence.

chapter 3

The Building of the Royal Military Canal (1804–1807)

Sir John Moore—cutting the canal begins (October 1804)—reports of progress—woman sold at Hythe—Rennie's visit (February 1805)—causes of delays—the sluice at Shorncliffe—bankruptcy of contractors—the prime minister intervenes (June 1805)—Lt-Col Brown appointed Director of Works—1,500 men at work—assembly of Grande Armée—Napoleon at Boulogne—immediate threat of invasion—Lord Ellenborough's criticism—ten miles completed in April 1806—the commander-in-chief navigates the canal in August—construction of barges—valuation of land and compensation for damages—Royal Military Canal Act (1807)

On Sunday, 14 October 1804, John Brown left London with Rennie, stopped at Farningham to dine and slept at the Star Inn, Maidstone. On the 15th they met the contractors and dined at the White Hart at Hythe. On the 16th, after examining the line between Shorncliffe and Hythe, Brown called on Sir John Moore at Sandgate, dined with him the following day, and spent the 18th riding with him and David Dundas to explain 'the manner which I meant to adopt in laying out the line, flanks etc.' The general, who commanded the brigade at Shorncliffe and was responsible for defending one of the key positions of the coast, took a very keen interest in the defences being built. He had met Brown, if not in the West Indies, then almost certainly during their service in Ireland or on the Helder expedition and he may well have expressed the same views at dinner as he did when writing to Creevy from Sandgate on 27 August —

We understand that Government have positive information that we are to be invaded, and I am told that Pitt believes it. The experience of the last twelve months has taught me to place little confidence in the information or belief of ministers, and as the undertaking seems to be so arduous and offering so little prospect of success, I cannot persuade myself that Bonaparte will be mad enough to attempt it. He will continue to threaten, by which means alone he can do us harm. The invasion would, I am confident, end in our glory and in his-disgrace.'

It was, more likely to have been a deliberate leak on the part of government than an adroit reporter that enabled *The Times* to report on 18 October that 'without vouching for the the correctness of any of the particulars' it has been suggested to government by 'an able military officer of the quartermaster-general's department' that a canal should be constructed which would admit armed vessels of above 200 tons burthen and commented that —

The great merit of this plan is, that it combines defence with utility. It will act as a catch-water drain, and greatly relieve the waters below from the highland water. It will enable them to carry the produce of the country at a comparatively small expense to the sea coast. It will afford a ready means of conveying shingle and beach to the interior of the country, for the making and repairing of roads, which, throughout this district, are very bad. It will be of infinite use to the county of Kent, should ever the projected canal from Yalden Lees on the Medway, by Lamberhurst and Ashford to Canterbury, with a branch by Tenterden to the Rother, take place.

From Canterbury, a canal, on one level, has been projected to communicate with the sea at St. Nicholas Bay, in the Isle of Thanet, capable of carrying sea-built vessels, so that by joining these two canals, the whole interior of the county of Kent will have a ready and easy navigation to the sea coast, at Canterbury, Chatham, Rye, and Hythe.

It will also, by means of the river Rother, open a navigation into an important part of the county of Sussex, at Robertsbridge, from whence the timber, and other articles, may be conveyed at a cheap rate to His Majesty's dockyards at Chatham and on the Thames. It will be the means, in all probability, in bringing about the improvement of the harbour of Rye, so long in contemplation, and so much to be wished for. The old harbour of Lympne, the 'Portus Lemanus' of the Romans, will also be opened, and it is probable that the attention of His Majesty's ministers may, sooner or later, be drawn to Hythe, and a good harbour established there.

The *Sussex Weekly Advertiser* commented on 22 October that 'it is considered one of the greatest military works in this or any other kingdom!' ²

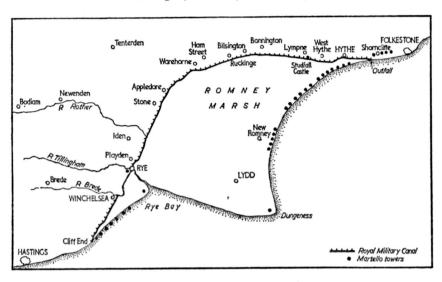

Line of the Royal Military Canal and road, 1810.

The line of canal was to stretch from beneath the cliffs of Sandgate through Hythe and along the edge of Romney Marsh until it joined the river Rother. Its channel was to be dug close by the ruins of St Mary's Church at West Hythe and to Studfall Castle where the castle of Lympne stood high above; then skirting the villages of Bonnington, Bilsington, Ruckinge, Ham Street, Warehorne, Kenardington, Appledore, and Stone to Iden. Here the channel of the Rother was to be used to form the defence work as far as the river's junction with the Tillingham at Rye, the channel of the Tillingham till its junction with the Brede and the channel of the Brede as far as Winchelsea. Then from Strand bridge the canal was to stretch across Pett Level to Cliff End where it was to terminate in the cliff face. A total distance of 28 miles, of which 22½ miles would be formed by the canal; 44 ft wide at bottom, 62 ft wide at the water's surface and 9 ft deep. The excavated earth was to form the banquette and parapet on the north side of the canal, and behind this was to be built the military road along the line of the canal except for small deviations at Rye and Winchelsea; on the south side were to be the tow-path and the wharves. On 23 October the *Kentish Gazette* criticised the line chosen on the grounds that it relinquished the whole marsh to the enemy. On 30 October work on the canal began. Brown recorded in his diary that 'a few of the contractors' people began to break ground near Shorncliffe,' and then went on to say that until 9 November 'the work continued with very few men employed.' The local papers were full of reports about the French:

ANNO QUADRAGESIMO SEPTIMO

GEORGII III. REGIS.

Seff. 2.

✻✻

C A P. LXX.

An Act for maintaining and preferving a Military Canal and Road, made from *Shorncliff* in the County of *Kent*, to *Cliff End* in the County of *Suffex*; and for regulating the taking of Rates and Tolls thereon. [13th *Auguft* 1807.]

WHEREAS a Canal called *The Royal Military Canal*, and alfo a Military Road and Towing Path, and other Works, have been lately made, from *Shorncliffe* in the County of *Kent*, to *Cliff End* in the County of *Suffex*: And whereas it is expedient that Provifion fhould be made for the maintaining and preferving the faid Canal, and the Ramparts and other Works belonging thereto : And whereas great Advantages will accrue to the Part of the Country through which the faid Canal and Road pafs if the fame is opened, under certain Reftrictions, for publick Ufe ; be it therefore enacted by the King's moft Excellent Majefty, by and with the Advice and Confent of the Lords Spiritual and Temporal, and Commons, in this prefent Parliament affembled, and by the Authority of the fame, That the Speaker of the Houfe of Commons, the Lord High Treafurer of *Great Britain,* the Firft Lord Commiffioner of the Treafury, the Chancellor of the Exchequer, His Majefty's Principal Secretaries of State, the Commander in Chief of His Majefty's Forces, the Lord Warden of the *Cinque Ports*, the Secretary at War, the Mafter General of the Ordnance, and the Quarter Mafter General of His Majefty's Forces, for the Time being refpectively, fhall be Commiffioners for the carrying on, completing, maintaining, regulating, and managing the faid Military Canal and Road,

and

(Lewes, Oct. 29) Saturday se'nnight towards dusk, an armed French vessel hove in sight off the town of Brighton, and captured two brigs and a lugger in the road — One of the battery guns being fired, and signals of an enemy made by the telegraph one of His Majesty's cruizers soon appeared and retook two of the captured vessels. The Frenchman by superior sailing we understand, escaped, with the other of her prizes into Dieppe;[3]

and

(Deal, Oct. 30) I have this instant received a note from an Officer off Boulogne, dated the 27th, in which he says 'We can now perceive at Ambleteuse twenty four brigs and luggers just returning with the tide, also a convoy of small lugsail boats etc. The enemy's craft cut a miserable figure in a swell, if they were three miles out, I think they would hardly make a knot an hour.'[4]

The direction and management of the canal was placed in the hands of the Quartermaster-General (Robert Brownrigg) with full powers to enter into contract for its execution. On Rennie's advice, Hollingsworth, Bough & Dyson, who had only recently executed the London Docks, were invited to excavate the whole line in six months. On 15 November the total cost of the canal to Cliff End was estimated at £200,000; and that it would be built from Shorncliffe to Hurst, 3 miles west of Lympne Hill by 1 March 1805, and the whole by 1 June 1805. The contract, which excluded making the military road and Iden lock, specified the measurements of the canal, how it should be constructed and the fact that all materials, horses and workmen except steam-engines had to be supplied by the contractors. There were some stiff clauses insisted upon by Rennie. The contractors were to be held responsible for all drains to be made to dispense water pumped out of the works by any steam-engine without additional payment. Brown was charged with its immediate superintendence. On 20 November, Pitt in his capacity as Lord Warden, wrote to Brown saying that as soon as he was advised of 'the particular parcels of land on which works are proposed to be carried on, I shall be ready to give the necessary certificates required by the Defence Act.'[5]

John Rennie was retained as chief engineer with instructions to supervise, with the assistance of a resident agent and a military-director — any one of whom had power to stop the work if it was being done unsatisfactorily until the contractors had put right the deficiency and if they did not, Rennie was empowered to discharge the contractors. Brown was charged with its immediate superintendence. The delegation of responsibility is not

4. Sir Robert Brownrigg.
Sir Robert Brownrigg
(1759-1833) quarter-
master-general 1803,
governor of Ceylon 1811,
general 1819.

clear in spite of the commander-in-chief's instructions, and this became increasingly apparent over the next few months.

Advertisements for canal diggers now appeared in the local press in various parts of the country. The attempt to attract labour from the Bristol area met with a spirited rebuff from Thomas Thatcher, who had been engaged to improve Bristol Harbour. An advertisement in the *Kentish Gazette* of 6 November contained the following footnote:

> There now appears in a Bristol paper an advertisement for 2,000 men to be employed in Kent. I hereby inform the workmen that it is my intention to give greater price for the work than has or may be offered by any contractor for work of this kind in Kent; for good hands by 1/- per day, be the price there what it may.

Thatcher was also quick to point out that his 'workmen may go to their breakfast or dinners in the regular time allowed them, but it is very different in Kent — the workmen there have at least 4 or 5 miles from their work to go to their lodgings'.

5. John Rennie 1803.
John Rennie (1761-1821) great
civil engineer. Designed canals,
docks, Waterloo Bridge etc.

The tremendous influx of troops and canal builders into the district
brought mixed blessings. The *Sussex Weekly Advertiser* commented on 10
December that —

> However calamitous the periods of war may be, they are not without
> their partial benefits — in large maritime countries, where a great
> number of troops are of necessity stationed, for the defence of the coast,
> the circulation of money they occasion is immense, and of course, have
> paid for hay, straw and oats only, delivered within the last ten months,
> between Brighthelmston and Rye, upwards of 30,000*l*.

The weather during the latter half of December delayed the work. There
was a considerable fall of snow on the 17th, followed by severe frost,
which continued until Christmas Day when a thaw set in. From the 26
December to 12 January the weather was very variable, and with the wind
in the north-east it rained and froze alternately.

On 8 January 1805 the *Kentish Gazette* reported that the canal through
Romney Marsh was being executed —

with unexampled activity, at various places along the whole line; and great numbers of labourers, lately employed at the docks and public works of the metropolis are arrived to assist in effecting it. The expense of cutting [only] is estimated at £150,000. In addition to this line of defence Mortella Towers are to be constructed on the edge of the sea, three of them equidistant between Hythe and Romney. Those near Dymchurch will be placed immediately behind the wall; for the purpose of building these, large quantities of stone are already collected, and twenty vessels, freighted with bricks are arrived; besides which three millions more have also been contracted for, to be made near the spot, as soon as the season will permit. One consequence of these works, together with the expensive repairs of Dymchurch wall, have been an increase of population hitherto unknown in that part of the country.

On 5 February the same paper mentioned that 'such is the ardour with which it [the canal] is prosecuted that the workmen are employed even on Sundays.

In spite of the impression gained from the local papers of feverish activity, wintry weather, heavy rain, constant flooding of the works, and a degree of disorganisation on both the army's and the contractors' part caused the work to fall behind. Entries in Brown's diary record: 20 January, 'raining and wet both day and night'; 21 January, 'rain and snow at night', 23 January, 'severe frost with snow'; 25 January, 'frost and strong east wind, very cold'. Frost and snow with intermittent thaws continued into February. In the meantime General Moore had returned to Shorncliffe — Brown dined with him on 24 January — after having been absent six weeks on a rather fruitless expedition to reconnoitre the defences. On 29 January the *Kentish Gazette* announced that a troop of the Royal Waggon Train was under orders to march from Canterbury to Hythe for the purpose of assisting with the works of the new canal. 'Thirty carts are expected from London, in addition to the waggons.'

There were, of course, also social problems. It was both expensive and difficult to find accommodation for wives. The *Kentish Gazette* reported on 15 March 1805 that:

Last week, the wife of one of the men employed in cutting the canal at Shorncliffe, was conducted by her husband to the market place, at Hythe, with a halter round her neck and tied to a post; from whence she was purchased for sixpence by a mulatto, the long drummer belonging to the band of the 4th regiment, lately in barracks at that place — She was a young woman, apparently not more than 20 years of age, tall, and of a likely form and figure; her face, however, exhibited evident marks of incompatibility of temper; vulgarly, she had a pair of black eyes; notwithstanding this, the new partner led her away, with much apparent satisfaction from his bargain.

The first serious setback occurred in making the culvert for the Seabrook millstream under the beach and rampart at Shorncliffe. This trunk of brick and stone was to be 90 ft long and 6 ft in diameter and required to be laid 20 ft below ground. Early in the new year (3 February) a storm had threatened to breach the bank where this was being constructed and the sea had threatened to inundate the countryside. Sixty men had to spend three days on a coffer dam, after which, wrote Brown, 'the whole is to be repaired at the expense of the contractors by order of the quartermaster-general'. Brown reported to Brownrigg on 4 February from Sandgate that the failure 'seems to have originated from want of skill on the part of the contractors, principally by placing the sluice, or top gate at the wrong place'. Of this work Rennie commented:

Whether the methods followed by the contractors were the best that could have been devised, I am unable to say, the work not having been under my direction; but the beach is so loose and the sea so boisterous at the time the work was executed that I have little doubt what was done at one tide would be deranged in the next and therefore, many parts of the work would be to do twice over. Difficult, however, as the work must have been and uncertain as the expense, I am decidedly of the opinion that it might have been executed without any hazard to the country.[6]

In the second week of February Rennie, accompanied for part of the time by Lt-Col Brown, 'inspected the state of the works and reported that "in respect to the contractors, I am sorry to say they have greatly disappointed my expectations, founded upon the diligence and accuracy with which I have seen other great works done by them".'[7] There were also allegations of overcharging. 'There are many charges in the accounts which have been delivered for the trench at Shorncliffe unreasonable and which in my opinion do not belong to government and of course ought not to be paid;' and of failure of the army to provide enough steam-engines for the pumps:

The steam-engine for the drainage of that district of the canal lying between West Hythe and Hurst, which ought to have been erected about Xmas, or at least early in January, is not nearly ready; of course the benefit which would have been derived from it is entirely lost and their men have been working to great disadvantage from the obstructing arising from the water which has sprung out of the ground and from that on the surface — silty and sandy soils of which much in the bottom of this canal has turned out to be — can never be worked with any advantage, unless it is thoroughly drained of water — which has not been the case here; good therefore as their workmen are, and much as such men will perform when the work is properly prepared for them, they must have been working hitherto both to their own disadvantage and greatly to the loss of the contractors and delay of the work.

On the last day of Rennie's visit (19 February) Brown wrote in his diary —

> This day in consequence of Mr Rennie's interference I came to a full explanation with him respecting his orders and interference on the work — after which he departed in a huff for London. On this occasion I directed the overseer [George Jones]*, not to receive or execute any orders without first acquainting me or the officer charged with the superintendence.

At the close of his lengthy report Rennie defended himself against any imputation that he might have been in any way responsible for the delays:

> The contractors cannot have the least pretence to excuse themselves from any neglect imputable to them by reason of their attention having been drawn off to other works in which I am engaged; so far as these have been concerned, they have been perfectly at liberty the whole time — except Mr Hollingsworth once and for that day only; with this single exception, I have not taken any of them away for one minute; therefore on this ground they can plead no excuse, which I think necessary to state for my own justification and in order that no part of the blame of the delay that has happened in this national work may be transferred to me.

This report was dated 12 March, but he apparently held up sending it till 14 April when he wrote that because some of his designs, sent on 14 March for comment, had not been returned and 'as the casting of the culvert pipes cannot admit of delay I have judged it proper to transmit this report without waiting longer for the return of the plans'. So it would seem that Rennie's comments to the quartermaster-general on the work of the contractors were withheld for some two months. Nevertheless, Brown must also have

---

*George Jones was a former army engineer who had served under General Craddock on the "Invasion of Ireland" and had been recommended by Rennie in 1802 to replace Joseph Hill to be in charge of building the ill-fated Salisbury & Southampton Canal. The company ran out of money and in June 1804 Jones issued a writ for his salary and advertised for 'his navigators' to join him working on the Royal Military Canal. (quoted by Charles Hadfield, *The Canals of South and South East England*, 1969 p. 185).

advised Brownrigg of the position, and it is clear from Brownrigg's letter to Brown on 28 February, which began — 'The variety of new and unforeseen circumstances, which have daily occurred respecting the mode of carrying on the Romney Canal has hitherto prevented me from conveying to you the commander-in-chief's final instructions,' that administrative chaos prevailed in Whitehall as a voluminous correspondence passed between the various government departments. Not until 12 May did he come down from London to see the works for the first time. Moore joined them on the 14th — to visit Rye and Winchelsea; on the 15th Brown met Moore at Cliff End and they 'walked along the foot of the heights to Rye, dined together and explored Playden Heights and the Rother beyond Boons Bridge.'

About 450 men were employed at the beginning of March and the weather had improved. However, Brown reported that the steam-engine would not be ready in less than five weeks. And so, after struggling with the work until the end of May less than 6 miles had been begun; 'not a twentieth part of the whole was executed and that in a slovenly manner' reported Rennie. The contractors having failed, the work was abandoned, the labourers began to disperse and the prime minister was advised of yet another crisis.

Pitt in fact, may not have been altogether surprised. He had on several occasions ridden over from his nearby home at Walmer Castle, to watch the progress of the work and in view of Rennie's earlier comments, it is perhaps surprising that action was not taken sooner. At any rate, on 6 June the Duke of York held a meeting at the Horse Guards at which Pitt, Lord Camden (the Secretary at War), Brigadier-General Hope (deputising for Brownrigg, who was ill), and George Harrison (counsel to the War Office, commander-in-chief's office and barrack office) attended, and at which it was agreed that no time should be lost in taking the work out of the hands of the present contractors, but that the penalties incurred by them under the contract should not be enforced if every facility in their power was afforded for the work being agreed on by others, without unnecessary delay. It was further agreed that the sole conduct of the work should now be entrusted to Lt-Col Brown under the authority of the commander-in-chief and the control of the quartermaster-general. Brown was to complete the work already begun and find a contractor for the remainder. Brown was called in and interrogated by the commander-in-chief and the prime minister as to the expectations that might be entertained of the successful progress of the work under his direction, and expressed himself free from any apprehensions.[8]

A further possible reason for taking the superintendence of the work out of Rennie's hands could be deduced from the following incident. According to Smiles, Rennie did not accumulate a large fortune and was apparently satisfied with a comparatively moderate rate of pay. However,

Mr Rennie's charge of seven guineas for an entire day's work was objected to by General Brownrigg — 'Why, this will never do,' said the general looking over the bill, 'seven guineas a day! Why it is equal to the pay of a field marshal!' 'Well,' replied Rennie, 'I am a field marshal in my profession, and if a field marshal in your line had answered your purpose, I suppose you would not have sent for me!' 'Then you refuse to make any abatement?' 'Not a penny' replied the engineer and the bill was paid.[9] If this was so, it is interesting to record that Thomas Telford when appointed principal engineer of the Caledonian Canal received only 3 guineas a day plus travelling expenses.[10] Be that as it may, Rennie had claimed £516 (also Giles £911 and Grantham £252) for surveys made in 1804 and 1805 of Romney Marsh, Pett Level, Pevensey Marsh and Rye Harbour[11] 'and the amount for these services appearing to the commander-in-chief to be large — and there being no means of having the charges examined under his authority,' Brownrigg asked that Lord Castlereagh, the Secretary of State for War, should obtain the Treasury's authority for their examination and instructions as to 'whether they are to be defrayed or not.'

Much of Brown's success at this stage was due to the support he received from his former chief, General Sir David Dundas, who was now in command of the Southern District and provided men from two militia regiments, the Cambridge and the Royal South Lincoln from whom small working camps were formed during the summer. Back in January Brown had recorded 'Wrote Sir D. D. applying for two horse carts, and to know if sheds would be built for horses, also to put me in communication with storekeeper for undertaking tools and also for working parties.' The building of bridges, culverts and other works was carried out by such part of the Staff Corps as remained at their headquarters at Hythe. Brown at once set to work using the material and machinery purchased from the contractors and by employing 'as he may find most advisable, labourers at day-work, or inferior contractors for small portions of the work and soldiers which will be stationed at Hythe for that purpose.' Brown was now given complete authority to certify payments for the whole expenditure.

Defence works had to be paid for in either of two ways. The cost of works small enough to be executed by soldier labour (who were allowed small additional gratuities), could be recovered on application to the Secretary of State and paid through the commissary's department. Large fortifications, normally tendered for by contractors, were paid for by the district commissioner from funds placed at his disposal by the Treasury. This was known as the fieldworks fund, and it was from this source that the cost of the Winchelsea section was met. For the remainder Brown was made entirely responsible for the accounts of expenditure. As might be imagined the responsibility for ensuring the correctness of the accounts was frightful, and following an inquiry from the Treasury requesting that every item be substantiated by a certificate to the effect that no more than the lowest market price had been paid for materials, Brown wrote to Brownrigg from Hythe on August 1805: 'I have all along seen the difficulties and dreaded the embarrassment of having the charge of public accounts, and I have used every endeavour to avoid it because it is impossible for me to conduct the work properly and give up a sufficient portion of my time to them.' Brown begged for a 'short general instruction' from the comptroller of accounts which would explain clearly the various procedures to 'relieve me from the heaviest part of my duty and leave me more time to apply to the essential parts of it where it will be more usefully employed.'

Brownrigg then wrote to the secretary of state conveying HRH's earnest request that this be done 'in order that the mind of this officer who is little accustomed to the duties of acacmptant may as far as possible be relieved from the height of responsibility'. Instead of a certificate of market price for every item purchased Brownrigg's suggestion that this be provided only for expenditure of over £100 was agreed.

Brown's control of expenditure was most exact. The troops were employed either by task work or by the day at regulation prices. The former practice was found to be the most economical and in these cases Brown approved, the price or rate, an officer of the Staff Corps measured the work done and confirmed that it was properly carried out, and Brown examined the account which was sent to the accountant for recalculation; payment was ordered by Brown initialling the account, without which it was stated no expenses were incurred or payments made. Any man found being idle or absent was mulcted of a day or half-day's pay by Brown — which method superseded the necessity of any other description of punishment.[12] A staff sergeant of the Corps acted as storekeeper for all the tools, and Alexander Swan as accountant, the Treasury having approved his appointment on 19 January 1805 at a salary of 15s a day. Swan did well. His reliability can be gauged from the fact that when the comptrollers of army accounts examined the accounts for the first four months of 1805, they reported that all the vouchers were regular '(except for a small error of eight pence in one of them)'. On 12 June Brown wrote in his diary 'Fine, but a bitter windy excursion to Dover for a screw pump. Swan applied to have his brother-in-law appointed a clerk. Refused'.

The Royal Waggon Train carted materials and dragged barges on to newly finished stretches of the canal. In addition, Brown engaged several hundred civilians previously employed by the contractors. When it was discovered that the contractors had only had tools and equipment for 200 workmen a further very large quantity, together with several small steam-engines for pumping, were immediately ordered.

On 14 July Brown reported from Hythe that he had 960 men at work between Shorncliffe and Hurst, exclusive of the Staff Corps and Waggon Train. Seven hundred were cutting the canal, 200 laying sods and dressing the rampart and 60 employed in day and night shifts working hand pumps. Another cargo of wheeling plank had arrived from the Rother and 'we shall shortly be in a state to employ any number that may offer'. The soldiers were mainly employed in forming the 3 ramparts and turfing the banks and were paid 2s a day. Labourers were paid 5s 6d a day, those engaged on the sluice at Shorncliffe 4s 6d a tide, and these frequently worked two tides in 24 hours.[13] Even in midsummer, water was a great hindrance to their work; not only were there few places where the canal could be excavated to its full depth but between Hythe and West Hythe the water had stopped work altogether 'until the portable engines, so anxiously expected arrive'. The trunk at Shorncliffe was completed in July and Brown considered that the canal from there to Hurst would be defensible by the middle of September except for the gravel bank at Hythe, and that work would be in progress perhaps as far as Bonnington or Ruckinge. Dumouriez had more optimistically stated in August that 'Romney and Rye have a defence prescribed and arranged in advance and supported by the excellent camp at Oxney'.[14] At the same time Brown was glad to report that no one had yet offered to take on the western end of the line —

> You have already had sufficient specimen of civil engineers, contractors and surveyors, and we have no reason to look for better treatment from amongst that description. The heavy expense of materials, sufficient to complete the whole line, has already been incurred, and you may rest assured that from the advantages we possess of employing the troops by task-work 20 per cent cheaper than any contractors could undertake it, and that we give no higher wages or prices than that given by the late contractors to the navigators, with which they are perfectly satisfied. I have no hesitation in saying, that under these circumstances, and as we are now fairly embarked in the business, and the energy and character of your department pledged, that we should go on with it without looking for other assistance.[15]

In view of Brown's comments the commander-in-chief wrote to Lord Castlereagh seeking the government's authority to allow Brown to finish the job,[16] to which Castlereagh replied on 18 July from Downing Street that His Majesty's ministers were in agreement with his proposal. By the middle of August, 1,500 men were at work — a huge number when compared with those engaged in similar canal undertakings* — but in the event this was the moment when the canal was most likely to have been put to the test. In July Napoleon had told Marshal Berthier, 'Every moment presses; there is no longer an instant to lose'. On 20 July it was reported that the whole of the enemy's forces were concentrated at Boulogne, Wimereux and Ambleteuse. Stores of every description had been collected. A total number of 2,340 flat-bottomed transports were available at the Channel ports for 167,000 troops, of whom 93,000 were already at the waterside. The English were fully aware of the preparations. Coastal craft kept the flotillas of barges moving under cover of the shore batteries from Dunkirk to Boulogne under constant observation and attack. On 26 July Napoleon wrote to Villeneuve 'Make us the masters of the channel for the space of three days and with God's help I will put an end to the career and existence of England. 150,000 men are embarked in 2,000 vessels'.

Pitt, however, was all for attacking the enemy and not for waiting to be attacked. The Secretary of State for War was asked to produce some figures and on 1 August 1805 the commander-in-chief advised Lord Castlereagh in a 'most secret' despatch that there were 20,613 rank and file infantry and 13,689 cavalry in Great Britain, who were all now stationed 'upon the coast between Harwich and Portsmouth except for two regiments at Weymouth Camp during the King's residence there but can be brought back again at any moment'. All these men were ready to leave for France from within one to five days. If this force was embarked advised the Duke of York, the number of troops, including militia but excluding volunteers, left to defend Great Britain would total 79,991 infantry and 5,335 cavalry.

On 3 August Napoleon reached Boulogne. 'They little guess what is in store for them,' he wrote to Decrès, his Minister of Marine. 'If we are masters of the straits for twelve hours England is no more.' Only two things were required — a calm sea and Villeneuve's fleet. On 7 August he summoned the Imperial Guard to Boulogne. Next day he countermanded the order. Nelson was reported from Cadiz to be back in Europe and to have been sailing north. For once Napoleon was in two minds. Talleyrand, convinced that he would have to face a superior British concentration in the Channel, was urging him not to risk a crossing. Yet Napoleon felt that no better opportunity might present itself for invading England. The indecisive Battle of Finisterre between Calder and Villeneuve claimed by both sides as a victory prompted instructions to the French Admirals Villeneuve and Ganteaume to hurry north.

Until the middle of August Napoleon seemed set on invasion, then learning that Villeneuve had entered harbour at Ferrol and that Ganteaume had failed to leave Brest, he altered the plan of his campaign and ordered the Grande Armée to strike camp and head for Austria.

---

*For example, in 1816 200 navigators were employed in excavating 18½ miles of the Wey of Arun Junction Canal.

6. Painting of Hythe by unknown artist *c.*1806.
The barracks built 1808-1810 are not shown, but the house, garden and land purchased
from the Board of Ordnance in 1809 for the use of the commandant of the Royal
Staff Corps can be seen below the church. The newly built martello towers, no's 10,11
and 12 were demolished in the nineteenth century. No. 10 stood near the present day
Imperial Hotel. Scanlons Bridge is visible in the foreground.

The greatest moment of danger had passed but the emperor's victory
at Ulm in September did nothing to reduce the uncertainty and because
of the seriousness of the situation, some 1,500 navigators continued to be
employed on the Hythe Canal until October when the weather turning
wet, it became impossible to keep the troops under canvas. Recourse was
then had to employing navigators or professional canal diggers under
the direction of George Jones, the civil superintendent, who had been
recommended by Rennie at the start of the work and having proved himself
'highly useful', continued to be employed at a salary of £400 per annum.

The fear of imminent invasion having evaporated, Fox wrote to Grey
on 28 August confidently remarking 'The alarm of invasion here was most
certainly a groundless one, and raised for some political purpose by the
ministers,' and Lord Ellenborough writing from Ramsgate on 20 October
to his friend Viscount Sidmouth, the former Prime Minister, Henry
Addington, commented that he felt the money being spent on defence
schemes an appalling waste of public money.

I have just taken a ramble along the coast, and see the great dyke, or canal,
near Hythe, of which about fourteen miles are completed out of thirty six.

It will cost an enormous sum of money, and be, in my poor judgment, of no adequate use. An invading enemy will, by means of fascines, get over it in any part they please in a very short time. The martello towers may be of some use, but the expense of the various works, barracks &c. &c in every part of the county, is perfectly appalling. The wanton waste of public money which presents itself to view in every direction must soon undo us in point of finance, as some late measures have irretrievably done in point of fame.* I long to resume my personal communications with your Lordship on the most critical and interesting situation of public concern both at home and abroad. The gloom of the present moment is not illumined with a single ray of comfort. God send us a better fate than we, I fear, deserve.[17]

Although Nelson's victory at Trafalgar in October crushed Villeneuve's fleet, Napoleon's decisive victory at Austerlitz early in December, left Britain's position as serious as ever. On 13 January Hawkesbury and Castlereagh reported to the dying prime minister the seriousness of the situation and the need to recall the army from Germany. Eleven days later Pitt was dead and the news from abroad was one of unrelieved defeat.

Work on the canal proceeded during the greater part of the winter with tolerable success. Notwithstanding, however, that three steam-engines were kept constantly pumping it became impossible to keep the canal free of water. In March 1806 heavy rain so flooded the whole excavation that work had to be abandoned for several weeks. In spite of the setbacks the eastern and most vital section of the canal was bottomed and 10 miles of navigation established by April 1806 but not for long apparently, for Lieutenant-General Alexander Todd later wrote that 'the whole of the excavation from Hythe downwards lay dry for many months'.[18] The fine weather enabled work on the remainder of the excavation to proceed rapidly and the 20 miles of channel from Shorncliffe to the Rother was completed in July.

Immediately after Napoleon had marched for Ulm and Austerlitz, Moore was asked to report on the possibility of landing near Boulogne to destroy the invasion fleet. On 29 September 1805 Moore was on board the *Antelope* off Boulogne with Sir Sidney Smith, and consequently reported to Pitt that any attempt of landing would have been attended with too much risk to justify the experiment.

During March 1806 Moore now promoted Lieutenant-General, had been complaining of inactivity. 'You know how tired I have for some time been of my employment here,' he wrote to his mother, 'I see little prospect of England ever being occupied in any manner more important. I never believed

---

* Neglect in providing adequate defence measures was a main cause of the collapse of Addington's administration.

in invasion and now less than ever.' Some weeks later Moore was appointed Military Adviser to General Fox, and in June he left England for Sicily. Brown was not to meet him again before his death at Corunna on 16 January 1809.

At the end of August the commander-in-chief, the Duke of York, together with his brother the Duke of Cambridge, inspected the canal from Hythe to the coffer dam at Iden, a distance of some 18 miles — in a small boat towed by relays of horses in 2¾ hours — an average speed of nearly 7 mph. Although the rampart and military road had still to be built, in the space of twenty-two months from the cutting of the first sod, the canal had been filled and a tolerable work of defence established.

While the military canal was in progress, the Ordnance had been building a line of fortifications along the shore but by 1806 only six had been completed. The construction of the martello towers had created a tremendous demand for bricks and building materials and consequently 'the few bricks which would be procured from London at an enormous price were applied' to building culverts to carry streams and drainage ditches beneath or into the canal. As a result the wooden bridges over the canal had had to be built without brick abutments.

As the work proceeded it became essential to fence the canal on both sides. This was done partly by an oak paling (purchased of Mr Waddell of Warehorne), partly by fence drains and completed as far as the Rother by the winter of 1806.

The canal's water supply was controlled by means of an oak trunk of great dimensions between the canal at Shorncliffe and the sea. This trunk was laid lower than the bottom of the canal. It was 25 ft in diameter, 300 ft long and made of 4 in oak plank strongly secured with piles and furnished with double draw gates to allow salt water into the canal and let off superfluous water.

During the summer of 1806 the carpenters of the Royal Staff Corps constructed at Hythe eight flat-bottomed barges and two boats of fir plank to enable 200 to 300 tons of shingle a day to be transported from the beach at Hythe to cover the military road and tow-path. The canal could not be opened to the public until this work had been completed and by the autumn of 1807 only 10 miles of wood and 12 miles of tow-path had been covered. There was also the need to link the canal to the Rother Navigation and Rye Harbour. The building of Iden lock (or as it was known locally the Royal Military lock) was begun in October 1807. Quoin and coping stones were procured from Dundee but great difficulty was experienced with the foundations, 300 loads of timber in piles from 25 to 30 ft long were required. Elm trees bought from Russell & Wilmot of Lewisham began to be planted on the banks in November.

The canal from Winchelsea through Pett Level to Cliff End was executed as a field work under the direction of Lt-Col William Nicolay of the Royal Staff Corps at a cost of £28,975 up to 30 June 1807. Although useable by barges, it had no navigable connection with the river Brede at Winchelsea. Nicolay had served as an engineer in India under Lord Cornwallis and in St Lucia under Sir John Moore. Having broken his thigh while in the West Indies, he had been obliged to return to England, and for nearly two years he remained unfit for duty; and then in 1801 he was made a major in the Staff Corps, being promoted Lt-Col in April 1805.*

The greater part of the land was taken under the powers of the Defence Act. Within the boundary of Romney Marsh 262 acres had been taken and seven landowners, including William Deedes,† Sir John Honeywood and Colonel Mackenzie, had each lost over ten acres. This proved a troublesome duty in view of the number and various descriptions of people who had to be dealth with, 'and not without serious apprehension of vexatious opposition as it was not always practicable to obtain in due time the requisite certificate, a circumstance most particularly felt in the Sussex part of the line'. Some property also had to be demolished in Hythe. In December 1804 Brown reported that he had entered into agreements with several persons for their premises in Hythe to be paid for before the 15th 'provided the houses are cleared away by this time'.

No payments were, however, made and in June 1806 the owners and occupiers, anxious for payment, assembled at Hythe to discuss the position with Brigadier Hope, the Deputy Quartermaster-General, and Mr William Harrison, the government's counsel. Brigadier Hope explained that due to the great delay, trouble and expense which would arise in summoning so many juries to ascertain 300 or 400 claims from individuals lying in different jurisdictions

> the government had determined at their own expense to employ a surveyor of respectability to value the whole and to estimate the damages, which valuation would be offered to each individual claimant. In the event of acceptance, the money would be immediately paid. On the other hand those who might object to the valuation would ultimately have their claims referred to a jury, but it was hoped these cases would be few.

---

* Nicolay had a distinguished career. On returning from the Peninsular War in 1808, he remained the Commanding Officer of the R.S.C. at Hythe until April 1815 when he took five R.S.C. companies to the Netherlands and was present at the Battle of Waterloo. He became Maj-Gen in 1819 and Lt-Gen in 1837 when he was knighted.

† The Deedes family had long been associated with Hythe. His epitaph in the parish church reads "When the Coast was threatened with invasion, he remained at his post in the fearless discharge of all his public and private duties".

7. Sandling Park, Hythe, 1829, the seat of William Deedes Sandling Park (Sandlands) possessed 1,400 acres. The mansion, designed by Bonomi in the late eighteenth century was badly damaged by enemy action in 1942 and later demolished.

The meeting agreed this proposal but many principal proprietors were not present although 'it was conjectured that they tacitly acquiesced'. Mr Wickens 'a surveyor of great respectability' was employed and the valuation completed in January 1807. In April the quartermaster-general was authorised to offer the valuation to each proprietor for immediate settlement with interest of 5 per cent on the purchase money calculated from the time the land was occupied in lieu of rent. One-third of the proprietors accepted the award and Brown was authorised by the lords of the Treasury to satisfy their claims, but the solicitor employed to inquire into the title deeds, not being satisfied, no sums had been paid on account of land at the time the commissioners were appointed.

On 30 April 1807 a meeting took place at the Guildhall in Hythe of those landowners, being two-thirds of the most opulent, which resolved that a list of points should be raised with the quartermaster-general. There were complaints that the wet and dry fences bordering the canal were in many places insufficient, and that as a result cattle had been frequently impounded, and that adjoining landowners should be allowed full and free use of the tow-path and military road. A further meeting was held on 16 July at which some 30 people agreed that they should appoint their own valuer to meet Mr Wickens and that a third person should act as arbitrator. To this proposal the government agreed and hoped that 'this

$\mathcal{A}$T a numerous Meeting of the Owners and Occupiers of the Land, taken for the use of the ROYAL MILITARY CANAL, and others, interested therein, holden at the Guildhall, at Hythe, this Day.

The following RESOLUTIONS were unanimously agreed to:—

Resolved, That the wet and dry Fences on each side the line of the Canal, are in many places insufficient, from the circumstances of the Cattle having been frequently impounded.

Resolved, That the Owners and Occupiers of the Land adjoining to, or near the Canal, ought to have the free and full use of the towing Path and Military Road, for the purposes of the occupation of such Lands; and that in cases where the Parties are deprived of all communication with their Land, Government should provide them with a Road.

Resolved, That agreeable to the assurance given by Mr. Pitt, at the first Meeting at Dymchurch, that the Lords of the Level of Romney Marsh, and the Commissioners of Walland Marsh, should be indemnified for the loss of Scots arising from the Land occupied by the Canal; and that Parishes and Tythe Owners should be also indemnified for the losses they may sustain.

Resolved, That it appears necessary to this Meeting, that a Culvert be put down to the Westward of Bonnington, on the North side of the Canal, to take off the Water from the Hills; and that provision be made for the occasional supply of Water from the Canal, for the use of the Marsh, when it does not interfere with public purposes.

Resolved, That all expences arising from making out the Titles and Conveyances of such Lands, should be at the expence of Government, and in case any delay should arise from the consideration of the Titles, or otherwise, interest should be allowed up to the time at which the principal is paid.

Resolved, That provision should be made for reducing the Land Tax, charged on those Districts through which the Canal passes, in proportion to the Sum charged on the Land taken for the Canal.

Resolved, That it is the opinion of this Meeting, that the remuneration offered to the Occupiers for the damages they have sustained, is generally insufficient.

Resolved, That it is the opinion of this Meeting, that it is impossible to give any answer to the proposal made by Government, to the Owners and Occupiers of Land, as a remuneration for the Land taken, and damages sustained by them, until they are informed of the sentiments of Government on the foregoing Resolutions.

Resolved, That the Chairman be requested to transmit these Resolutions forthwith to Colonel Browne; and to call a Meeting whenever it appears to be necessary.

WM. DEEDES, Chairman.

April 30th, 1807.

Bristow and Cowtan, Printers, Canterbury, 1807.

most troublesome and vexatious part of the business may be finally adjusted'. The proprietors apparently 'although many of them highly respectable, appeared to be of a mind to obtain remuneration far beyond the damages they have actually sustained.'

This then was the position when the government decided to pass an Act to establish the maintenance and preservation of the canal and road and to authorise rates of toll and their collection. Presented in July, the Bill passed both Houses without amendment in less than a month and received the Royal Assent on 13 August 1807. Up to 31 August the total expenditure had been £143,081 excluding compensation for damages to property, etc.; but although partially complete as a work of defence, the

WILLIAM DEEDES Esquire.	A.	R.	P.	A.	R.	P.
Part of Two Fields lying on the East Side of the Ladies Walk, near Hithe, in the Occupation of George Portwine	1	3	38			
A Part of a Field close to the Town of Hithe, on the East Side of Marrowbone Park, Mr. Andrew Tenant	1	1	16			
Marrowbone Park, adjoining the former, including the new Road, occupied by Mr. Eaton	1	1	17			
Part of Two Fields, commonly called the Duke's Head Fields, occupied by William Winter	3	1	17			
Adjoining to Mr. Harrison's Barn, lying on the West Side of Ditto, and occupied by William Harrison	1	2	15			
Part of a Field joining the last, on the West Side, occupied by Thomas Marshall	1	1	5			
Part of a Field bounded on the East by Mr. Fenner's Field, and on the West by that of Filmer Honeywood Esquire, commonly called the Long Field, occupied by William Harrison	6	2	17			
Part of a small Field lying near the Road to Butterbridge, occupied by William Shingleton	0	3	20			
Part of a Field lying on the South Side of the Butterbridge Road, occupied by Mr. William Harrison	2	1	0			
Part of a Field near West Hithe, in the Parish of Lymne, occupied by Henry Tilbey Esquire	2	3	30			
Part of a Field lying on the West Side of Honey-pot Lane, occupied by Mr. Mount	3	2	0			
Part of a Field near Jigger's Green, Henry Tilbey Tenant	3	1	4			
Part of a Field adjoining to Mr. Dunk's Property, in the Parish of Bonnington, Henry Tilbey Esquire Tenant	1	2	33			
Acres Roads Perches				32	12	0

August 1807

Royal Military Canal was as yet unlinked to Rye Harbour and unfortified. At the same time the Emperor Napoleon was at the zenith of his power, engaged in securing the Peace of Tilsit (7 July) with the Tsar of Russia, and anxious to revive his crippled navy. The defeat of Trafalgar could be mitigated by the Danish fleet being at his disposal in which case the danger of invasion would not have passed. However, Britain's newly-appointed Foreign Secretary, George Canning, forewarned of the Tsar's intentions, at once dispatched an expedition to Copenhagen to offer our alliance to Denmark. The Danes refused. Copenhagen was bombarded and for the second time her fleet was carried off by force. Meanwhile, Decrès had been sent to visit all the ports where the invasion flotilla was still lying and had found the harbours badly silted and no more than 300 of the multitude of boats in a serviceable state.[19]

Napoleon's plan for securing the Danish navy having been frustrated, he ordered Junot to capture the Portuguese fleet in the Tagus. But on the very day that Junot arrived, the fleet set sail with the royal family and 18,000 Portuguese. And so the means with which Napoleon might have regained a navy had disappeared by the end of November 1807, and with it even the contemplation of an invasion of the British shore.

8. Charles Abbot.

chapter 4

The Completion of the Royal Military Canal (1807–1809)

Meetings of the commissioners—appointment of Rickman as secretary—
details of work to be completed—dispute with Hythe Corporation over
removal of beach—the Winchelsea section—construction and completion
of military road—opening of Iden lock (1808)—movement of troops
by barge—great storm of 18 November 1808—building of barracks at
Hythe— 'red tape' and the appointment of a barrack master—attack on
public conduct of Colonel Brown—problem of wives and children—
disputes over compensation—High Knock Channel—cannons and side
arms—summary of building costs.

The commissioners appointed to administer the canal included the Speaker
of the House of Commons, the Prime Minister, the Chancellor of the
Exchequer, the Principal Secretaries of State, the commander-in-chief of
His Majesty's Forces, the lord warden of the Cinque ports, the secretary at
war, the master-general of the Ordnance and the quartermaster-general for
the time being. No canal in history was ever controlled by so distinguished
a body of men. Six of them attended the first meeting on 15 September
1807. Spencer Perceval,* Chancellor of the Exchequer and future Prime
Minister, Lord Hawkesbury, Principal Secretary of State, Lord Warden of
the Cinque Ports and future Prime Minister, His Royal Highness Frederick,
Duke of York, Sir James Pulteney, the Secretary at War and Major-General
Brownrigg, the Quartermaster-General. Charles Abbot, Speaker of the
House of Commons took the chair.

---

* Perceval became Prime Minister in 1809 but continued to remain Chancellor of the
Exchequer. He was assassinated in 1812 in the precincts of the House of Commons.

9. Spencer Perceval.
(*Above left*) Spencer Perceval (1762-1812) supported Pitt in Parliament, chancellor of the Exchequer 1807, prime minister 1809, assassinated 1812.

10. Lord Hawkesbury, 1808.
(*Above right*) Lord Hawkesbury (1784-1851) later third earl of Liverpool, MP Sandwich (1807-12), undersecretary for Home Department (1807-9).

11. The Duke of Wellington.
(*Above left*) Duke of Wellington (1769-1852) MP Rye 1806, commanded army in the Peninsula (1808-1814), won Waterloo 1815, commander-in-chief 1827-8,1842-52, prime minister 1828-30, lord warden of Cinque Ports 1829-52.

12. George Canning.
(*Above right*) George Canning (1770-1827) foreign secretary 1807-9, prime minister 1827.

The meetings of the commissioners were held once a year either at the Speaker's house or at Horse Guards (except for one occasion in 1829 when the Duke of Wellington was present and they assembled at 10 Downing Street), and sometimes more often until 1832 after which they were only held biennially. Some of the most famous politicians of the time, including seven Prime Ministers, gave their advice on how to run the canal. A glance at Appendix C on page 209 reveals the names of Liverpool and Wellington, Castlereagh and Canning, Palmerston and Peel. The former Prime Minister, Henry Addington, now Lord Sidmouth, also regularly took part from 1812 to 1821 when Secretary of State for the home department. The Duke of York attended very meeting until his death in 1827 except for the two years when he was forced to temporarily relinquish his position as Commander-in-Chief over the Clarke affair.*

John Rickman was appointed secretary to the board for the purpose of keeping an account of the proceedings of the commissioners and it is largely due to him that the early part of the canal's history is so well documented. Another of his duties was to present the account of the tolls received each year to both Houses of Parliament. Rickman (1771–1840) was a statistician, who after taking his BA at Lincoln College, Oxford in 1792, became secretary to the speaker and had been employed in preparing the first census report of 1801. More relevant to his new duties was the fact that he had been chosen in 1803 to be secretary to the parliamentary committees for the making of roads and bridges in Scotland and for the construction of the Caledonian Canal. Rickman received a not ungenerous £150 p.a. for his services; the remuneration of the accountant, Alexander Swan, was fixed at £400 p.a.

The first meeting of the commissioners was devoted to listening to the quartermaster-general's account of the formation of the canal and military road, together with an estimate of the expense for their completion. There was still much to be done — so far only a third of the military road and the tow-path had been covered with shingle — to cover the remainder of road to a depth of 12 in and the tow-path with 6 in would entail moving 158,400 tons of shingle at a cost of around £12,000. There was a need, they thought, to fence the road from the parapet by a paling fence on the edge of the banquette (see plan) for which the estimate was £5,000. The tendency of the sandy banks to crumble — particularly between Appledore

---

* Colonel Wardle, M.P., furnished with information by a vindictive and disreputable woman, Mrs Mary Anne Clarke, who had been the Duke of York's mistress, accused the duke of corruption which was in reality practised by Mrs Clarke herself, and a committee of the House of Commons acquitted the duke of the charges. Public opinion, however, was so deeply stirred that the duke felt it necessary to resign in 1809. (G. Grant Robertson, *A History of England—England under the Hanoverians*.)

and the Rother — made it expedient to secure them with wicker work for which £2,000 was allowed. £8,000 was required for barracks and stabling at Hythe. Guard houses (known as station houses) were required to be built at each bridge to prevent smuggling and to protect the banks from willful injury. A culvert had to be laid beneath the canal between Bonnington and Bilsington to carry the muddy water from the hills as the present channel was found to be silting up the canal. The twenty or so temporary timber bridges had also to be replaced and a substantial bridge was also required to carry the military road over the Rother. The government granted financial assistance of £63,393 for 1808 and £20,800 for 1809 to meet the cost of this work.

The expense of maintaining the canal was initially higher because of the time required for the rampart to settle, the road to become hard and the banks to become consolidated with reeds, rushes or wicker work. Future annual expenditure on maintenance was provisionally put at £6,000 per annum.

The beach for covering the road and tow-path was only freely available,* until the opening of Iden lock, in the vicinity of Hythe and this had been taken from the waste ground without difficulty until a letter arrived from the town clerk of Hythe on 16 June 1807 drawing attention to the fact that this land belonged to the corporation and demanding compensation of 1d a ton for the shingle. A tactful letter from John Brown drew attention to the fact that 'the commissioners of public roads and others had been taking beach from the same place time out of mind without remuneration' and that as they had been doing so for over two years without obstruction, he had not imagined that 'any feeling of this sort could exist on the part of the corporation and I take this opportunity of assuring them that omission on my part was from a sense of public duty and no way meant disrespectful to them'. This was followed by a stiff letter from the Treasury solicitor on 5 September offering to negotiate on proof of title of the beach in question and threatening to resort to the Defence Act if need be 'as the liberty of taking this gravel cannot be dispensed with'. The town clerk replied on 8 September supporting their rights. The commissioners agreed to acknowledge these rights and left it to Colonel Brown to decide how best to procure future supplies of shingle. He reported in December that he had purchased a 7-acre beach field close to the canal at Hythe for £105.

A report dated 30 August 1807 from General Lord Charles Somerset, who then commanded the Sussex district, indicated that a very strong line of defence had been formed by the canal and the river Brede between

---

* The cost of delivery to Scots Float Sluice in 1808 was 1s 3d a ton.

Winchelsea and Rye, but that the right appui of this defence had not been completed. 'At present I could very easily ride over the bank where the work commences.' And when Brown took charge of this section in November 1807 he found that the canal was in a 'very rough and unfinished state', that part of the rampart had slipped in and that part of the road and tow-path had still to be made. A further problem was the ruinous condition of Rye lock at the entrance to the river Brede which was, however, repaired in the autumn of 1808.

The military road between Scots Float Sluice and Rye and the bridge across the Rother by Iden lock were completed in the spring of 1808. In June the commissioners had approved the building of ten intermediate stations for alternative detachments of infantry and cavalry and the purchase of seven or eight half-acre plots for building wharves on the opposite side of the tow-path. The tedious operation of making and covering the military road from Iden to Shorncliffe with shingle continued throughout the year. Ten barges — two more had been purchased in London — carrying from 20 to 30 tons were employed throughout the summer. Between June and October 25,000 to 30,000 tons of beach were transported from Hythe. The farther the road from Hythe, however, the more difficult and extensive its execution. Huts were constructed at Appledore for one officer and fifty men of the Lincoln Regiment, who were stationed there and at Iden, to unload the barges and spread the beach on the road. A detachment of the Royal Waggon Train was also stationed at Warehorne to relieve the horses and forward the barges to Appledore. By October when the drafts from the Waggon Train were sent to assist Sir Arthur Wellesley in Portugal half the width of the road for its whole length had received one coat of beach 10 in deep. During 1809 the full width of 30 ft was covered for 10 miles 'which has employed the boats and horses that could be spared the greater part of the summer,' and the remainder with a thinner coat by raking over the covered half; 20 miles of oak fencing from Hythe to Scots Float had been erected. The road was opened to the public during the latter part of the year but Brown pointed out that it would be a great while before it became a good road, and advised that tolls should not be initially demanded as 'beach roads are for a long time very soft and heavy, and are only made hard and smooth by use'.

The completion and opening of Iden lock in September 1808 linked the canal with the Rother Navigation and Rye Harbour. One immediate benefit was the availability of a more convenient source of shingle for the military road around Appledore, and this could be obtained near Rye without payment. The lock at Iden consisted of three pairs of large gates — an unusual number necessitated by the rise and fall of the Rother

Navigation. The two pairs of gates adjoining the river could act as lower or upper gates as required. A swivel drawbridge crossed the lock to avoid the tow-path being interrupted. The quartermaster-general reported that the completion of the lock did credit to Captain Todd and the artificers of the Royal Staff Corps who built it. 'It also affords a satisfactory proof,' added Brownrigg, rather pointedly, 'that difficult works may be executed without the assistance of a civil engineer;' Six months later the quartermaster-general advised the commissioners that

> government barges are now passing and repassing from Rye Harbour to all parts of the line as occasion requires. The advantages of the Navigation Sluice, as connected with military operations, are great as the facility with which the canal can be supplied upon any emergency with sea water, is now quadrupled from the capacities of the lock gates; the canal may be overflowed in one quarter of the time which it could have been by means of the trunk at Shorncliffe alone, and the sea now acting from both ends, there is no doubt entertained, that the effect of one spring tide, would make an island of Romney Marsh an advantage which was originally foreseen and fully appreciated, by the great and ever to be lamented, promoter of the work. (William Pitt.)

The battle of Corunna had taken place in January 1809 by which time over one hundred vessels, escorted by a dozen men-of-war, had arrived to evacuate the British troops from Spain. On 16th January, Sir John Moore while supervising the rearguard on horse back at Elvina, was struck by round shot and died that night in Corunna. An eyewitness reported that when the companies marched to embark straight from the battlefield, the soldiers with their uniforms all in tatters, hollow-eyed and covered in blood and filth, had so terrified the onlookers as they passed through the streets that they made the sign of the cross.

Captain Harry Smith of the Rifles said on his arrival at Portsmouth that, so exhausted were the men on his ship that they had fallen asleep and not woken during the three days and nights of their hazardous passage.* The troops returned at irregular intervals at almost every harbour between Falmouth and Dover. Those landed at Rye bound for Hythe or Dover were fortunate as the canal now afforded the means of conveying large bodies of troops between Kent and Sussex. Brownrigg reported in April 1809 that 'part of the troops, recently returned from Spain, on their march from

---

* Carola Oman, *Sir John Moore*, 1953 p. 605.

Sussex into Kent, have with their baggage, been conveyed in four hours from the lock on the Rother to Hythe, thus performing the march from Rye to Hythe in one day which before always occupied two'. He went on to add that 'if extraordinary expedition is at any time required troops from Dover can reach Hastings or Battle (a distance of forty miles) in one day, being conveyed twenty miles of that extent by the canal'. Brown, giving oral evidence to the commissioners of military enquiry in July 1809, stated that this facility saved the public expense and was a convenience to the neighbourhood by relieving a large district from having to provide quarters and carriages. Troops leaving Dover early in the morning reached Rye the same day 'with great ease' instead of taking three days.

Compton & Carr-Gomm have included a chapter in their account of *The Military on English Waterways* (see bibliography) giving details of troops carried on the canal. In 1809 they totalled 4,740 of whom 1,427 were from the King's German Legion and 852 from the Shropshire Militia. The number fell to 2,919 and 1,285 in the following years but in 1813 the figure rose to 1,644 with the need to transport Irish militia between Dover and Portsmouth to assist the Duke of Wellington in his Peninsular Campaign. After the departure of Napoleon to the island of Elba no major movements of troops used the canal and only occasional use is identified. Altogether a total of over 11,500 troops movements are recorded between 1809 and 1818.

There was nearly a major disaster in the autumn. During a great storm in 18 November 1808, the sea broke in near Shorncliffe and flooded the country as far as West Hythe. The south bank of the canal was destroyed — in some places by as much as 4 ft — for nearly 2 miles, as a wave of water 5 ft high entered the canal and rushed westwards. Colonel Brown was at once alerted of the danger by the detachment at Shorncliffe and a messenger sent post haste to warn the lockkeeper at Iden. He arrived just in time for the gates to be opened to allow the water to pour into the Rother. The most troublesome part of the work was removing the immense quantity of earth and rubbish which had been washed into the canal, and for this purpose 'scoops of large dimensions were contrived and wrought by means of portable cranes placed on the banks'. As each scoop could hold half a ton and they were worked in sets of two or three by teams of men the enormity of the operation can be imagined, yet within months the canal was back in working order. The government bought the land where the sea broke in, and built the present sea embankment between Marine and Town Bridge, Hythe, but before it could be finished the sea broke in again on 30 January 1809; great quantities of beach were thrown into the canal but the half completed embankment prevented more serious damage.[1]

At the end of 1808 the director of works dispensed with the services of George Jones. His work was now done. After the canal had been dug he had continued to assist Mr Wickens and later the arbitrator, with the task of assessing compensation for loss of property, as well as making occupation roads.

In 1805 the commander-in-chief had decided that to lessen as much as possible the future expense of maintaining the canal, the Royal Staff Corps and part of the Royal Waggon Train should be stationed at Hythe. A site was found on the borders of the canal but in consequence of some flaw in the Defence Act, the lord warden of the Cinque ports could not give the necessary certificates and the proprietor having refused to treat, no progress could be made 'and the troops had to be lodged in hired barracks at a very heavy expense'. The commissioners granted the order for compulsory purchase in September 1807 and in January 1808 £2,641 was paid for the land on which to build the barracks at Hythe, whose cost was now estimated at £12,000 due to the 'extravagant price of memel timber'. The design of the building was on similar lines to the infantry barracks at Canterbury and was chosen as being 'airy, convenient and suitable to the ground'. The work was carried out by men and artificers of the Royal Staff Corps assisted by masons, bricklayers and labourers. In June the roofs were covered in with Bangor slates brought from Rye by barges.

The soldiers' barracks were completed early in 1809; each room contained twelve men and was equipped with bedsteads 'of a new construction' and furniture made by the Staff Corps. However, they could not be occupied 'because the commissioners for the affairs of barracks declined to make the usual issue of coals, candles and straw unless the buildings were delivered over exclusively to their charge. The correspondence dragged on for nine months. Then on 21 March 1810 the commander-in-chief himself proposed a plan for the issue of barrack stores which he hoped the lords of His Majesty's treasury would sanction. As a result a barrack master was appointed to be responsible for all issues including the repair and cleaning of bedding and since Alexander Swan the accountant was 'a proper person' and resided at Hythe, he was appointed to do the duty of barrack master in April 1810 for all barracks and stations upon the line of the canal. For this work he was granted an allowance of house rent, an extra £100 per annum salary and allowed to draw coals and candles at the rate of 5s a day. Swan, once described by Brown as a 'respectable officer and man of business', had been a trifle unlucky in March when there had been an inquiry over a supposed duplicate payment for land purchase; the commissioners were 'satisfied that no criminal negligence is imputable to Mr Swan in this supposed mistake' — but that seeing nevertheless that mistakes like this could occur unless some effectual check was established, Mr Swan had now to introduce a system of

13. Turner's painting of the Royal Staff Corps Barracks, Hythe.
J. M. W. Turner's view of the Barracks in 1824. Two lines of troops are ranged for
inspection while others ascend the hill to Saltwood Barracks. The cannon at the bottom
right of the picture appears to be aimed at the point where the Ashford road joins the
military road.

charge and discharge. Moreover, the Commissioner thought fit on this
occasion to caution Mr Swan about transmitting incomplete vouchers.

The officers' barracks were begun in May 1809 and completed twelve
months later. Their accommodation consisted of apartments for two field
officers, eight captains and twelve subalterns 'with a mess room, room for
drawing and kitchens behind; also store room, guard house, black-hole,
engine house etc'.

The delay in occupying the barracks caused more than usual mortification
for on the night of 9 January the regimental stores housed in a temporary
building on Hythe beach were burnt down. The officers lost much of their
baggage and the clothing of the companies on foreign service. The loss of
public property was put at £600.

It had been agreed in 1808 that the commandant of the Staff Corps
for the time being should be *ex-officio* the director of the Royal Military
Canal. Now John Brown had been in complete charge of the project since
Rennie had retired from the scene in June 1805 and since the remuneration
of a civil engineer had been saved, and perhaps more particularly because
'of the extraordinary zeal, ability and integrity with which Brown had
conducted the execution of the work,' the commissioners decided in April
1809 that he should be paid the very substantial sum of £3,000 for his work
in superintending the execution of the Royal Military Canal and for the

responsibility of acting as a public accountant from 1805 to 1808. This was a generous sum compared with his military pay and allowances which totalled £826 net in 1809, but the delay in authorising this payment may have had something to do with Robert Brownrigg's comments about his behaviour in April 1808. Writing to the Deputy Quartermaster-General, Sir Alexander Hope, about the whereabouts of martello towers, Brownrigg added

> by the bye I am very sorry to hear from more quarters than one of Brown being in a very uncomfortable state of health, that he is dejected and complains of nothing being done for him. I am concerned at this because I consider him a most valuable officer and have a high regard for him, and if I knew how to satisfy his expectations I would do my utmost to have them gratified if they appeared reasonable. His health is the first consideration and I wish you would see that he is well advised about it.

Until the barracks were ready, Brown was also granted a lodging allowance of £136 p.a. and £50 p.a. for stationery and postage. In 1809 a house and garden and a small field valued at £1,730, formerly belonging to the Board of Ordnance and adjoining the barracks was purchased for the residence of the commandant of the Royal Staff Corps. Here Brown took up residence in June.

What the quartermaster-general termed 'a most unjust and unmerited attack on the public conduct of Lt-Col. Brown' took place during the winter of 1808. Richard Shipden, a shopkeeper and magistrate of Hythe libelled the conduct and character of the director of works in an announcement inserted in the *Canterbury News*, but on the advice of the Attorney-General proceedings against Shipden for his libel were 'abandoned upon public motives'. The commissioners directed that all law charges should be paid by the Crown. I can find no reference to Shipden's allegations. It seems possible that Brown may have been inclined to treat the town of Hythe as more of a military depot than a market town and that such an attitude was resented by some of its citizens, in spite of the fact that Britain was at war.

The canal's first income came from cutting the hay along the parapet which was sold in 1807 for £100, but this did not pay half the expense of making and collecting it. Several used steam engines and a considerable amount of builders' paraphernalia was disposed of for £853. In 1808 and 1809 the parapet was mowed several times and sold on the ground and large quantities of stable dung sold for a total of £220.

In March 1808 the Ham Street road commissioners' request that beach gravel might be carried along the canal for their use was refused by the commissioners on the ground that only military barges were to be used until the work was perfectly finished and protected. It was, however, arranged that 200 tons should be deposited at Ham Street bridge for which £25 was paid. A delivery of 100 tons was also made to Appledore for £15. In 1808 shingle, timber and other articles were conveyed in military boats or boats hired for the purpose, which produced a revenue of £130. Brown, when giving oral evidence to the commissioners of military enquiry in July said that 'generally speaking neither the canal nor the road has yet been open to the public, but permission has been given to some individuals to convey beach and other articles by the canal, they agreeing to pay the tolls when fixed by the commissioners'.[2]

In April 1809 the first guard house was erected at Hythe bridge under the charge of a sergeant to serve both as a town guard and station on the canal and others built at Appledore, Ham Street, Ruckinge and West Hythe. However, this work had gone slowly due to a large number of Royal Staff Corps artificers being withdrawn for foreign service and also to the extraordinary high price of memel timber due to the general supplanting of Baltic by North American timber as a result of the Napoleonic blockade. Each of the intermediate stations could accommodate one nco and eight men 'they are of course, small but sufficient for the purpose' observed the Quarter Master General. In 1810 the commissioners agreed that guard houses for infantry only should be erected at all bridges across the canal from Hythe to Iden, where a subaltern was stationed to superintend the Cliff End section. A stone quay 40 ft long was also built for landing timber and other heavy articles at Shornecliffe.

A major problem was the question of compensation to those whose lands had been taken or interfered with by the building of the canal. So slow, however, was the payment of money for land purchase and damages that it was estimated in 1807 that over one-third of the total amount was still outstanding. William Deedes, MP, who lived at Sandling, proposed to the commissioners that payment of 5 per cent interest should continue to be paid after 1 January 1808 to the date of actual payment, but this they thought would involve a claim of considerable magnitude and was 'totally unnecessary, nor expected or looked for by the parties'. Consequently, both Mr E. J. Curteis and the trustees of Colonel Mackenzie went to court and lost their cases for interest payments. There were numerous disputes over the amounts of compensation payable, but in one or two cases, however, landowners asked to take a lesser sum than was offered. Lord Lownes asked to receive £199.95 for certain land instead of £213.15 to avoid a 'large expense in petitioning the court of Exchequer and in producing marriage settlements and deeds of entail' as was laid down in Section XXXVIII of the Act for payment of sums exceeding £200.

The military road from Iden lock to Rye passed under Playden Heights. Parts of the old toll road were raised 18 in as they were flooded at

Guard houses erected and to be erected at the Bridges

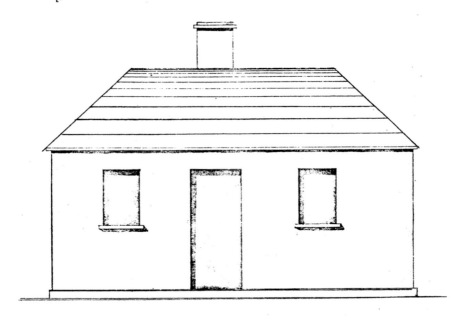

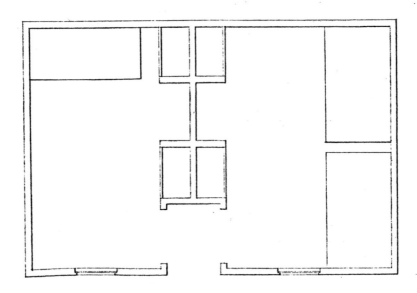

Scale 4 feet to an Inch.

spring tides, and at the same time widened from 14 to 30 ft. With the
military road completed, the owner of the former toll gate, Mr Curteis,
claimed £8,000 damages which 'appearing to Mr Wickens so excessivly
extravagant he declined giving any opinion'. The quartermaster-general
felt that £200 plus the value of the land taken for the road would be liberal
enough. Curteis also demanded remuneration for a ferry near Winchelsea
which Mr Wickens did not feel was entitled to any consideration. This
dispute like several others, dragged on and was eventually decided
by a jury in 1809 who awarded £2,900. There was, however, further
'disagreeable correspondence' with Curteis alleging injustice done him by
the commissioners but it appears that this was settled satisfactorily for the
minute ends 'He, in his individual capacity menaces no further hostility'.

A long correspondence also ensued between William Deedes and the
Director regarding the measurement and purchase of a large quantity of
oak timber from his estate. Deedes referred the matter to the commissioners
who offered £920 in compensation which he refused. Deedes then brought
an action against them. The trial was heard before Lord Ellenborough by
a special jury at Maidstone at the summer assizes in 1809 and a verdict
obtained in the commissioners' favour.

A total of £24,000 had been paid up to 1 June 1808 although at the
end of 1810 claims to the amount of nearly £5,000 were still unsettled
but as the delay was 'entirely attributable to the parties themselves, arising
from family disputes, the want of proper titles and other causes, many
years may elapse before these payments are finally closed'. In 1814 Sir
Edward Knatchbull finally accepted the offer made for his land taken in
1805 but still claimed an occupation road. The account presented to the
House of Lords on 24 May 1816 indicated that the total sum expended
in the purchase of land and for damages up to 30 April 1816 amounted
to £64,236. Not until 4 November 1822 was payment made of £1,169
to the estate of Mr J. H. Franks for 14 acres of meadow-land lying in Pett
Level 'on account of an Exchequer process' and the difficulties arising in
establishing a title; it was also reported that there were still remaining many
outstanding claims.[3] These still totalled £955 on 1 January 1830 so that the
total sum for purchase of land and compensation was probably £66,000.

The canal, had, of course, cut across a number of streams as well as
ditches and sewers, which had formerly drained into the marshes from the
hills. These had either been culverted or turned into the canal. In the case
of High Knock Channel, which drained the extensive tract of flat country
behind Appledore towards Woodchurch to the east and Small Hythe to
the west and which the canal had cut twice between Appledore and the
Rother, a new channel had been made at the back of the military road. The
commissioners of the Upper Levels of Romney Marsh, whose chairman at

that time was Sir Edward Knatchbull, complained in the summer of 1809 that this drain was insufficient and that it should be frequently cleared of weeds to prevent choking. A similar memorial was received from the commissioners of the Sussex Levels regarding the drainage of Pett Level. Col Brown replying that it would be extremely difficult to satisfy the 'extravagant expectations of the commissioners', proposed a lump sum payment to terminate the military's liability. This the commissioners refused and Brown gave orders for the channel to be cleared and widened throughout. The Royal Military Canal commissioners further agreed to pay 'scotts' from 1 January 1808 on condition that the commissioners for the Upper Levels maintained the channel. The commissioners for the Upper Levels held a meeting at Tenterden on 20 June 1810 at which the Royal Military Canal commissioners' proposals were rejected and further complaints registered, including one that the military breastwork had caused a dangerous bulge in Scots Float Sluice. The commissioners knew that the new complaints were 'utterly without foundation and arising from an individual always hostile to the Royal Military Canal' — the decay of Scots Sluices was notorious — but they wisely decided to obtain professional advice and invited Mr Rennie to report (see Chapter 5).

In April 1809 the Royal Military Canal could be said to be completed for the purposes of navigation and defence; the cannon emplacements had been prepared and only required to be armed for the defensive works to be in a state to meet any emergency. As has been described the canal and its parapets were built so that gun positions were provided at the end of each length to flank the crossings. The quartermaster-general had proposed that some 180 twelve- or eighteen-pounders should be placed in the depot at Hythe and Rye so that they would be available to arm these positions. At Iden it was intended that a battery should be set up with two cannons, one flanking the lock and the reach of canal leading to it, and the other the river Rother from the opposite bank. By 1810 74 martello towers had been built along the shore from Folkestone to Seaford.

Cannon and side arms were requested in April 1809 for the ramparts from the Board of Ordnance but they appear to have ignored the request for it had to be repeated the following year and on 14 September 1810 they claimed they had mislaid the letter. A copy was sent on 26 September to which the Ordnance replied on 10 July 1811 to say that they had ordered 80 Danish guns with their carriages and side arms to be supplied for the canal.

In the meantime, the inspector-general of fortifications was asked to prepare a project for closing the flanks of the canal at Shorncliffe and Cliff End. On 6 September the Ordnance wrote proposing to land the cannon at Rye but Brown suggested that they should wait until the spring as the season was thought to be too far advanced to land them at Shorncliffe.

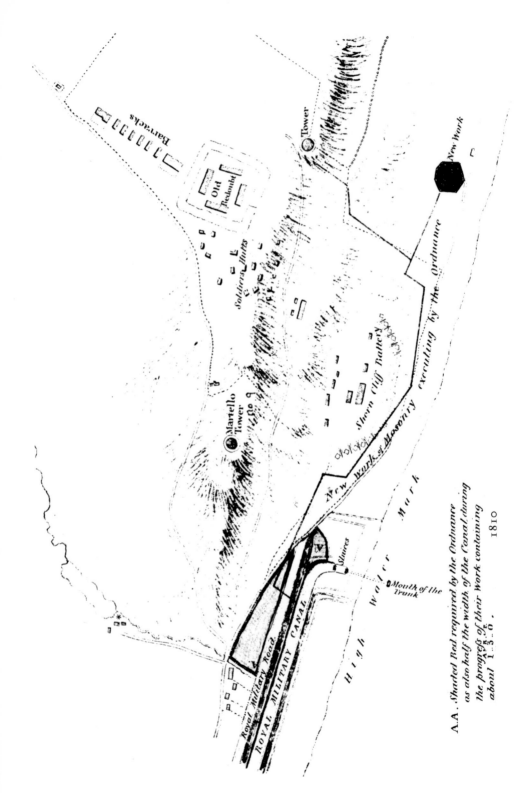

Plan of Shorncliffe Camp, 1810.

They were eventually delivered in July 1812 but the side arms and round shot were still awaited. In 1812 the defence of the left flank at Shorncliffe was completed by excavating the canal under a projecting escarpment to a depth of 22ft; a drawbridge was then built to carry the Hythe-Folkestone road across the cut. However, the contiguous battery begun by General Twiss in 1809 and intended to have twelve 24-pounders was left incomplete on the termination of the war.

The right flank at Cliff End was protected by martello towers 37 and 38 and the canal itself was scarfed into the cliff face so that the beach could only be reached by means of a wooden bridge. (This bridge was taken down in 1817 and an embankment made to carry a road over the canal to Dymchurch Wall.)

It seems strange that there should have been this difficulty but now that the threat of imminent invasion was over, artillery could be more usefully employed elsewhere. Admiral Gambier's victory at the second battle of Copenhagen in 1807 had resulted in the capture of the Danish fleet and it was their cannon which were eventually provided to defend the canal.

The actual cost of constructing all the works including the canal, towpath and military road from Shorncliffe to Cliff End, as well as such items as the building of the barracks at Hythe, but excluding the basic pay of the troops employed up to 31 December 1808, was as follows:

Expended by the contractors November 1804 — May 1805	10,500
Expended by Lt-Col. Brown 12.1.1805 to 30.6.1807	101,395
Expended by Lt-Col. Nicolay before 30.6.1807	28,975
Expended by Lt-Col. Brown 1.7.1807 to 31.12.1807	9,628
Expended by Lt-Col. Brown during 1808	17,812
Cost of land and payment of damages	66,000
	£234,310[4]

In November 1804 when it had been hoped to complete the canal by 1 June 1805, the commander-in-chief had estimated the total cost at £200,000, of which the expense of cutting was estimated at £150,000. It will, therefore, be seen how well Colonel Brown had succeeded in keeping within this rough estimate; if the works had been carried out by a civilian contract or the cost would have been nearly double.

For one fleeting moment in 1811 Napoleon did revive the idea of invasion by planning to spend two millions francs on repairing the flotilla;[5] but nothing was done and after his return from Moscow little more than the ruined frames of prams and pinnaces, half-buried in mud along the river banks of Northern France, remained as evidence of the emperor's wishful plans.

Appendix,
(No. 68.)
28° *Julii.*

ACCOUNT of Sums expended in the Formation of The ROYAL MILITARY CANAL, from Shorncliffe, in the County of Kent, to Cliffs End, in the County of Suffex, to the 30th June 1807.

To Amount of Difburfements for the various Services of that part of the Royal Military Canal, extending from Shorncliffe to Rye, within the under-mentioned periods refpectively; per Abftracts and Vouchers of the fame, fubmitted Monthly to the Comptrollers of Army Accounts; viz.

	£.	s.	d.
From 12th January to 28th February 1805 inclufive	1,208	2	—
From the 1ft to the 31ft day of March — —	121	4	7
From - 1ft to the 30th day of April — —	33	19	1
From - 1ft to the 31ft day of May — —	768	19	7
From - 1ft to the 30th day of June — —	1,042	—	2¾
From - 1ft to the 31ft day of July — —	9,906	16	3
From - 1ft to the 31ft day of Auguft — —	8,560	14	10¼
From - 1ft to the 30th day of September —	5,541	3	4¼
From - 1ft to the 31ft day of October —	6,984	3	3
From - 1ft to the 30th day of November —	6,147	13	4½
From - 1ft to the 31ft day of December —	2,524	14	11
From - 1ft to the 31ft day of January 1806 —	4,915	5	11½
From - 1ft to the 28th day of February —	2,311	19	4¼
From the 1ft to the 31ft day of March 1806 inclufive	3,695	4	1
From - 1ft to the 30th day of April — —	2,269	10	1¼
From - 1ft to the 31ft day of May — —	5,101	14	3
From - 1ft to the 30th day of June — —	7,637	7	11
From - 1ft to the 31ft day of July — —	6,040	3	4¾
From - 1ft to the 31ft day of Auguft — —	9,801	15	6¾
From - 1ft to the 30th day of September —	4,556	10	9¼
From - 1ft to the 31ft day of October —	3,649	16	4½
From - 1ft to the 30th day of November —	2,299	9	11¾
From - 1ft to the 31ft day of December —	4,404	2	8
From - 1ft to the 31ft day of January 1807 —	176	8	1½
From - 1ft to the 28th day of February —	702	13	6¼
From - 1ft to the 31ft day of March — —	356	2	11½
From - 1ft to the 30th day of April — —	529	7	8¼
From - 1ft to the 31ft day of May — —	133	8	8
From - 1ft to the 30th day of June — —	882	6	—¾
£.	101,892	19	—¾
Deduct therefrom the Amount received for a ufed Steam Engine, certain Tools and Beds fold to the Workmen, &c. already accounted for to the Public	497	10	3
Sum Total expended under the Direction of Lieut. Colonel Brown, between Shorn Cliff in Kent, and Rye in Suffex	101,395	8	9¾
Expended by the Contractors Meffrs. Hollinfworth, Bough, and Dyfon, before the Work was placed under the Direction of the Quarter Mafter General of the Forces	10,500	—	—
Expenditure on that part of the Canal and other Works beyond Rye, and from thence to Cliffs End, executed (under the Direction of Lieut. Colonel Nicolay) under the Head of, Field Works	28,975	11	—¾
The Price of the Ground is not finally fettled, but it is conjectured that it cannot exceed, and may fall confiderably fhort of	50,000	—	—
£.	190,870	19	10½

Horfe Guards,
July 27th 1807.

Robt Brownrigg,
Qr Mr Gl.

chapter 5

The Development of the
Royal Military Canal
(1810–1816)

Meetings of the commissioners—opening of navigation to the public—
toll rates—tour of inspection by the Speaker (1810)—report by Rennie
(1810)—introduction of passage boat service (1810)—the Royal
Staff Corps—the barracks at Hythe—the Royal Waggon Train—tolls
introduced on the military road—navigation tolls—the Winchelsea
section—Brown's promotion—leases a house in Sloane Street—rebuilding
of temporary bridges—smuggling—angling—dispute with Knatchbull
(1815)—the Staff Corps at Waterloo—death of Major-General Brown.

Now that the threat of invasion had passed away, the commissioners
took steps to earn what revenue could be obtained from the waterway
while ensuring that it was maintained as a defence work. They officially
authorised the canal to be opened to public navigation at their meeting
on 18 April 1810 when they also approved the toll rates to be charged.
The canal had, however, been used for some commercial traffic since the
previous year when tolls had begun to be collected, and already the wharf
established at the end of the canal at Shorncliffe was proving a 'landing
place for timber and other bulky articles from the westward for the supply
of the dock yards of Sandgate, Folkestone and Dover, as well as for coals
and all articles coming coastways to go up the country, and where coal
yards and other stores will of course be built'.[1]
    It was agreed that the toll on unburnt limestone and on beach gravel for
the repair of roads should not exceed 1d a ton-mile. Timber was charged
3d and coal 2d a ton-mile, the provisional charge of 3d a ton-mile on coal
having excited some complaint. Corn, which had initially been charged at
2d a load, was increased to 2½d. Other commodities were to be charged

3*d* a ton-mile unless the director of the works felt a lower rate should be charged, in which event the commissioners had to be advised. It was also agreed that no toll should be imposed for using the military road (except between Rye and Scots Float) until the beach surface had been consolidated. In June details of these rates were presented to both Houses of Parliament. Because the majority of the traffic was from Rye or Hythe the collection of tolls was a simple matter; two collectors — nco's — were employed; one at Iden lock and the other at Hythe; both were paid 1*s* a day for their trouble. The quartermaster-general did not feel it advisable to farm the tolls since the commissioners were empowered to close the navigation for any reason and every stoppage of the navigation could lead to a claim to abatement of rent and possible law suits.

On 16 August 1810 the Speaker, Charles Abbot and the Quartermaster-General Robert Brownrigg, accompanied by Colonel Brown, made an official tour of inspection of the canal. It had been hoped that Rennie might have been able to meet them at Hythe but this had not proved possible. However, in his absence they raised with Brown such matters as the state of the temporary bridges and the provision of armaments for the canal and agreed that the public road in front of the barracks at Hythe should be diverted. It also gave them the opportunity to prepare more accurate instructions to Rennie who visited Kent with George Jones in October. Rennie's report[2] was sent to Brown for comment following which both report and comments were considered by the commissioners.

Rennie concluded that the Knock Channel was too small to drain 7,000 acres, to which Brown commented that it could be enlarged if requisite, and Rickman observed in the minutes that 'Mr Rennie seems not to have fully understood the instruction or to have thought the apprehension of the commissioners for the Upper Levels too absurd for refutation'. Rennie confirmed that the bulge in Scots Float Sluice had nothing to do with the rampart erected by the commissioners but to the decayed state of the sluice. The back drains in Pett Level and Wallsnd Marsh were a constant source of grievance and expense as they had to be cleared out every year or second year. 'Such is the laborious, unwholesome and dirty nature of the work that it is not desirable to employ soldiers upon it,' wrote Colonel Brown. A land flood did destroy Scots Float sluice in September 1812 and it was necessary to build an embankment to protect the lock gates at Iden, which also had to be raised several feet to prevent salt water entering the canal. The replacement of the sluice cost the commissioners for sewers £20,000.

Before the coming of the railways, passage boats were not an uncommon feature of canal transport. Besides passengers they carried a certain amount of light and usually perishable cargo. The first passage boat to use the canal belonged to Stephen Ward, and on 21 August 1810 began running daily from the Town bridge at Hythe to Iden lock. The fare was 7s return. The service ceased during the winter, ran for two more summers and was discontinued in September 1812. It was not until 1818 that another service was introduced (see p. 121).

The canal was managed by a company of the Royal Staff Corps and assisted by a detachment of the Royal Waggon Train. The history of this Corps has been rather neglected — the bibliography of military regimental history lists only one article and that describes their work overseas[3] — but it achieved many notable successes and several battle honours. The corps was formed at the express wish of the Duke of York in 1800 as a result of the previous difficulty in obtaining field engineers (who were the responsibility of the master-general of the Ordnance), to take part in the expedition to the Helder. Its main purpose was to execute all fieldworks as opposed to fortifications and consequently much of its work was devoted to bridge building over rivers and road building over marshes, demolition and the surveying of military positions. None of its officers had purchased commissions and most had been recruited from the Artillery and Engineers and some from the College at Marlow; other officers were examined by Brown in drawing, trigonometry, surveying and the principles of field fortifications before being given appointments. The soldiers consisted of artificers of every description. The officers received cavalry pay and forage for their horses of 1s 6d per horse. The third-class privates received threepence a day less than the horse allowance but the six first-class privates in each company were paid 2s and the twelve-second class 1s 6d a day. The individuals comprising these classes were selected by Brown according to their abilities and good character upon the recommendation of the captains of companies. However, the companies were seldom up to strength.

Brown pointed out when giving evidence to the commissioners of military inquiry in July 1809 that the RSC saved public expense when executing fieldworks and the QMG had readily available in cases of emergency a trained body of officers and men capable of carrying his orders into effect. The commissioners accepted the very considerable saving to the public by using the Staff Corps in preference to troops of the line on fieldworks, but observed that the pay and allowances of the officers had not been taken into consideration; nevertheless 'we can entertain no doubt that this establishment must be attended to a considerable degree with the advantages pointed. out by. Lt-Col Brown', and added, 'It will rest of course, on the discretion of government to reduce or keep up this corps as the circumstances of the country may require'.[4] Gleig, in his *Military History* relates that His Royal Highness determined to establish a corps

14. The Royal Waggon Train
Barracks, Hythe, 1829.

which should be absolutely at the disposal of the Horse Guards; and as HRH held office in times when the thoughts of statesmen were bent rather to render the means of the country's defence complete, and to aid other nations in opposing the aggressions of an arrogant and unscrupulous power, than to effect savings in the public expenditure, he found no difficulty in consummating his wishes.

On the other hand if the commander-in-chief had had to wait until a company of the Royal Sappers & Miners could have been made available, a start to the canal project would have been considerably delayed. By May 1802 when Brown was appointed Commandant, the original company had been augmented to four companies of 100 men, whose officers had mostly come from the disbanded Irish Engineers. The corps had been reduced in number at the peace in 1802 but in 1804 consisted of 8 companies of 48 men commanded by a captain or major. In 1809 additional companies had been attached.

The Royal Staff Corps barracks at Hythe was the main depot of the military canal. They contained within their walls all the accommodation, living facilities, materials, stores and workshops for the use of the corps. There was a library and the Duke of York directed that coals 'not exceeding the allowance for three rooms' should be issued to the topographical drawing rooms in which officers of the Royal Staff Corps were employed in copying plans for the Horse Guards in Whitehall.

Besides accommodation for the officers and men, there was a regimental hospital built in 1810, which was large enough to accommodate forty patients with four wards, kitchen and nurses' room, 'which will not be too large as it is also intended for the sick of the Royal Waggon Train employed on the works of the canal'. A brick store house 152 ft long with slated roof, known as the gun shed, was built in 1811 to contain the small arms and stores belonging to the cannon. There was also a smithy, timber, and coal yards, wheelbarrow and straw sheds, stabling for the officers' horses, as well as for the thirty barge horses belonging to the Royal Waggon Train.

The Royal Staff Corps was more stationary than regiments of the line and the men, who had volunteered for it from the militia, were mainly all married. In consequence, there was a greater proportion of women and children than usual; in March 1810 there were 150 women and children living a hand-to-mouth existence outside the camp, since they were excluded by barrack regulations from all regular barracks and precluded from the advantages resulting from the normal barrack establishment. Brown brought their distressed and miserable situation to the attention of the commissioners so that instead of the wretched shacks, which married soldiers were generally permitted to build at their own expense in the vicinity of the barracks, 'which are at all times a great nuisance', some sort of accommodation could be provided for the 'most deserving' of the married soldiers for 56 families, 'consisting of not less than 200 persons'. Neat brick huts with slate roofs were built and each family received a small allowance of fuel as approved by the commander-in-chief.

The Royal Waggon Train was the predecessor of the Royal Army Service Corps.[5] Originally formed in 1799, it was responsible for supplying transport of every description — bread and hospital waggons, forge and forage carts — to assist overseas expeditions. Detachments were stationed at Hythe and Ham Street to move troops and army stores. The men and horses employed were generally of the lowest order; the horses which towed the army barges in relays, were 'those cast from cavalry or transferred when regiments were reduced, taking the worst first'. By July 1812 the number of horses employed on the canal numbered 55. Stabling for 30 horses was provided at Hythe, for 12 horses at Ham Street and later (1819) a smaller stable was built at Iden. Every year until 1830 up to £40 was spent on providing extra forage for the horses at 'hard work'.

Tolls were introduced on the military road between Rye and Iden on 9 July 1810 and another tollgate established on the Rye to Winchelsea road on 22 August 1812. This latter road, completed early in 1809 was now in

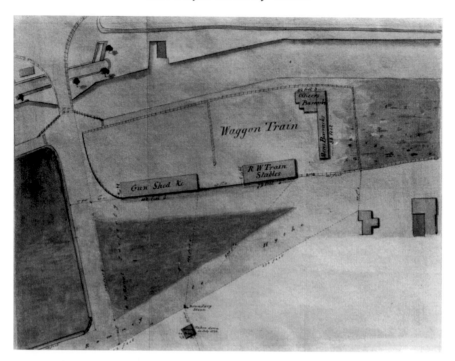

15. The layout of the Royal Waggon Train Barracks Hythe, 1833.
The barracks had a slate roof and provided accommodation for one staff sergeant and fifty men. The gun shed was 112 feet long, the stables 79 feet and the men's barracks 88 feet.

16. The Royal Staff Corps Barracks, Hythe, 1971.

excellent condition, and due to the destruction of the bridge over the Brede, which carried the old road running along the south side of the Brede and was a mile longer in length, it had become the only coast road between Rye and Winchelsea and Hastings.[6] As the tolls charged were only half those taken at the gate between Rye and Scots Float, Brown recommended an increased toll 'which would I am persuaded, be cheerfully acquiesced in'. The commissioners agreed to increase the tolls to around two-thirds of those charged at the toll gate between Rye and Scots Float sluice.[7] As might have been expected the inhabitants of Rye protested and asked for relief from the military tolls. There was no doubt that the number of private tolls about Rye and Winchelsea were a real grievance to the inhabitants for even foot passengers were obliged to pay tolls within 200 yards of those villages, but as the commissioners pointed out to the town clerk of Rye, the remedy was in their hands; the tolls for the military road were in themselves quite reasonable.

The cost of maintaining the canal was not as expensive as had at first been contemplated. Besides tolls from the navigation and the military road, the sale of grazing rights along the parapet, of dung from the stables of the Royal Waggon Train, and of shingle from the beach field contributed to revenue. Brown wrote on 24 June 1814 'that future annual expenses will be very moderate and as far as can be foreseen may be estimated at about £2,000 p.a. for four years'. Indeed, no grant was made by government towards the cost of maintaining the canal after 1809 except for sums of £8,000 in 1813 and £9,000 in 1815.

Traffic on the canal during 1810 — the first year the canal was open to the public — exceeded 15,000 tons and tolls totalled £542 compared with turnpike tolls of £87, but in 1811 the former dropped by over 25 per cent to £421 while the latter almost doubled. However, in 1812, revenue from the navigation rose to £576, a figure which was never to be exceeded; turnpike tolls totalled £194 and the total revenue exceeded £1,000 (see appendix E for details). Nevertheless, the canal's income had fallen 20 per cent by 1815. Although the turnpike receipts had improved with the imposition of higher toll charges on the Rye to Winchelsea road, those from the navigation had dropped to £426 in 1813 and were still declining when the Secretary to the Treasury, Mr Lushington, suggested that the tolls on the canal should be lowered; Brown did not agree and wrote on 24 June 1814 that 'I am fully persuaded that such a measure cannot at this time be adopted without loss to the concern of the canal, and that the proper time for raising the tolls will be when the Weald of Kent is made'. Nevertheless, the commissioners took into account several objections which had been communicated to Mr Lushington and on 4 July the tolls were revised as required by Section 94 of the Weald of Kent Canal Act. However, on the collapse of this canal scheme and as barge traffic continued to decline, the rates were again adjusted in July 1817. The table below gives the various toll rates.

| Article | Pre 1814 per ton mile | 1814–1817 | | Post 1817 per ton mile |
		passing Iden lock	not passing Iden lock	
Sea beach or shingle	1d*	1d	1d	1d‡
Chalk and manure	1d*	1½d	1d	1d†
Coal, culm and coke	2d*	2d	2d	2d§
Corn	2½d*	3d	2d	2d†
Timber	3d*	3d	2d	2d†
Other merchandise	3d	3d	2d	2d†
Other merchandise	3d	3d	2d	2d

* Minimum charge of 6 miles passage if Iden lock used
† 50 per cent surcharge if Iden lock used for up to 6 miles
‡ Surcharge of 1d per ton for using lock
§ Surcharge of 2d per ton if using lock

The toll charged in 1814 for the 18 miles from the Rother to Hythe was, therefore 1s 6d a ton for shingle, 2s 3d a ton for manure, 3s a ton for coal and 4s 6d a ton for timber, corn and other goods, and altered to 1s 7d, 1s 9d, 3s 2d and 3s 6d respectively in 1817.

There was never any commercial traffic on the section of the canal from Winchelsea to Cliff End. The only barges to use these waters were the military ones which were initially engaged in moving shingle from the beach for building the military road for which purpose a wharf was built at Cliff End. When the military road had been completed, regular navigation was discontinued and in 1810 Brown reported that there was no navigation on this detached piece of waterway. By 1814 the swivel bridge and flood gates at Winchelsea had become unserviceable and it was decided that to improve the drainage — at high-water spring tides the water of the Brede rose higher than the meadows — an oak trunk should be built into the canal over which a road and dam should be carried; this, of course, prevented boats from using this section unless they were portaged.

John Brown had been made a full colonel in July 1810 and on 19 July 1811 was appointed Deputy Quartermaster-General. Palmerston, in the name of the Prince Regent, appointed him a commissioner of the Royal Staff College at Camberley on 31 January 1812 and he was promoted major-general on 4 June 1813. He was appointed a member of the Clothing Board (15 July 1813) which was responsible for the inspection of the army's clothing. Brown never married; when he was only 25 he had written to his brother George, who was ten years his senior, congratulating him on his happy home life but giving no hint of his reasons for saying 'tho I am afraid I shall ever be deprived of the pleasure of enjoying a loving wife and children'. In view of the increasing need for him to spend more time in London, he decided to lease a house in Chelsea and on 8 March 1813 took possession of No. 82 Sloane Street, together with its furniture and such incidentals as 8 sacks of coal, 68 bottles of madeira and 204 bottles of port. Besides having his two nieces Isobel and Euphemia Gardner to keep house for him, he engaged Mrs Oakley as cook, Mrs Osborne as washerwoman and Bentley Malt as valet. He continued to use his house at Hythe on his regular visits to the depot. In 1814 he visited Holland; in 1815 he attended various meetings such as those held in London on 31 May and 18 June to form the Royal Military Club.

A new bridge (Marine or Ladies') was built by the Duke's Head public house in Hythe in 1813 and a wharf and crane established there for unloading timber. The temporary canal bridges, whose abutments, as well as their spans were made of wood, were rebuilt over a number of years. Major Todd's company of 3 subalterns and 62 men spent the summer rebuilding 11 bridges in 1814 with stone quoins from Yorkshire for the brick piers; 3 in oak plank was used for the roadway so that they could easily be broken down in an emergency. In August Todd left Portsmouth for New Orleans.

A problem of a different nature which the military authorities had to face was the demand from farmers to lay bridges across the back drain and thereby gain access to the military road for waggons, ploughs, harrows, droves of cattle and stock of every description. The commissioners left it to Brown to decide the rights of the matter and in most cases he allowed access on the grounds that the former occupation roads had been cut by the canal. However, when thirty years later the authorities proposed to stop the private use of certain parts of the military road, they were confronted with numerous problems over rights of way which did not appear to them to have been legally granted.

In some respects the canal was not as successful as its promoters had hoped. The belief that the canal would reduce, if not stop, smuggling had not been fulfilled; in 1816 Alexander Swan reported to the commissioners that 'there is reason to apprehend this expectation has proved fallacious; for it is known the smugglers have become extremely audacious, not only in the remote sequestered part of the works between Winchelsea and Cliff End but near Hythe'. It was suggested that more cavalry patrols might be set up to protect the Revenue.

Angling was a popular pursuit. According to county historian Ireland the canal was first stocked with fish in 1806 and abounded 'with large carp, tench, perch, pike, eels and every other species of freshwater fish'.[8] The field officers and some of the country gentlemen were furnished with fishing permits during the summer to angle from the tow-path side only. However, in 1815 Sir Edward Knatchbull asked leave to fish in the canal by hauling nets and Sir Edward 'with that intent and without waiting the result of his application, placed a small boat in the canal at Bilsington Bridge without a licence. General Brown felt bound to point out that from this mode of angling 'idle people would be collected, the works and the banks of the canal destroyed, the ornamental trees damaged and the fish speedily exterminated'. The commissioners agreed that while angling was permissible, fishing with nets would not be allowed, Sir Edward ignored the commissioners' decision and they decided to serve a legal notice upon him to prevent future trespass rather than levy the penalty of 10s authorised by the Canal Act.

At the same time, thinking to increase their annual income by letting the fishery on lease, advertisements were inserted in the London and Kentish newspapers inviting proposals to rent the fishery with right to grant annual licences at not less than £1 a year, or for a shorter term than one year and that they should be countersigned by the Director of Works who should be at liberty to grant licences of his own to any commissioned military or naval officers. The attempt to let the fishery met with no success and Rickman wondered whether the contingent facility afforded to smuggling by suffering boats to be kept on the canal might not countenance the expected revenue. Nevertheless, in 1817 the commissioners agreed to let the fishery between Winchelsea and Cliff End to a Mr Shadwell but postponed letting the remainder until they had ascertained whether fishing boats in the canal would aid smuggling. Of the success of this venture, however, no more is heard.

The Royal Staff Corps were quite active during the Peninsular War. Two companies sailed to Portugal in 1809 and two more joined Wellington in Spain in 1812. These four companies remained with the duke until the end of the conflict and returned to Hythe in July 1814. The capture of Paris and the abdication of Napoleon in April 1814 brought temporary peace to Europe and Brown's return to London. But on the Emperor's return from Elba in March 1815, Wellington was ordered to Brussels where the British Government was feverishly trying to re-create an army. In April five companies of the Royal Staff Corps marched from Hythe to Dover under the command of Lt-Col Nicolay where they took ship to the Netherlands; On 18 June some of the officers but none of the men were present at the battle of Waterloo. However, they must have been in the vicinity since the corps was awarded 'Waterloo' as a Battle Honour. Ten Royal Staff Corps officers were present on the battlefield of whom three were wounded and another had three horses shot from under him.[9]

On 24 June 1815 Major-General Brown wrote his last report. News of the victory would have only just been received at Hythe. During the previous week he had inspected the whole line of the canal. Few officers and men had been left at the depot* but in spite of that he reported that the works were in as perfect a state of repair as could be expected for so extensive a line of defence. A fitting conclusion to the work of a fine soldier who nine months later was to suddenly die, and who by his unremitting and zealous attention to the works had ensured its completion and successful maintenance. The defence of the canal had not been put to the test but there is no doubt that it would have proved a good second line of defence and if the flooding of Romney Marsh had been successfully accomplished, might well have proved an effective barrier against French forces landed between Folkestone and Hastings.

John Brown died on 20 March 1816 at his house in Sloane Street after a six-hour illness at the age of 59.[10] His brother George was greatly shocked by his death 'I have been in so debilitated a state for some time,' he wrote to his attorney, 'that I have been able to do nothing; the severe loss of so valuable and respectable a kind brother, in so unlooked for and unexpected a manner, must cut deep with me in mind and spirits'. He was in truth a man of great ability, 'beloved by numerous acquaintances' who had 'made himself by his merit, without any other funds or interest'. His brother described him as a 'thin slender made man, most sober in living both in eating and drinking, and as unlikely a man to be carried off by apoplexy as most men'. Yet he obviously enjoyed wine — his cellar fetched the substantial sum of £397 19s 11d on his death. He was a benevolent man as witnessed by his interest in his nephew George, for whom he obtained at the age of 24 a half colonelcy and the position of assistant quartermaster-general, and by his attachment to his brother and his family. It was brother George's fond hope 'that he would have been a protection to them all after I was gone, having always expressed an anxiety to have a home near me when he should retire.[11]

---

* Major Todd's company ordered back from New Orleans reached Portsmouth on 5 June and after reforming at Hythe left Dover on 22 July to reach Paris on 8 August to join Army Headquarters. Lt-Colonel Sir William Nicolay, (1771-1842) left Hythe to serve at Waterloo. He kept in touch with John Brown writing him four informative and confidential letters totalling 14 pages. The first dated 17 May from Brussels and those dated 2 July, 21 August and 12 October describe his experiences in Paris and his distaste for the French. Appointed Governor of Dominica 1824-31, Antigua 1831-2 and Mauritius 1833-40. (Burgess Browning, Blue Ball Yard SW1, Bulletin No. 11, December 1987).

General Brown left over £20,000 of which nephew George inherited some £7,000 as well as a number of his choice possessions; his six other nephews and nieces received £11,000 in equal shares and the balance went to his sister's two daughters, who had been keeping house for him. His personal effects — clocks, watches, wines, telescopes, maps, turning lathes and 'mathematical instruments' — reflect well enough his bachelor habits. His notebooks reveal his study of astronomy, his sketch books his delight in drawing and his library his great interest in books, 'too numerous' said his brother, 'for any private man' but so beloved by his nephew George that he had them sent by boat to the family home at Linkwood in Morayshire. Brown himself wrote that 'although it has not fallen to my lot to have been employed on more splendid services, still they have been varied, laborious and without intermission for thirty-four years leave excepted'. And today the Royal Military Canal remains a lasting monument to his engineering skills.

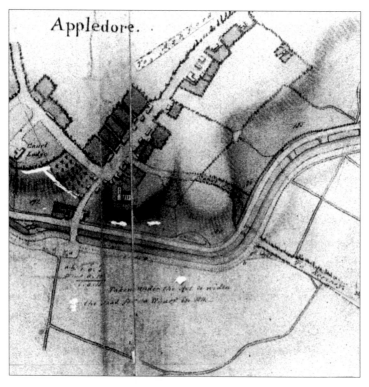

The site of Appledore Wharf, 1811.

chapter 6

The Weald of Kent Canal Project (1800–1815)

Survey by Alexander Sutherland (1800)—proposed Kent & Sussex Junction Canal—Survey by Francis and Netlam Giles (1802)—Report by John Rennie—Bills introduced in 1811 and 1812—Weald of Kent Canal Act (1812)—extension of time Bill (1815)—project dropped.

The Thames & Medway Canal Act 1800 had authorised the building of a canal from Gravesend to Frindsbury. This encouraged proposals to link the rivers Thames and Medway with the river Rother and Rye Harbour and make a through waterway from London to the English Channel. In September 1800 a plan for such a canal, surveyed by Alexander Sutherland, was deposited and on 31 July 1801 a meeting of promoters, held at the Bell Inn, Maidstone, with Sir William Geary, MP for Kent, in the chair and attended by both the Earl of Romney and Earl Camden, decided that it was a practicable proposition.[1]

The distance from London to Rye by sea was 140 miles. By road it was 63 miles and by the proposed Kent & Sussex Junction Canal 85½ miles. By road it took 60 hours — by water it was hoped that the voyage could be accomplished in little longer. Two coasters, and sometimes three, were employed exclusively in the London trade but owing to the dangers of the passage by the Nore and the Goodwin Sands and of delays of up to six weeks due to contrary winds, three stage waggons went weekly by road. Land charges were 1s 10d a ton-mile which it was hoped to reduce to 8d per ton-mile by inland water carriage.

The canal was planned to take 40-ton Medway barges and to run 28 miles, from the Medway between Brandbridges and Yalding to the tideway at Scots Float Sluice on the Rother through a 1,200 yard tunnel near Fosten

Green to the north of Tenterden. There were also to be three branches; one by making the river Teise navigable for 11 miles to Lamberhurst and the others to Headcorn and to Cranbrook, 1 mile and 3¾ miles respectively from the main line. The total cost was estimated at £118,167 of which £84,711 was for the junction canal. The chief objects were to connect London and Rye by 'avoiding a tedious, circuitous and dangerous passage by sea' and to carry beach, chalk, lime and coal into the Weald, and to bring out timber, hops, corn, wool and agricultural produce. In addition, Sutherland also concluded that 'oak bark, hop-poles, flax, seeds, tallow, hides, bricks, tiles, lead, iron and ironmongery, flour, ale, beer, porter, groceries etc. and provisions of all the different kinds that mankind make use of, may be easily transferred and mutually exchanged, to the great benefit of society in general, and more particularly to the labouring party of the community. Why might not supplies of livestock, or carcases, be sent by these navigations from the famous pasturage of Romney Marsh, and the equally productive marshes in its vicinity, as also from the Wealds of Kent and northern parts of Sussex, to the metropolis? Accidents from driving would be thereby prevented, and the meat not being heated by overdriving, would the longer resist putrefaction.'[2]

The revenue from carrying 41,500 tons along the main line was estimated at £6,241; a further 17,900 tons was expected from the Teise Navigation to increase the revenue by £1,808. Sutherland considered that there was 'every reason to expect' that the subscribers would receive 8 per cent on their investment.

Sutherland also pointed out the great value of such a canal in providing an 'easy, safe and expeditious conveyance of stores, troops etc. to the different military depots in and near the coasts of Kent and Sussex, points the most exposed and perhaps the most seriously vulnerable of any around the island of Great Britain; an object which merits the attention of, and will no doubt be considered by, the wisdom, prudence and vigilance of Government, as its great importance deserves'. Even after mentioning all the advantages and benefits, Sutherland was ingenuous enough to mention that 'many who are sanguine and warm friends to this scheme have expressed some doubts as to its practicability'.

A further meeting was held in Easter week 1802 at the George Inn, Cranbrook, when it was agreed that John Rennie should be commissioned to carry out a survey. In his report of 4 September 1802 Rennie suggested the idea of taking a different line to avoid the long tunnel through the hill near Tenterden and to extend the advantages 'into a much greater tract of country'. This was approved and Francis and Netlam Giles were employed to survey the line.

Rennie indeed confirmed Sutherland's main line and Lamberhurst branch on 8 August 1803 but added another to Ashford and Wye, so increasing the cost to £175,653. The tolls, however, were still estimated at only £6,241 to give about 3 per cent on capital but in spite of this discouraging forecast it was nevertheless hoped that Geary might be able to obtain the support of public-spirited landowners and traders in the project. The times were not now propitious, however, and the figures being so discouraging the scheme lay dormant.

The Royal Military Canal was begun and finished before the scheme was revived in 1809. Rennie addressed a second report[3] to Sir William Geary on 19 July stating that 'it appears that the county of Kent admits of an extent of canal navigation far exceeding what at first was imagined, and much of it through a country where the soil is most favourable for the purpose; where the roads for want of materials are almost impassable during the winter and spring, and where manure is much wanted'. Rennie's enthusiasm rose exceedingly high — 'no country therefore is more in want of canal navigation than this, and none that I have every seen is more practicable for such a work, or more amply provided with water for the supply of an extensive trade.' Rennie now proposed that the canal should terminate in the Royal Military Canal near Stone instead of in the Rother and that by extending the length of the main line to 33¾ miles, branches could be made to Lamberhurst and to Wye, Canterbury and the sea. Rennie would not have been 'surprised', if on the summit level alone 100,000 tons of manure were carried without passing a lock. The link with Rye by the Rother and with Romney Marsh and Hythe would enable the carriage of beach for the roads, 'a material greatly wanted through the most of the Weald' as well as goods, provisions and merchandise. The total cost of 87¾ miles of canal navigation was put at £381,358, of which £190,688 was for the main line from the Medway to the Rother.

The Weald of Kent Canal committee accepted most of Rennie's findings with enthusiasm but doubted the value and practicability of the branch to Cranbrook and considered whether it should be made on a smaller scale than the main line. Rennie reported in August 1810 that it must be made the same size and that although its length would only be 2¾ miles, it would rise 60ft and yet still be a mile from the town. The ground was unfavourable being porous sand rock which would have to be lined. The cost of £32,000 to save a distance of 1¾ miles could only be justified, wrote Rennie, if by its construction a sufficient amount of cargo went by water to the Medway via the canal instead of by land, and on this point Rennie pointed out that he did not have sufficient local information.[4]

The committee of the Weald of Kent Canal also had reservations about making use of the Royal Military Canal. Firstly because they feared that in case of a threatened invasion by the enemy, it was probable that the commander-in-chief might stop the navigation of barges on the canal, and

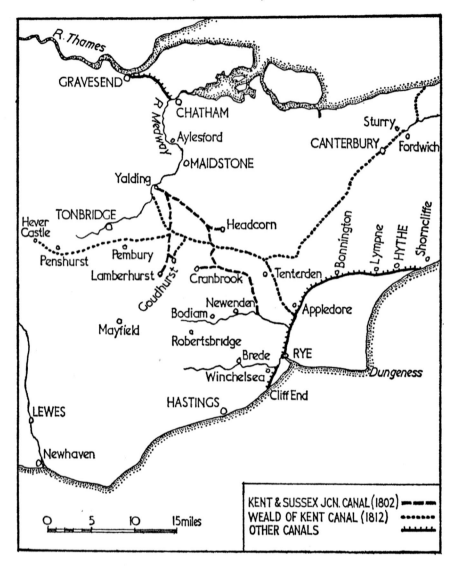

Line of the intended Weald of Kent Canal, 1812.

thereby prevent their trade from being carried on. Secondly, because long barges would not be able to pass through Iden lock which was shorter than the locks intended for the Weald of Kent Canal. They, therefore, proposed to the commissioners of the Royal Military Canal that the back ditch of the. Royal Military Canal between the junction of the two canals and the river Rother, should be made capable of conveying the barges from the Weald of Kent Canal into the river Rother. This the commissioners rejected, but they did agree that Iden lock might be enlarged on payment of compensation.

The canal promoters accepted these points but decided to withdraw their Bill from the coming session to await the progress of Rennie's scheme for a Grand Southern Canal from the Medway at Tonbridge to Portsmouth which allowed for a level line from Hever Castle to join the summit level of the Weald at Horsmonden. The petition for the Bill was presented to both Houses on 1 February 1811 and soon attracted numerous petitions both supporting and opposing the scheme. The second reading was postponed once and to avert disaster the promoters announced on 4 April that the commissioners had proposed that the Medway-Rother Canal should terminate in the Royal Military Canal. However, the second reading in the Commons was again deferred and on 8 April 1811 Rennie's Grand Southern Canal was decisively defeated in the Lords on second reading by 100 votes to 17.

The commissioners of the Royal Military Canal meanwhile had approved the idea that the proposed canal should terminate in their own waterway and consulted Rennie in February 1811 as to the best spot for the junction to be made.[5] He recommended either of two places.[6] One where the Old Knock Channel joined the back ditch of the Royal Military Canal, about 1,000 yards to the west of Appledore Bridge. The other about 2,050 yards to the west of Appledore Bridge and just over two miles to the eastward of Iden lock. The former junction was proposed with the view of keeping the Weald of Kent Canal entirely clear of the Knock Channel; the latter with the view of cutting off an angle of the Knock Channel; to fall in with the desire of several of the proprietors of land in the level, for the purpose of improving the drainage.

The scheme was reintroduced in April 1812 as the Weald of Kent Canal, 29 miles long with 25 locks (11 up and 14 down) from Brandbridges to Appledore with a 15½ mile level branch to the chalk hills near Wye (where there were to be feeder railroads) and another 3 miles long with one lock to near Hope Mill (Goudhurst). The width of the intended locks was to be the same as the one on the military canal. The estimate was £305,108, which included £37,114 for four reservoirs. But, only £83,500 had so far been subscribed, some of it by those, like Geary and Lord Romney, connected with the Thames & Medway Canal, who probably saw the new project as benefiting the older one. No connection was now proposed to the St Nicholas Bay Harbour & Canterbury Canal, though this navigation from Canterbury to the sea had been authorised in the previous year. Rennie perpetually hopeful about the most unlikely projects, told the Lords Committee that 'it is without exception the finest piece of country to cut a canal through I ever saw'. The Act was passed on 5 May 1812, authorising a capital of £320,000 and £160,000 more by mortgage if necessary.

The Act was lengthy containing no less than 137 sections covering 68 pages. An interesting provision was the authorization to make railways

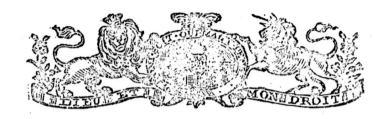

GEORGII III. REGIS.

Cap. 70.

An Act for making and maintaining a Navigable Canal from the River *Medway*, near *Brandbridges* in the Parish of *East Peckham* in the County of *Kent*, to extend to and unite with the Royal Military Canal in the Parish of *Appledore* in the said County; and also certain Navigable Branches and Railways from the said intended Canal.

[5th *May* 1812.]

WHEREAS the making and maintaining a Navigable Canal (with Basins and Reservoirs) for the Passage of Boats, Barges, and other Vessels from and out of the River *Medway*, near *Brand-bridges* in the Parish of *East Peckham* in the County of *Kent*, to extend to and unite with the Royal Military Canal in the Parish of *Appledore* in the said County, and also the Navigable Branches and Railways herein-after described, from the said intended Canal, will open an easy and commodious Communication, not only between the several Towns, Parishes, Districts, and Places, through or near to which the said intended Navigation will pass, but also between those Places and the Ports of *London* and *Rye*, the Towns of *Tonbridge*, *Maidstone*, *Rochester*, *Chatham*, and *Gravesend*, and the Arsenals and Dock Yards at *Chatham*, *Woolwich*, and *Deptford*; whereby the Conveyance of Coals, Timber, Sea Beach, Chalk, Lime, Manure, Goods, Wares, Stores, and Merchandize, to and from

wherever the company deemed it more expedient than a canal (III)*
in which case no carriage was to pass on the railway unless constructed
'agreeably to the orders and regulations of the company', (IV). It was laid
down that the committee of management was to consist of fifteen persons
(XLVI). Expenses of members of committees and subcommittees could be
borne by the company (VII). Committee members neglecting to attend four
successive meetings without sufficient excuse ceased to be members (LXL).
Tolls could be taken for horses (1d), oxen (½d), and sheep and swine (1s
4d) using the tow-path (LXXXII) but these could be taken only once a
day (LXXXIII). The promoters were prepared to lengthen Iden lock from
72 to 80 ft to accommodate Medway barges at their expense but to meet
the increased cost of maintenance the commissioners of the Royal Military
Canal were to be entitled to charge a toll rate of 4 miles instead of 3 miles
which was the actual distance from the intended place of junction to Iden
lock (XCIV). There was a restriction on vessels laden with hay passing
through locks unless the water flowed over the waste weir or the boat was
going to a colliery for a cargo of coal to be conveyed along some part of the
canal (XCVII). Where the canal crossed the military road, the company had
to build 'a substantial bridge of masonry, not less than twenty feet wide' as
well as a wooden horse bridge to link the tow-paths. No lock was to be made
within half a mile of the junction (CXI). Any person wilfully destroying
the canal banks or works could be convicted of felony and transported
(CXXVI). The Royal Military Canal commissioners were prohibited from
closing the canal 'save and except in the event of an actual invasion of the
coast of Kent or Sussex by His Majesty's enemies' or in the event of the
water level of the canal sinking unavoidably below 6 ft (CXII).

An unusual clause inserted into the Act on the petition of 57 subscribers
who had paid deposits before 25 December 1811 and who had withdrawn
their names from the list of subscribers before 25 February 1812 provided
that they could be refunded a proportion of their deposit (CXXX).
Apparently although these subscribers had informed the solicitors acting
for the promoters that they were no longer supporting the Bill, they had
been 'surprised to find' that they were listed among the 110 names of
those wishing to be proprietors of the Company. Indeed, many of these
had been the supporters of the Grand Southern Canal Bill in the spring
of 1810 and in view of the present depressed state of trade they found it
'most inconvenient' to advance further sums. No person could own more
than 100 shares of £100 each (LXVIII) and since work could not begin
until £308,800 of the authorised capital of £320,000 had been subscribed
within three years (LXIX) the committee had the difficult task of obtaining

---

*Figures in parentheses denote the section of the Act.

WEALD OF KENT CANAL.

52 George III. Cap. 70, Royal Assent 5th May, 1812.

It incorporates the subscribers by the name of " The Company of " Proprietors of the Weald of Kent Canal," and empowers them to raise amongst themselves, for the purposes of the act, the sum of £320,000, in shares of £100 each, of which sum, £305,800 is to be raised before the work is commenced, and three years is given to them to get this amount of subscription, which must be proved to have been done at the general quarter sessions. The company may raise a further sum of £160,000, if necessary, either amongst themselves, by creation of new shares, or by mortgage of the rates, and also take the following

TONNAGE RATES.

	d.		
For all Chalk, Lime, Marl, Dung, Compost or Manure, which shall pass any Lock............................	1½	per Ton,	per Mile.
If not passing through a Lock	1	ditto.	ditto.
For all Coal, Culm and Coke	2	ditto.	ditto.
For all Sea Beach or Shingle.............................	1	ditto.	ditto.
For all Timber and all other Goods, Wares and Merchandize, passing through any Lock.............................	3	ditto.	ditto.
If not passing through a Lock	2	ditto.	ditto.

And in proportion for any greater or less Quantity or Distance; but Fractions of a Quarter in both cases to be taken as a Quarter.

The company are also authorized to take the following tolls for passing on the towing-path.

TOLLS.

	d.	
For every Horse, Mule or Ass (not drawing a Vessel) passing through any Toll Gate	1	each.
For every Drove of Oxen or Neat Cattle	10	per Score.
For every Drove of Swine, Sheep or Lambs	5	ditto.

Vessels in Ballast only or light, to pay Three-pence per Ton per Mile; and all Vessels entering any Basins or Harbours, to pay Three-pence per Ton if they have not passed Ten Miles on the Canal.

This canal would open a communication from the River Thames at Gravesend, by the Thames and Medway Canal, and the River Medway, and by its junction with the Royal Military Canal, to all the places on the coast between Hythe and Winchelsea; thus avoiding the boisterous navigation round the North and South Forelands, as will be seen by reference to our map; but it has not been executed, and probably this delay arises from the restrictive clause which required a large sum to be raised before the work commenced.

Joseph Priestley's account of the Canal, 1831.

the support of some 500 or 600 people each willing to speculate £500 or more in this venture. It was this restrictive clause which more than anything else doomed the canal never to be begun.

I can trace no record of the committee's proceedings following the passing of the Act although in July 1814 the commissioners of the Royal Military Canal agreed to revise their tolls so that they met the requirements of Section XCIV of the Weald of Kent Canal Act (see p. 101).

However, in May 1815 the promoters were back in Parliament for an extension of time Bill; although they had received subscriptions for £103,500, there was also another petition from some subscribers of the original Act praying that provision be made for allowing them to withdraw their names. The Bill passed through the House of Commons but was amended and abandoned in the Lords.

Although the opening of the Wey & Arun Junction Canal in 1816 linked the Thames to the English Channel, the idea lingered on. In July 1823, for example, when the Thames & Medway Canal was nearly finished, a letter in the *Maidstone Journal* urged its building, so that hops could be more easily transported from Kent to the Midlands; others in 1824 saw a connection with the future Canterbury Navigation. And there the matter died and the failure of the only attempt to link the Royal Military Canal with another waterway left the canal to develop its own peculiar trade along the fringes of Romney Marsh. It is evident in the event, however, that if the money had been raised, the canal would have been a financial catastrophe so that once the end of the war had removed much of the speculative interest, the project was doomed.

chapter 7

The Royal Staff Corps at Work
(1816–1837)

Cuts in expenditure—reductions in salaries—John Rickman resigns—
Col Sir Benjamin D'Urban—two quartermasters create difficulty—their
respective duties—Col Sir Richard Jackson—more stringent economies—
analysis of road traffic—Cobbett's rural ride (1823)—purchase of
boats—the town of Hythe—improvements to the barracks—rebuilding
of bridges and establishment of wharves—problems relating to the
maintenance of the canal—passage boat services-storms and floods—
reduction of the Royal Staff Corps (1829)—character of the men—Royal
Waggon Train disbanded (1833)—transfer of canal proposed to Board
of Ordnance.

With the war won, the commissioners of the Royal Military Canal
promptly curtailed all works in progress other than reparations and looked
to ways of reducing annual expenditure. At their meeting in April 1816,
the director's allowance of £50 per annum for stationery and postage
was no longer regarded as necessary. Swan the accountant, had his salary
reduced from £400 to £150 per annum, but retained the office of barrack
master at £100 per annum and the usual allowances assessed by himself
at £30 per annum. Swan wrote a 'memorial' to the quartermaster-general
setting forth how inconvenient it was to have one's salary reduced and the
commissioners being 'sensible of his service' decided to raise him to the
higher order of barrack master with an increase in salary of fifty guineas.
Indeed, when Swan was ordered to survey the canal and report on the
works in 1816, Rickman suggested that it be entered in the Minute Book
since the quartermaster-general had characterised it as clear, comprehensive
and accurate, and as supplying a chasm in the Annual Reports occasioned

by the sudden death of General Brown. Swan was also a good bookkeeper and in 1819 the auditors expressed the view that his accounts were 'in every respect favourable to his accuracy, precision and attention'.

The commissioners also considered that £50 instead of £150 per annum was now sufficient salary for the secretary having regard to his diminished duties. Rickman, who had now risen to become second clerk assistant at the House of Commons promptly resigned and the commissioners appointed Edward Phillips, Secretary to the Speaker in his place. At the same time they placed on record

> their approbation of the services of his predecessor, who having been appointed to that office when the affairs of the Royal Military Canal required much regulation, not only accomplished that object, but has met and overcome many supervening difficulties with a zeal and ability always adequate to the occasion.

Indeed the commissioners had been well served for in the words of Sharon Turner, Rickman was 'a man of facts and realities, well adapted to all things that required close attention, investigation and continued mental labour', whose public fame as a statistician was founded on his efficient organisation of the population censuses of 1801, 1811, 1821 and 1831.* Phillips resigned in 1819 and Francis Dighton, the private secretary to His Royal Highness the commander-in-chief, was appointed.

On the death of John Brown, Colonel Sir Benjamin D'Urban was summoned from Portugal to become the new commandant of the Royal Staff Corps and deputy quartermaster-general. D'Urban, now aged 39, had already had a distinguished military career; he had served in all the great battles of the Peninsular War for which he had received a gold cross and five clasps for the nine pitched battles at which he had been present. He took up duties at the Horse Guards in April 1816. 'A new broom sweeps clean.' One of his first steps as Director of the Royal Military Canal was to have the allowance of coals and candles reviewed so that his men had more in winter and less in summer. The issue of candles was discontinued from May to September on a principle of economy. He also paid some attention to the officers' barracks, building them their 'necessaries', a forage barn for the supply of their horses, and 'some alterations in the adjutant quarters which were scarcely habitable'. The useless contents of an old store were condemned and sold. In this work he was ably assisted by Colonel John Pine Coffin, who had the general direction during the different periods that D'Urban was

---

* It is amusing to record Robert Southey's description of Rickman as 'being so careless in his dress as to have been taken by the press-gang for a common tramp'.

17. Sir Benjamin D'Urban, 1817.
Sir Benjamin D'Urban (1777-1849),
major-general in Portuguese army
1813, Director Royal Military
Canal 1816-19, Governor British
Guiana 1821-5, Barbados 1825-9,
the Cape 1834-8, Lieutenant-
general 1837. (From a miniature
painted after his return from the
Peninsular War.)

employed on other duties — and Mr Gott, the quartermaster who was the
executive superintendent of the works and who was paid an extra 3s 6d a
day while holding the post of storekeeper to the Royal Military Canal.[1]

The return from France of Quartermaster Heatly in December 1818
created a difficulty for Gott, who ceased to be regimental quartermaster
and was told on 23 December to confine himself to 'duties connected with
the canal works' and to 'take charge of the tool cart horses'. Nine days
later regimental orders explained rather more precisely that Heatly would
have charge of the regimental stores, magazine, ammunition, tools of the
companies, clothing, etc, and superintend the tailors, armourers and other
tradesmen. Also

> he will have the general charge and superindence of the barrack
> rooms, guard houses, huts and station houses, etc; the issue of barrack
> allowance to officers and be responsible to Mr Swan in his capacity of
> Barrack master. He will receive and issue to the companies all supplies
> of meat, bread and other general issues and be careful to report to the
> commanding officers if at any time those are of a bad quality.[2]

Gott, on the other hand, was storekeeper to the Royal Military Canal and
especially attached to the service of the canal. His duties were specified in
detail.

He will continue in the general superintendence of all the works, premises, plantations, road, barges, etc. belonging to and connected with the Royal Military Canal. He will assign and distribute the daily work, and working parties. He will have charge of all the stores, materials etc. for the use of the establishment, watch over the application and expenditure, make out the different estimates, make out and certify all bills, keep all books of entry, and make out all reports and returns, connected with the foregoing charges, communicating with Mr Swan in his capacity of Accountant of the Royal Military Canal upon them whenever it may be necessary. He will have the charge and superintendence of the work and all belonging to it, workshops, fabrics, tools, implements, etc. horses, carts and harness. He will be responsible for the whole to the commanding officer and to the Director of the Royal Military Canal.[3]

Eleven months later a further regimental order reflected some of the difficulties which had arisen during the year over the interpretation of their instructions. Heatly was now to be allowed to inspect four times a year the station houses and barracks occupied by different detachments. Gott, while continuing to superintend all repairs, was, however, to consult with the officer at Iden lock and point out any action to be taken regarding stores along the line from Iden to Cliff End, for which the officer was responsible; nor was he to give any directions for any work on which an officer was specifically charged. Gott had the responsibility for assigning the tasks and composition of the daily working parties of which details had to be passed to the adjutant before 7.00 pm every night. Particularly emphasised was the fact that neither the men nor their tools nor their horses were to be employed on any private work without the Director or Commanding Officer's authority.

Among other instructions were that the orderly officer in the barracks should twice a day at uncertain hours, 'go through the work yard and observe that all is quiet and ask the sergeant if all his party were present'; and that the officers when making weekly inspections 'will have the goodness to be very minute and careful in the execution of that duty; and proceeding along one side of the canal and returning along the other so that nothing material may escape their notice'.

The Barrack Board owned Saltwood Barracks at Hythe where the magazine and gun shed for the Military Canal was maintained, and when they 'rather suddenly' offered the barracks for sale by public auction in 1816, an 'active correspondence' ensued which resulted in the Treasury ordering these buildings to be transferred to the commissioners. The barracks were thereupon demolished by the Staff Corps and the materials used to rebuild the gun shed and magazine; in 1819 the 80 cannons which had been stored at Shorncliffe for the past seven years were deposited in the new armoury.

The receipts from tolls and produce from the canal and military road gradually improved from 1815 when they totalled £839 to 1820 when they reached £1,229; tolls from the navigation had similarly increased during this period from £305 to £536 and generally represented 30 to 40 per cent of the total revenue. Only between 1810 and 1812 had they represented more than 50 per cent. Quite a flourishing business had developed opposite the Beach Field at Hythe where several small wharves had been established and the shingle was sold to the boatmen at 1d per ton. The toll rates on shingle operated a little unfairly, however, and since the tonnage carried had dropped from 2,830 tons (1814) to 1,313 tons (1817) it was reduced in July 1818 by limiting the toll to 3½d a ton for any distance and charging 1d a ton for passing through Iden lock. As a consequence the traffic doubled — 3,846 and 4,514 tons being carried in 1819 and 1820. Besides shingle, the main cargoes were coal and hop poles from Winchelsea and Rye to Appledore, Ham Street, and Warehorne and corn from these places to Rye Market.

Increased rent from sheep grazing was obtained by allowing those parts which had for fear of injuring the trees, previously been mown, to be grazed. In 1816 rent from this source increased by £56 and in 1819 by £159 per annum compared with 1815. In the 1820s the commissioners agreed that tickets could be issued to 'respectable individuals' for riding along the towpath on horseback for an annual charge of 7s. In 1824 over twenty people were granted this facility. No grant was made by government towards the cost of maintaining the canal after 1815 and the Director of the canal was reminded in the minutes of every commissioners' meeting of the need for strict economy and that under no circumstances should expenditure exceed the revenue.

One obstacle to increasing the amount of traffic on the canal was the poor state of the roads in Romney Marsh which were 'nearly impassable in May and entirely so in the autumn, winter and spring, so that however desirous to avail themselves of the canal, the farmers are cut off, as it were, from all access to it at those periods of the year when it would be most useful to them'.[3] The Director of Works also felt that the parishes farthest from the beach fields at Hythe and Rye would be more likely to repair their roads if the tolls could be more equitably levied, and the commissioners agreed that from 1 August 1818 a further adjustment should be made so that the toll on shingle of 1d a mile should be limited to a maximum of 3½ miles or 3½d a ton. This particular distance was chosen as the trustees of the turnpike road from Tenterden into Romney Marsh obtained their supplies from Appledore for which the toll was already 3½d; consequently, within the next nine months the amount of beach carried trebled in quantity: 3,846 and 4,514 tons were sold in 1819 and 1820 while a similar amount was carried in the military barges. However, although shingle represented the largest item carried, it amounted to only 10 per cent of the total toll receipts. In 1821 it was agreed to allow coal toll free beyond Bilsington, the halfway point between Iden and Shorncliffe. In 1823 the drop in traffic was attributed to the 'low state of the hop trade in particular and of agriculture in general'.

In 1818 it was decided to change the road rather than repair the bridge at Cliff End — 'a very long and laborious operation and establish a permanent station house there for four men'. Although there was no commercial traffic on the Winchelsea to Cliff End section, it remained part of the defence works and for its repair a barge was employed to move beach from the shingle wharf. This wharf had been rebuilt in 1819[4] although it would appear that it was seldom in use since it was reported in 1823 that the west end of the canal was not 'apparently worse than it was, and as it does not deteriorate much from being left to itself, there is less reason to regret the absolute want of means to improve its condition'. A barge on this section was found unworthy of repair in 1823 and was condemned. The wharf itself was removed in 1830.

18. Passage boat at Hythe, 1829.
Mr Pilcher's boat left Hythe every morning at ten o'clock carrying passengers and goods to Appledore, Iden and sometimes Rye. The service which had begun in 1810, was discontinued in 1812 and restarted in 1818. In 1833 the director stopped it because of the damage caused to the banks by the boat's 'frequent rapid transit'. An iron passage boat was introduced in 1839 but was withdrawn after the opening of the Ashford and Folkestone railway in 1843. A passenger packet boat also operated between Ham Street and Shorncliffe in the 1850's.

By now the trees which had been planted along by the canal were in a very flourishing state and not only ornamental 'but by the spreading of their roots afforded great security to the parapet'. Hedges of thorn as well as elms, acacias and evergreens were planted along the edge of the banquette close to the parapet and also upon the outer side of the tow-path to save the expense of renewing the oak-fence; 110,000 plants were purchased from Mr Catbush of Ashford and from London, and seven miles of the banquette planted from Hythe to Bonnington and the nurseries established by the Royal Staff Corps provided a further 45,000 in 1819; 160,000 two- or three-year 'quicks' were also purchased from Leith in October of that year. In 1823, however, the utility of planting the banquette was considered doubtful.

At the same time, ways of increasing the canal's income were sought including the possibility of letting the fishing rights and the removal of the rail fencing from Winchelsea sluice gates to Cliff End (3 miles) — 'it having been found quite unnecessary since there is little or no traffic on that part of the military road' — to improve the grazing of this section of the parapet.

In 1819 it was reported that the new buoy and rope bridges invented by Lt-Col Sir James Colleton and Colonel Steergrove, both late of the Royal Staff Corps, which had been approved and used by the Duke of Wellington, and which had been used in the field by the Royal Staff Corps in their capacity as 'pontooniers', had accompanied the detachment from France and were placed in the magazine at Hythe. Regular training in their use was carried out on the canal.[5] In the same year a brickworks was established close to the banks of the canal between Hythe and West Hythe and a coal merchant's yard at Ham Street.

In 1820 Colonel Sir Richard Jackson became Colonel Commandant of the Royal Staff Corps and Director of Works in the room of Sir Benjamin D'Urban, who had been appointed Governor of Antigua.* The economies introduced in 1816 were now intensified. The commissioners were determined that expenditure should not exceed revenue. By 1820 this had been achieved although as a result it was not possible to maintain the works — especially the Winchelsea section of the canal and part of the military road — in such good order. Stone was used for common repairs instead of brick. Men of the Royal Staff Corps were taught riseheading instead of having this work done by contract. The making of fascines of various sizes from the loppings of the trees on the brow of the parapet was 'a source of instruction to the young soldiers'. An example of the measures taken is well illustrated by the report in 1824 that only the upper rails of the fences would be painted

---

* D'Urban became Governor of the Cape in 1842 and his connection with the occupation of Natal and its port is perpetuated in the name of Durban. In 1847 he took command of the British forces in Canada and died in Montreal in 1849.

white and that the remaining woodwork would be covered with a coat of coal tar. Other means of making the canal property more productive were examined; every station house had its own vegetable plot; nurseries were established for growing slips of hawthorn and patches of unused ground planted with red willows and osier. Sales of surplus 'quick' as the young hawthorn was called, increased revenue by £47 in 1824.

As a further economy it was decided in 1820 to relieve the canal funds of the cost of maintaining the 56 huts for married soldiers by the foundation of a fund for that purpose, supported by a 'very small contribution from each inhabitant in the manner practised by the Royal Artillery'. This would appear very cheese-paring but at least it enabled 14 shacks to be reconstructed in 1822 out of the hut fund.

A clothing fund was also established in June 1822 by a saving from the allowance issued for making up uniforms and by the sale of old clothing belonging to deserters. Its objects were to enable the soldier to have his uniform made in the best possible manner, added security against losses contingent upon it being made up at HQ; as an aid to the scientific and charitable establishments of the corps and for incidental acts of regimental charity. Apparently it had a wide range of miscellaneous uses of quite a different purpose, such as providing books for the regimental library, extra bounty for recruits, extra rewards for apprehending deserters, materials for the lithographic press, comforts and emergency medical assistance for married soldiers and their families, education of soldiers' children and adornments to the staff sergeants' clothing.

It was not until 1816 that it could be reported that the military road from Hythe to Winchelsea was in good condition. 'In parts upon which from local circumstances there is much intercourse, there cannot be a firmer road'. There were ruts needing attention, however, between Kenardington and Appledore and it could not yet rival the old and more circuitous road from Hythe to Rye by New Romney. Indeed, it never did. Rather surprisingly, it was less successful as an artery of commerce than the canal. Its upkeep was costly and as an experiment 500 yards of road between Ham Street and West Hythe were covered in 1820 with mould obtained from dredging the canal, for a sheep walk. The following year it was admitted that the road was bad where it was used by only the heavily laden narrow-wheeled waggons of the farmers, but the opinion of McAdam* was sought. He commented rather unfavourably saying that

---

* John London McAdam (1756-1836) gave his name to the surfacing of roads with stone broken small enough to make a hard smooth surface suitable for traffic. In 1816 he successfully 'macadamised' the road around Bristol and was appointed Surveyor-General of metropolitan roads in 1827.

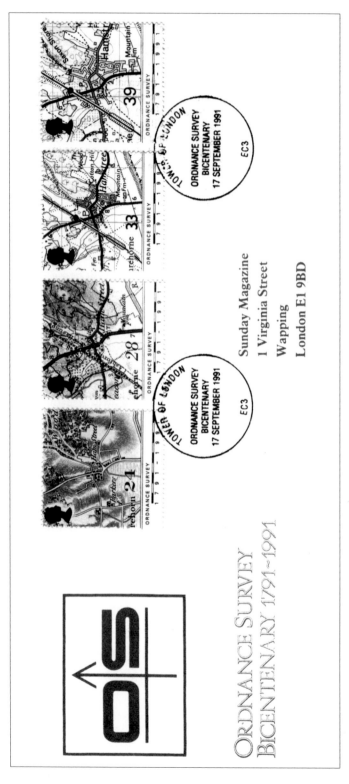

Ham Street was marked on postage stamps issued to commemorate the bicentenary of the Ordnance Survey in 1991. The four different editions illustrated were issued in 1816, 1906, 1959 and 1991. The Royal Military Canal is located below Mountain Farm at the bottom right hand corner of each stamp. (Courtesy of the General Post Office)

the existing road would never be good unless the shingle was broken up; also that a much narrower road could not be made for under £12,000 and that such expenditure could not be justified since the interest on this sum could not be repaid from the tolls.

In 1822 further consideration was given as to whether parts of the road should be closed to the public or tolls introduced. A very detailed traffic survey was thereupon carried out during the first week of every month for a year between 5 am and 10 pm. In July 1823 Swan reported the results of his estimate of monthly traffic passing along the Royal Military Road:

	Horses	Asses	Carts	Waggons	Oxen	Estimated Tolls £
Iden lock	1,927	111	449	797	957	109
Appledore	3,335	104	1,039	921	1,030	160
Kenardington	2,267	141	279	514	702	73
Ham Street	2,318	188	304	787	85	92
Bilsington	2,507	596	307	1,493	1,198	121
Eldergate	1,974	355	25	259	233	46
Hythe	2,716	631	69	545	91	67
						£668

Jackson, in his annual report to the commissioners, recommended that tolls should be introduced on the road from Iden to Ham Street by establishing gates at Appledore and Warehorne bridges. One reason advanced for their introduction was to make the canal more competitive with the road. It was not practicable, wrote Jackson, to attempt to levy tolls beyond east of Warehorne because of the numerous lateral communications and the facility for evasion.[6] He also pointed out that the road itself was not in good order as a result of it being used by narrow-wheeled country waggons and timber drays, particularly at the most unfavourable seasons for the purpose of saving the parish roads. The commissioners, at the meeting in July 1824 were the Rt Hon Charles Sutton, Speaker of the House of Commons; HRH the Duke of York, Commander-in-Chief; the Rt Hon the Earl of Liverpool, Prime Minister and Lord Warden of the Cinque Ports; Major-General Sir Willoughby Gordon, Quartermaster-General; the Rt Hon Earl Bathurst, Secretary of State for the Colonies and the Rt Hon Frederick J. Robinson, Chancellor of the Exchequer. They approved the director's recommendation but to the historian's annoyance the reason why no further action was taken is not recorded.

In September 1823 William Cobbett took one of his 'rural rides' through Sussex and Kent to Dover. The sight of the military canal and line of martello towers stretching along the coast caused Cobbett to give full vent to what he felt was the squandering of public money. 'From Dimchurch to Hythe you go on the sea-beach,' he wrote,

and nearly the same from Hythe to Sandgate, from which last place you come over the hill to Folkestone. But, let me look back. Here has been the squandering! Here has been the pauper-making work! Here we see some of these causes that are now sending some farmers to the workhouse and driving others to flee the country or to cut their throats! I had baited my horse at New Romney, and was coming jogging along very soberly, now looking at the sea, then looking at the cattle, then the corn, when, my eye, in swinging round, lighted upon a great round building, standing upon the beach. I had scarcely had time to think about what it could be, when twenty or thirty others, standing along the coast, caught my eye; and, if anyone had been behind me, he might have heard me exclaim, in a voice that made my horse bound, 'That Martello Towers by. . . !' Oh, Lord! To think that I should be destined to behold these monuments of the wisdom of Pitt and Dundas and Perceval! Good G——! Here they are, piles of bricks in a circular form about three hundred feet (guess) circumference at the base, about forty feet high, and about one hundred and fifty feet circumference at the top. There is a doorway, about midway up, in each, and each has two windows. Cannons were to be fired from the top of these things, in order to defend the country against the French Jacobins!

I think I have counted along here upwards of thirty of these ridiculous things, which, I dare say, cost five, perhaps ten, thousand pounds each; and one of which was, I am told, sold on the coast of Sussex, the other day, for two hundred pounds! There is, they say, a chain of these things all the way to Hastings! I dare say they cost millions. But, far indeed are these from being all, or half, or a quarter of the squanderings along here. Hythe is half barracks; the hills are covered with barracks; and barracks most expensive, most squandering, fill up the side of the hill. Here is a canal (I crossed it at Appledore) made for the length of thirty miles (from Hythe, in Kent, to Rye, in Sussex) to keep out the French; for, those armies who had so often crossed the Rhine, and the Danube, were to be kept back by a canal, made by Pitt, thirty feet wide at the most! All along the coast there are works of some sort or other; incessant sinks of money; walls of immense dimensions; masses of stone brought and put into piles. Then you see some of the walls and buildings falling down; some that have never been finished. The whole thing, all taken together, looks as if a spell had been, all of a sudden, set upon the workmen; or, in the words of the Scripture, there is the 'desolation of abomination, standing in high places.'[7]

The military barges which had been constructed by 'common carpenters' needed frequent repair. Two good barges were needed at all times for maintaining the works, Stone, timber, beach for the works and other heavy materials were conveyed almost daily from Hythe for repairs along the line of the canal. In 1820 only one was serviceable out of twelve craft and while six barges were repairable the other five were totally unserviceable. Jackson considered them unwieldy and ill-adapted to the canal. This indeed was true for although they had adequately served their original purpose their length made it difficult for them to be turned as the canal had been built with no special turning places. It was, therefore, decided to keep only two barges for dredging and weed cutting and to purchase condemned smuggling luggers and other craft from the Custom Houses at Dover and Rye. In 1821 one lugger, four long boats and two small boats were accordingly purchased for a very small sum. A replacement barge was purchased at Rye in 1827 for £170 and its life estimated at from 15 to 18 years. Purchase of a second barge was deferred and in 1829 only one barge and two boats remained serviceable. A special boat was built for tarring the bridges.

Hythe in the 1820s was a pleasant little town. It contained, according to Ireland,

> a neat little theatre, [closed in 1837] some good and spacious inns, a subscription reading-room and an excellent public library. The shops, as well as the dwellings belonging to the superior classes of inhabitants, speak the opulence, respectability and commercial importance of this place. There are many pleasant houses and extensive views both of the sea and neighbouring country, as well as numerous convenient habitations appropriated for the use of strangers during the bathing season. Others are occupied by the families of officers of rank in the army stationed at this place, who greatly contribute to enliven and improve the society constantly frequenting the town of Hythe.

Bathing machines 'and the mildness of the sea breezes on this shore, invite a very early attendance of bathers in the spring, and encourage them to protract their stay in the neighbourhood further into the autumnal season than is usual elsewhere.'[8]

Regular repairs had to be carried out to the barracks at Hythe; there was trouble from damp in the south wall, new kitchens had to be installed. Early in 1819 the return of the companies from France caused an unprecedented number to be housed. The blacksmith's and tailor's shops were rebuilt. In 1821 improvements were made to the Drawing Rooms and the resiting of the room for the lithographic and metallic presses. 'A room was also appropriated to the use of the officers and men in making models of useful inventions,' such as military bridges, carriages, telegraphs, and also locks and sluices of the Royal Military Canal. In 1822 it was agreed to 'remove the soldiers' privies from the front of the barracks (close to the public road) where they prove a nuisance to the town of which the Mayor and inhabitants have frequently complained'.

A curious case arose in 1815 which at the time of Waterloo really had no bearing on the battle nor the RSC. It only merits a footnote in this history as it concerned the barracks at Hythe and the Lord Chief Justice.[9]

In 1823 a canteen 'essential to the good economy and discipline of all troops' was established from which the military authorities received a rent of £50 per annum out of the profits.* In 1824 a school was built for the daughters of the NCOs and soldiers out of 'charitable contributions of the officers and the earnings of the children', and a schoolmaster-sergeant put in charge. Ireland pointed out that besides the officers' apartments there were 'accommodations for about 300 men and various comfortable rooms for married soldiers. Near the spot is also a remarkably pleasant and commodious house, occupied by the Deputy Quartermaster General and Commandant of this respectable corps'.

The barracks at Winchelsea 'where men were occasionally stationed', the officer's quarters at Iden, the toll houses on the military road, the station houses along the canal and the stables at Ham Street were the subject of regular repair. The eleven stations and toll houses along the line of canal, including the officer's quarters at Iden, were originally constructed of brick noggin, and by the early 1820s were fast going to decay. Between 1822 and 1825 these were rebuilt in stone. In 1819 the station house at Shorncliffe, which was built over the canal by the sluice just above the surface of the water, had to be rebuilt on dry land as its location was 'extremely prejudicial to the health of the soldiers'. The drawbridge carrying the Sandgate road was re-planked in 1831 and removed in 1840.

Marine Walk bridge at Hythe was rebuilt in 1818 and Twiss bridge in 1821 when it was also raised 'to admit the passage of barges laden with cargoes of all descriptions'. In the same year West Hythe bridge was rebuilt under the direction of Captain Mann 'with only one day's interruption to the passage of traffic owing to his judicious arrangements'. Eldergate bridge was reconstructed and the swing bridge over Iden lock replaced in 1825.

---

* These regimental canteens were normally hired out by tender to contractors who as often as not charged the men exorbitant prices for beer and spirits. According to W. S. Miller (1892) the Hope public house served as a canteen and the row of buildings standing back to the right were used as stables by the Waggon Train before their barracks were built. A small house on the left was used as a hospital and the two houses facing were the married mens' quarters.

19. Town Bridge, Hythe, c.1850.

Altogether twenty-two bridges had to be maintained, and these were all rebuilt again between 1827 and 1835.[10] The low headroom of some of the bridges caused inconvenience to barge traffic when laden with hop poles and straw. Several, including those at Eldergate and Jiggers Green were raised by 14 to 21 inches. There is little doubt that the canal was still kept up in an altogether extravagant manner although those responsible emphasised the difficulties. In 1819 the establishment at Hythe had totalled 517 officers and men, of whom 57 were employed along the canal (42 labourers, 5 carpenters, 4 blacksmiths, 3 bricklayers, 2 sawyers and a blacksmith).[11] However, in 1820 the company intended for clearing the Winchelsea section was sent to the Mediterranean and the corps, 'from a variety of circumstances, was subsequently too weak to effect it'. The following year the return of a company from the banks of the Mississippi and New Orleans was awaited before parts of the canal could be cleared of weeds and dredged. In 1822 it was reported that 'the weak state of the Royal Staff Corps at Hythe during the last two years has rendered it impossible to keep the whole of the works in a state of substantial repair'. However, plenty of men were available during 1825 and 1826 so that much of the outstanding work was completed although the 'great augmentation of the Corps' at Hythe necessitated the adjutant moving out of the crowded barracks into a newly bought cottage at the eastern extremity of the barracks.

Sir Richard Jackson's report of 20 June 1827, however, began on a dismal note: 'The year that has elapsed,' he wrote, 'has been one of much difficulty and embarrassment to those entrusted with the care of the Royal Military Canal'. Repairs were already in progress when the means of carrying them on were crippled by the departure of one company of the Royal Staff Corps and the entire detachment of the Royal Waggon Train for service in Portugal. This occurred at a time when in addition to the repairs being carried out, great danger was threatened to the canal by the defective state of the sluice at Winchelsea. Mann, now a major, was stationed at Winchelsea to reconstruct this sluice, but 'unfortunately the season proved so unhealthy in the vicinity of Winchelsea as to retard the progress of the works;' of the 107 men employed on this work — 98 had to be admitted to hospital and many of the cases were of a bad description'. The minutes record that great credit was due to Major Mann and the officers and men of this detachment for their 'perseverance in the execution of this trying duty'. Jackson might also have referred to the death of the Commander-in-Chief Frederick, Duke of York on 6 January. A man of many faults in private life but an admirable servant of the public. His interest in the work of those maintaining the canal remained as diligent and painstaking as it was when he proposed the scheme to Pitt twenty-three years before.

In 1828 the parapet in front of the barracks at Hythe was removed so that the road could be rebuilt along it, the ditch ('which could be very offensive at certain periods of the year') bordering the barracks filled in and the parade ground enlarged. In 1832 Jackson referred to the complaints of proprietors of adjoining land regarding the drainage, 'sometimes well-founded, but more often very unreasonable' and to the constant care needed to 'secure the public property for the injurious consequences of struggles between conflicting private interests'.

In 1831, Joseph Priestley published his historical account of the waterways of Great Britain (see Bibliography) and made reference to the 'Royal Military or Shorncliff & Rye Canal'. He went on to state that "the purposes for which it was originally constructed having become no longer necessary, it was deemed expedient by government, that the canal and towing-paths should be turned to some account in a commercial point of view, whilst they were likewise kept in repairs, in case they should be wanted as a means of repelling an invading force." He concluded his account stating it "is well calculated for the warlike, no less than for the commercial purposes, of the country." Unusually for Priestley no details were given of tonnage and wharfage rates.

A certain amount of inter-station traffic developed between Iden and Hythe for which toll was not always received by the collectors. To remedy this loss Jackson decreed in 1833 that the keepers should check the indices of barges loaded at their stations independently of the collectors, and that the toll collectors were to exercise the greatest possible vigilance in levying the tolls as henceforth they would 'be called upon to make good any deficiency of toll which may accrue from negligence or misconduct on their part'.

The toll collectors on the military road were paid by the commissioners; although no suspicion had become 'entertained of their honesty', no check could be 'devised upon their conduct'; so it was agreed in 1827 that the turnpike tolls should be let by tender and the salaries of the collectors saved. Romney Marsh is famoue for its rich pasture and great flocks of sheep. A glance at the old ordnance survey six inch maps reveals how numerous were the sheep folds marked in the fields bordering the waterway. The Royal Staff Corps, and later the Board of Ordnance, received a tidy income from letting the parapet, military road and towing-path for grazing. More than twenty lots between Cliff End and Shorncliffe were offered for tender. In 1833 annual rents exceeded £300 compared with turnpike tolls of £370 and canal tols of £453.

In 1833 it was reported that the part of the military road between Appledore and Hythe no longer open to the public (amounting to some 80 acres), had now become a sheep walk and was let with the parapet on a three-year lease. For the three years ending 10 October 1839 the annual rental had increased from £348 to £499. Six patches of land — formerly shingle beds at Hythe — were filled with earth and silt from the canal; some were let and others retained as plantations for growing quick, elms and potatoes. The forage barn of the Royal Waggon Train was a common country barn of wood, lathe and plaster and a thatched roof. It became more and more dilapidated but to save the cost of rebuilding it in stone part of the gun shed was turned into a store. Iden lock was fitted with new gates and in 1834 it was agreed that the two houses occupied by the toll collectors at Hythe and Iden should be completely rebuilt. The reduction in military barge traffic to Hythe caused the wharf at Romney Road bridge no 1 to be lent to the town of Hythe in August 1837 for experimental use as a cattle market.

In 1833 the Director, Sir Richard Jackson approved revised 'Rules and Regulations for the Guidance of Owners and Masters of Barges'. This booklet set out the licensing requirements for all craft using the canal; also penalties for non observance. Barges had to be brought to Hythe where graduated indexes to show the tonnage were affixed to the head and stern. These had then to be painted black, the tonnage marked in white, the boats weighed when both loaded and unloaded. Toll collectors were told to check indexes and to exercise the greatest possible vigilance in levying sums payable since any negligence on their part would need to be made

ROYAL MILITARY CANAL.

RULES

AND

REGULATIONS

For the Guidance of

OWNERS AND MASTERS

or

BARGES.

1st October, 1833.

WITH

AN ABSTRACT OF A PART OF THE

CANAL ACT,

IN A NOTICE BY THE COMMISSIONERS,

And INSTRUCTIONS for Checking the NAVIGATION.

APPENDED THERETO.

with Instructions for Collectors of Rates.

W. Tiffen, Printer, Library, Hythe.

good. Indexes defaced by tar or obscured by 'the lading of straw or hop poles' made the owner liable to a penalty of five pounds. Miscreants lacking sufficient 'distress' were to be committed to the 'common gaol or house of correction' for up to three months. Alexander Swan, the accountant at Hythe, included in the new booklet details of the tolls payable to any of the 14 stopping places listed between Iden and Shorncliffe. The charge for the total distance rose from 1s 9d a ton for beach, to 1s 11d for manure, 3s 6d for coal and 3s s

The business of keeping the canal free of silt was a major problem as all the waters from the lands on the north bank, with the exception of a culvert near Warehorne, passed into the canal. These streams brought with them not only silt but quantities of weeds collected by the farmers from the lands and ditches connected with them. Indeed it had so accumulated that it stretched for 8 miles from Shorncliffe and was some 2 ft in depth. An improvement had been carried out by making a reservoir near the junction of the Seabrook at Shorncliffe in 1827 for catching the silt. An indication of the quantity can be gauged from the fact that over 1,000 cartloads were taken out of this reservoir in 1832. Similar shoals formed on the Winchelsea canal, which in 1830 was 'obstructed throughout by silt and overrun with reeds and rushes'.

A regular passage boat service had been introduced in July 1818 when Mr Pilcher's small boat plied between Hythe and Rye charging 7s for the journey in either direction; a few weeks later a weekly charge of 15s was introduced; from 1 November this was reduced to 5s. The service to Rye did not prove popular — it must have been a very tedious journey — and from 26 June 1819 it went no farther than Iden lock although the 5s weekly charge remained the same. After three years there was a further curtailment when the service was restricted to running between Hythe and Appledore and the fare increased to 7s 6d a week. This packet boat also carried Government letters free of charge in return for being allowed to operate the service. This service continued successfully from 9 August 1822 for rather more than ten years. An illustration of a passage boat — it

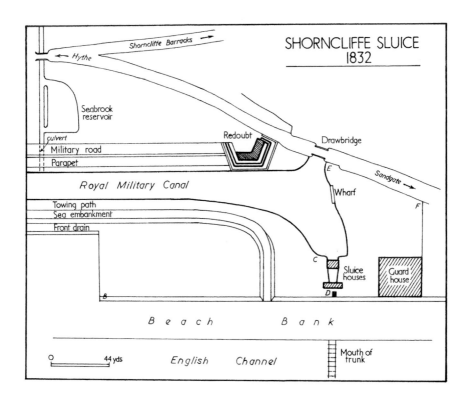

20. The military road, parapet and canal, Ham Street, 1971.

may have been Pilcher's — is to be found in Westall's print of 'Hythe from the Canal Bridge' published in 1829 (see p. 109).

The service was stopped in 1833 on the orders of Major-General Jackson, because of the great damage being caused to the banks by the 'frequent and rapid transit of the boat'. The damage had been particularly severe at the numerous angles of the canal. The director recognised that this boat was of great convenience to the public and 'it was with great regret that its continuance was found incompatible with due regard to the preservation of the works. It was found that no toll a boat of this kind could afford to pay would in any degree compensate for the injury done by it to the works — the damage was estimated at £150 in materials alone — and the proprietor (who died in 1834), had in fact applied for a reduction of one-third of the toll previous to the termination of the agreement.[12]

Alexander Swan had been asked by Captain White to provide details of the service on 3 June 1833. Swan reported the position up to 31 May 1833 and this information had been forwarded to the director on 30 June 1833. From this I would assume that the agreement with the proprietors was terminated at the end of July or August. A memorial 'respectably signed' in favour of the late proprietor was submitted by the director to the commissioners at their biennial meeting in August 1834. This memorial was refused and the director's report for 1836 refers to the continued

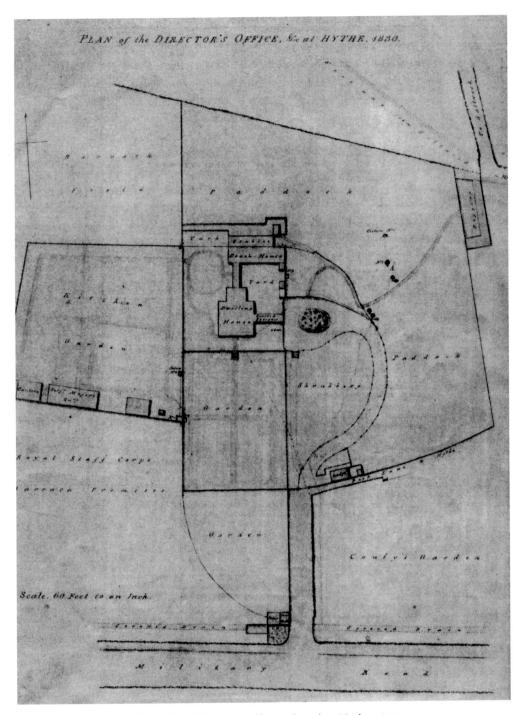

Plan of the Director's office and garden, Hythe 1830.

suppression of 'rapid passage boats of small dimensions'. Not until 1839 was a service reintroduced.

The canal was exposed to the danger of accidents peculiar to itself. On the one hand because of its contiguity to the sea at the Shorncliffe end or the other by its connections with the tidal Rother and Brede rivers, which form the Harbour of Rye, whose commissioners' 'local interests' would appear to be always at variance with those of the commissioners of the Levels of Romney Marsh. 'This supposed opposition of interests', wrote Jackson in 1830, 'has led to long and expensive contests and has given rise to repeated acts of violence from which the canal property has suffered and is suffering without any apparent means of redress.' Sluices placed on the Brede river by the commissioners in 1817 were destroyed by the people of Rye and the canal commissioners were involved in 'a very heavy expense' as a consequence of damage to the river banks by the tides. In April 1830 a similar group of people destroyed Scots Float sluice and caused an almost total loss of toll from barges passing to and from the canal with the result that tolls for 1830 fell by £70 to their lowest figures since 1809.[13]

Revenue did not begin to exceed the cost of maintenance until 1824 although no provision was made for the expense of the company of the Staff Corps whose cost was provided for in the army estimates. For the remainder of the 1820s income and expenditure showed no material difference. Total revenue increased during the 1830s rising from £1,058 in 1830 to nearly £1,501 in 1835 when expenditure on the works totalled £1,241, £1,536 in 1836, and may have risen higher in 1837, 1838 and 1839 for which years the accounts are missing.

The canal was also exposed to many natural hazards; the sea end of the wooden tunnel at Shorncliffe was often choked by shingle but this was easily cleared by opening the sluices at low water. What was not so easy was to carry out repairs to the banks. In February 1814 ice and floods destroyed the brick culvert west of Hythe which conveyed some streams into the canal. Todd put in a dam at General Brown's direction at the place 'where the old road to Romney passed' and although they secured with coffer dam piles

as we thought beyond risk, yet the weight of the water found its way through the shingle underneath and undermined and blew up the whole. I tried a second time at the bridge next to the Ladies Walk bridge but when the water rose a few feet on the higher side it began to ooze through the gravel underneath, and around in so alarming a manner that I was glad to destroy the dam as fast as I could.[14]

Consequently, the military road rampart had to be removed and the water let out before the repairs could be carried out.

ROYAL MILITARY CANAL.

AN ACCOUNT of all RATES and TOLLS, and RECEIPTS of MONEY and DISBURSEMENTS, and BALANCES remaining of any such RECEIPTS of RATES and TOLLS, for the Year ending 31 December 1833, of the ROYAL MILITARY CANAL.

CASH RECEIVED IN 1833.

		£. s. d.	£. s. d.
BALANCE in hand, 31 December 1832 - - - - - - -		- - -	108 4 8½
Drawn from Mr. Swan's Account at Messrs. Hoares - - -		50 - -	
Canal Rates received at - { Hythe - £. 90 5 - ½ / The Lock - 363 2 5½	£. s. d. 453 7 6		
Turnpike Tolls received for { Gate, No. 1 - 201 - - / Gate, No. 2 - 170 - -	371 - -		
Toll Tickets of leave to ride on Towing Path - -	5 12 -		
Rents of - - { Parapet and Land - - 306 6 8½ / Houses, &c. - - - 81 12 -	387 18 8½		
Produce of Land cultivated (Quicks.) - - -	5 12 3½		
Manure sold - - - - - - - -	3 3 1		
Beach sold from Property of Hythe Corporation -	72 11 9		
Old Stores - - - - - - -	5 4 7½		
Miscellaneous Receipts - - - - -	7 3 6		
Amount arising from the Works - -		1,311 13 5½	
TOTAL RECEIVED - - - - - - -			1,361 13 5½
£.			1,469 18 2

CASH EXPENDED IN 1833.

	£. s. d.
FOR Labour - - - - - - - - - - -	104 17 8
— Timber - - - - - - - - - -	87 18 9¾
— Tools and Ironmongery - - - - - - - -	31 - 9½
— Iron and Steel - - - - - - - - -	16 3 11¼
— Building Materials - - - - - - - -	61 1 -½
— Paints and Glazier's Materials - - - - - -	5 18 10½
— Plumbery - - - - - - - - -	7 18 7
— Rise Heading and Wicker Work - - - - - -	4 2 9
— Mixed Supplies - - - - - - - -	29 14 8¼
— Barrack Expenses - - - - - - - -	198 15 4
— Salaries - - - - - - - - -	318 12 6
— Miscellaneous Services - - - - - - -	106 13 -
Amount expended on the Works - - - - - -	972 17 11¾
Balance in hand, 31 December 1833 - - - - - -	497 - 2¼
£.	1,469 18 2

Hythe, } 9 April 1834. }

Alexr Swan, Acctt to the Commissioners R. Military Canal.

Fig. 1.

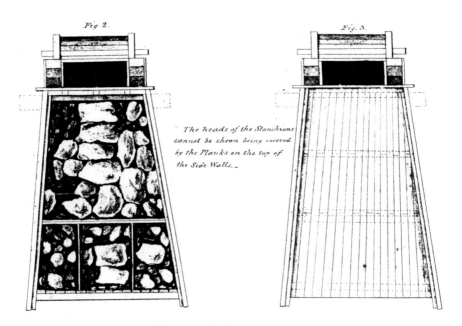

Fig. 2.

Fig. 3.

The heads of the Stanchions cannot be shewn being covered by the Planks on the top of the Side Walls. —

Scale. — One Eighth of an Inch to a Foot.

Fig. 1 – The Mouth of the Trunk as seen at Low Water.
Fig. 2 – Shows the State of the Stone Apron, with the holes where the Stones
    are sunk or washed away.
Fig. 3 – The Apron as it would appear when filled up with Stones, well puddled
    with clay and planked over.

Besides the floods of autumn and ice of winter, the canal's proximity to the sea was the cause of much concern. In the winter of 1824 'a violent storm occasioned the removal of a considerable part of the great bank of shingle near Hythe and the sea, after inundating the intermediate country, nearly forced an entrance into the canal'.* Considerable injury was done to the towing-path and to the southern bank of the canal and the sluices belonging to the Corporation of Hythe were destroyed.[15] Heavy rain in the autumn of 1829 caused floods which inundated most of the land south of the canal, as well as large tracts to the north. A strong south-west wind prevented the sluice gates operating at Shorncliffe and the canal began to overflow its banks. A fracture was reported at Kenardington and a serious threat to the locality arose. A strong force of the Staff Corps were rushed to the spot and succeeded in saving the banks. The local farmers were immensely relieved, the 'most respectable' fearing that half a million of money would not have covered the loss'.[16]

In 1829 the secretary of war announced a reduction in the size of the army by 8,000 men. On 21 January the quartermaster-general was advised that the Queen had agreed to the Royal Staff Corps being reduced from a total strength of 762 to 418, that three companies were to be disbanded, five companies abroad were to be attached to the Ordnance and the three companies retained at home.† By June 1830 only the company at Hythe remained and 'this I suppose one cannot get ride of' wrote one staff officer. Jackson drew attention to the effects this would have on maintaining the canal, mentioned the likely loss of £100 per annum in rent from the canteen in the barracks and the fact that there was no painter left on strength. However, the house formerly occupied by the commandant was let from Lady Day 1830 for seven years at £40 per annum.

The company which managed the canal during the 1830s was commanded by Captain Edward White and consisted of 60 rank and file,

---

* John Bishop in his History of the Brighton Chain Pier, 1897, p. 24, records that 'on 24 November 1824 there arose at daybreak one of the most violent storms that ever occurred on this coast, and it was all the more owing to its being at the period of the highest spring tides. At high water the storm was at its worst. Dr Mantell, the eminent geologist, who was then in Brighton, says that at one time the water rolled over the Towers of the Chain Pier and dashed with violence on the Steine, and many large masses of cliff were thrown down. Torrents of water poured across the carriage road of the Pier esplanade casting their spray upon Marine Parade. The wind blew directly ashore on the flood the rain at the same time descended in torrents, and the scene that the beach resented seemed to verify all that the most romantic could form of sea-side horrors'.

† Captain Dumaresq's company was disbanded in New South Wales. Ten years later the Board of Ordnance tried to discover what had happend to their arms and equipment! (MS Major E. P. White to Colonel Fox, Hythe, 6 December 1837).

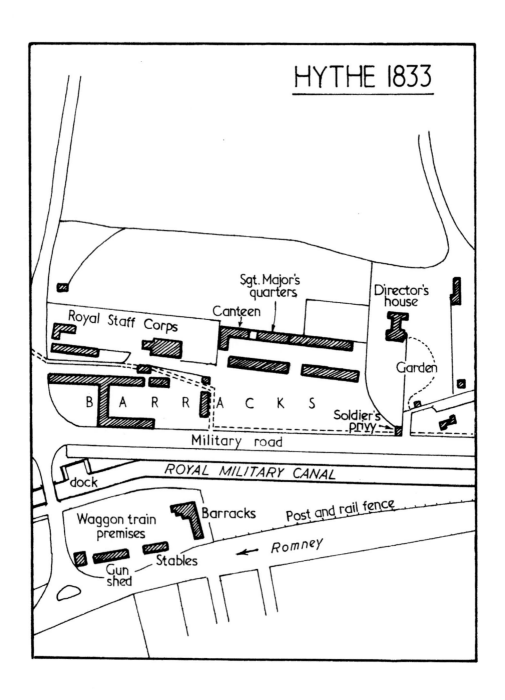

HYTHE 1833

Sgt. Major's quarters

Canteen

Director's house

Royal Staff Corps

Garden

B A R R I A C K S

Soldier's privy

Military road

ROYAL MILITARY CANAL

dock

Barracks

Waggon train premises

Post and rail fence

Stables

Gun shed

Romney

3 officers and 1 drummer. Of this number 27 were posted at the various canal stations. White had been commissioned into the Staff Corps in 1812 and was promoted regimental captain on 25 June 1830 when he took charge of the company.

The senior NCO was Sergeant Wilcockson. Herbert Wilcockson was 6 ft tall, had been in the army since 1821 and had, according to White, an exemplary character as well as a good wife. He was also a 'fair scholar', wrote a good hand and was considered to be particularly competent to superintend the workmen from Ham Street to Cliff End.

The men in the company worked a variety of trades. There was Walter Travener, the blacksmith, 'a man of excellent character and abilities, and although a blacksmith is a sober man'. John Conran the gardener, who looked after the plantations was sober, willing and hardworking, and William Gill the file cutter was 'a very useful man, a good bench man and a handy smith', Private Egerton was a very good tailor with 24 years service. Carpenter Will Taylor was a sober, steady bachelor. Dublin-born Hugh Arnold was a top sawyer of a very good character and wrote an excellent hand. Peter Breman the bricklayer, was a first-rate workman, who found his marriage 'to a woman of an extremely irritable temper', by whom he had a family of six children, his one drawback to happiness. Large families, however, were common. Clunan the tailor had seven and Wilcockson eight children.

There were, of course, some bad soldiers like Privates (3rd class) Emmat and Powers, 'idle, worthless characters', and Private Isaac Austin who was employed as a groom, and after 12 years' service was still termed 'a very bad character, who had lately returned from desertion'. Henry Hurst had a fair character but was occasionally 'rather loose'. John Crow the carpenter, could read and write and was a fair arithmetician, but although a good workman, was 'rather irregular'. Labourer Will Bailey was not strongly recommended — he had been six times in the defaulters' book, the last time absent from his quarters for two days when he married a woman of questionable character without leave, which had been refused; however, for the past two years he had behaved very well. The character of George Crowther after 24 years' service could only be described as 'very indifferent and James Lambert, who had served two years longer also had a doubtful character and was recommended for discharge. On the other hand, John Broom of the Royal Sappers & Miners was singled out as 'a most excellent man and good workman'.

In May 1832 the headquarters and principal part of the Waggon Train were moved from Croydon to Hythe. Jackson reported that some alterations in the interior arrangements of the stables and addition to the smith's forge had become necessary as a result of the increased number of horses. The following March, however, it was decided to disband the Corps and this was completed at Hythe on 10 July 1833. The men at Hythe were dismissed or transferred to the Royal Staff Corps. Of the eighty and more horses only ten remained employed on the canal; thirty were transferred to the Royal Artillery and the rest sold by auction at Canterbury. As a result of this sweeping away of the last remnant of the Waggon Train all the accumulated experience of the last war in matters of supply and transport was lost and consequently no transport organisation was available for general service when the Crimean War broke out in 1854.

A survey of the canal in the autumn of 1832 revealed that 26,000 cubic yards of mud needed to be dredged from the canal, a task requiring 100 men for 2 years. Jackson suggested that a portable steam-engine might be the answer and three estimates were received for a boat and dredging machine with a 4 hp engine, which varied from £960 to £1,650. The commissioners, however, being in no hurry to approve such a measure, suggested that a coffer dam built longitudinally so as not to obstruct navigation, might suffice and deferred a decision until the balance of revenue over expenditure was sufficient to meet this expense. Meanwhile, Colonel Freeth sought the advice of Major Alexander Todd, who was stationed in February 1834 at Loftus in Yorkshire. Todd replied that clearing out the mud from the bottom of the canal 'is a serious affair and I fear that manage it how you will must involve a considerable expense'. He confirmed that the new ballast engine 'will unquestionably be the best and most economical, notwithstanding the cost, provided that it could discharge the silt over the top of the parapet or towing path', but that if it only discharged into a boat he saw little advantage save the interruption to the navigation by emptying the canal and wheeling out the mud. Todd, who saw the navigation in 1806 when the 'whole of the excavation from Hythe downwards lay dry for many months', thought there was little danger of the banks falling in when the water was let out.[17]

In 1836 the commissioners noted that there was now sufficient money for a steam-dredging machine but decided that as the silting appeared to be little worse than it was before, the purchase could be deferred; they did agree, however, that in the meantime a Royal Staff Corps officer should be sent to see how the dredgers worked on the Grand Junction Canal.

Another serious danger to the canal's safety occurred during the hurricane which struck on the afternoon of 26 February 1835. During the morning the wind had been blowing with increasing vigour from the south-west causing the water to be driven violently to the eastwards towards Shorncliffe. By one o'clock it stood 18 in higher at the sluice than at Iden lock. Captain White, noting that no water was passing into the canal through the culverts from the sewers (which had recently been

21. The School of Musketry's boat-house, Hythe, 1971.
A view of the boat-house, (now demolished), and the concrete gun emplacement which was erected during the Second World War between the canal and the barracks.

cleared out), and that the freshes in the Rother were above the level of the canal, threw open the gates at Iden and admitted 18 inches of water on one tide. This dangerous operation was successfully accomplished for commented White —

> if the gates are not opened and closed simultaneously with those at Scots Float, for when they are first struck during the great floods the rush of water up the river is so great as to force the canal gates and when they are opened to let the water retire the flow is so excessive that if the gates at Iden are not instantly: closed, they would be in great danger of being carried away.

In 1836 Major-General Jackson was appointed to another post — he was later to command the British Forces in North America before dying in Montreal in 1845 — and it was agreed in November that Lt-Col James Freeth* the senior assistant in the quartermaster-general's department should be nominated director; an unexpected honour for Freeth — who had served in the Staff Corps since becoming an ensign in 1807 and with

---

* Quartermaster-General 1851-5, died 1867.

distinction under Wellington in the Peninsular War — but the Secretary at War commented that it 'seems absurd to have an officer employed in all other respects on civil duties in London, made responsible for visiting from thence a permanent military work'.

Indeed, now that the Corps had been reduced to only the one company at Hythe it was clearly a sensible arrangement to try and transfer the management of the canal to the Board of Ordnance, who controlled the Royal Artillery and the Royal Engineers and were charged in any case with the maintenance of fortifications. The Secretary at War, Sir John Hobhouse, had accordingly written to the Board on 30 June 1832. The Master-General, Sir James Kempt, replied on 28 July that he had not been aware that he was a commissioner of the canal until he had received Hobhouse's letter, but that he had had the question of the canal fully investigated both by the quartermaster-general's staff and his own, and that on balance he felt that it was being conducted in as 'economical and judicious a manner as the liabilities and nature of the service to be performed will admit of', and that 'the public will consequently derive no advantage by its transfer'. Hobhouse commented that he could see no reason whatever for the present arrangement and wished for another attempt to be made to put the canal under the control of the Ordnance.

However, five years were to pass before a new Secretary of War, Lord Howick, was able to persuade a new Master-General, Sir Hussey Vivian, to take over the canal, albeit with reluctance:

22. Ballast barge at Hythe *c.* 1905.

It will be troublesome and not a very profitable concern. The work was of as little advantage as a canal as it was absurd as a means of defence [he told Sir Andrew Hay] and if we take it [he exclaimed], I will take the earliest opportunity of going down to Shorncliffe to look thoroughly into the matter. One might have thought that a ditch which ought never to have been dug might with propriety be filled up; not so the military canal — for although if the water flows out of it half a million of damage may be done, yet if the earth is thrown into it a pestilence may ensue and more than half a million be required to empty it again, so little does this evil admit of any palliative that parliament would feel some difficulty even in raising a sewer rate.[18]

The Master-General did as a last gesture point out that an Act of Parliament would be required to effect the transfer and to empower the Board to assume the responsibilities of the commissioners but by then the secretary at war had already made the position of a *fait accompli* by announcing that the Royal Staff Corps had been excluded from the next year's army estimates and would be disbanded.

chapter 8

The Board of Ordnance Takes Charge (1837–1855)

Second Act of Parliament (1837)—transfer of Royal Military Canal to the Board of Ordnance—Royal Staff Corps disbanded (July 1838)—Major Thompson's economies—withdrawal of sappers and miners—passage boat services restarted—barge licence fees introduced and toll rates reduced (1840)—Kelly's quarterly reports—tolls and traffic—sheep grazing—sales of property—the School of Musketry occupies the barracks at Hythe—reassessment of the canal's value as a work of defence—the Duke of Wellington's opinion (1846)—Lord Raglan's view (1853)—attempts to purchase the canal.

It took less than a month for the Bill to be introduced and the Act granted for transferring the management and control of the Royal Military Canal to the master-general and the principal officers of the Ordnance. On 30 June 1837 the Royal Assent was received. The new Act was very brief, contained only two sections and simply mentioned that it had been deemed expedient to place the management and control of the canal and military road under the charge of the Ordnance.

Colonel Sir Andrew Hay, the clerk to the Board of Ordnance, was appointed director in September; he also took over the responsibilities of the former secretary to the commissioners. John O'Neil, the confidential clerk to Willoughby Gordon, had been the secretary to the commissioners since Dighton resigned in March 1828 on his retirement from public life. Although the salary was only £50 a year, when the transfer to the Ordnance was agreed the quartermaster-general thoughtfully wrote to the secretary at war drawing attention to the fact that the loss of this comparatively small salary would be an object of serious importance to

ANNO PRIMO

VICTORIÆ REGINÆ.

✶✶

C A P. XX.

An Act for transferring and vesting the Royal
Military Canal, Roads, Towing Paths, and the
Ramparts and other Works belonging thereto,
and all Estates and Property taken and occu-
pied for the same, in the Counties of *Kent* and
Sussex, and also the Rates and Tolls arising there-
from, in the principal Officers of His Majesty's
Ordnance.   [30th *June* 1837.]

WHEREAS an Act was passed in the Forty-seventh Year of
the Reign of His late Majesty King *George* the Third,
intituled *An Act for maintaining and preserving a Military*   47 G. 3. c. 70.
Canal and Road made from Shorncliff *in the County of* Kent *to* Cliff
End *in the County of* Sussex, *and for regulating the taking of Rates
and Tolls thereon*, whereby it was among other things enacted, that
the Speaker of the House of Commons, the Lord High Treasurer of
Great Britain, the First Commissioner of the Treasury, the Chancellor
of the Exchequer, His Majesty's Principal Secretaries of State, the
Commander in Chief of His Majesty's Forces, the Lord Warden of
the Cinque Ports, the Secretary at War, the Master General of the
Ordnance, and the Quartermaster General of His Majesty's Forces,
for the Time being respectively, should be Commissioners for carrying
on, completing, maintaining, regulating, and managing the said
Military Canal and Road, and Cuts and other Works thereof or belonging thereto, and then made or which might thereafter be made : And

U u

whereas

O'Neil; consequently compensation for loss of office was made.

For twenty years the canal had been managed more like an old-established trading company than a military defence work. Its troops were engaged in a variety of un-soldier-like duties and their occupations not unlike those employed on any country estate. There were gardeners to care for the plantations of ash, elm and quick; labourers to clean ditches and maintain the tow-path; station keepers each with his own plot of vegetables, the responsibility for trimming the hedges and keeping an eye on the property; blacksmiths to shoe the horses and forge the ironwork; sawyers and carpenters to cut the timber and repair the barges and fences; bricklayers and masons to tend the bridges and painters, plasterers and slaters the buildings; a wheelwright to maintain the carts, barrows and carriages; a millwright, two tailors, grooms and all these men instead of being ordinary craftsmen and labourers, were soldiers paid by the state with a pension to boot. Clearly it was time for the situation to be reappraised.

The changeover in responsibilities took effect from 1 October 1837 and initially, at any rate, life on the canal continued much as before, and it was not until December that the board decided to replace the Royal Staff Corps with 'steady, efficient, old soldiers' from the Royal Sappers & Miners and the Royal Artillery.[1]

The gradual demise of the Royal Staff Corps was a sad business for their last Commanding Officer, Edward White. The Master-General himself, Sir Hussey Vivian, had come down to Hythe and asked him on the evening of 3 December how he would manage the canal if it was his own. Three days later White wrote a guarded and diplomatic reply suggesting certain economies, and recommended that the sappers should be 'brought into training for their duties, which are very different from anything I as a military man have been acquainted with either at home or abroad'. The board decided that Major White should continue in charge until July 1838, that an officer (directly responsible to the inspector-general of fortifications) from the Royal Engineers, should at once be sent to Hythe to become the future manager of the Royal Military Canal, and that the establishment should be reduced to two sergeants, two corporals and forty privates. 'In order not to make the change immediate and thus bear hard on those who have served long and meritoriously' the master-general proposed the immediate discharge of only those unfit for duty. The men in charge of the horses and the horses themselves were to come from the Horse Artillery.

In March White advised the Brigade-Major at Woolwich that 'the sooner the detachment of one sergeant, one corporal and nineteen privates from the Royal Sappers & Miners can be sent to Hythe the better'. This first detachment arrived at Hythe Barracks on 6 April and three days later

White reported that 'I have lost no time in furtherance of the master-general and board's wishes in preparing the discharge document of eighteen men whose services on the works of the Royal Military Canal can now be dispensed with'. Some of the old soldiers became pensioners at Chelsea, some were simply discharged; others like Corporal George Luxford emigrated to New South Wales while Private Austin was not entitled to a pension 'nor any other indulgence which his service would have given him had he not deserted'.

In May ten men volunteered for service in the Royal Sappers & Miners — four of whom were anxious to join the companies employed in the survey in Ireland. At the same time White requested that five men experienced in the management of draught horses should be sent to Hythe with as little delay as possible with a view to their being instructed by the men attached to his company from the late Royal Waggon Train, for the particular duty of drawing boats on the canal with horses driven tandem on a narrow tow-path having water on each side. The five men of the late Waggon Train would then be discharged, 'as they are old soldiers and not disposed to remain longer in the service'.

It was now decided that the Commander Royal Engineers at Dover should assume the responsibility for the direction of the canal. In July Major Ringler Thompson of the Royal Engineers took over command from White and Richard Kelly took over the position of Barrack master and accountant from Alexander Swan. Swan was granted a 'retirement allowance' of £220 per annum on the abolition of his office which the Lords of the Treasury refused to increase in spite of Swan's appeals in 1838 and 1842. Swan had been the canal's accountant for 33 years, and as his salary had been fixed since 1816 at £332 10s 0d this pension does not seem unreasonable. White stayed on until he retired in March 1839 — his last act being to arrange for the guardians of the National School at Hythe to receive the balance of the Royal Staff Corps hut fund — £9 0s 1d. Toll collectors Baker of Hythe and Barnes of Iden were also retired and granted an additional pension of £11 per annum.

The 15 lock and station houses were now all manned by pensioners and provided with a fuel allowance of £3 during the winter months. Medical services were provided by Mr Fagg of Hythe, who received 1½d a week for each man, woman or child stationed between Shorncliffe and Jiggers Green. For £15 p.a. each Mr Houghton of Brooklands looked after those between Bonnington and Kenardington, and Mr Haden Banks those from Appledore to Winchelsea. Emergency payments for attention presented problems. White reported in March 1838 that one man's life would have been in danger 'if removed before the leeches had been applied' but that Staff Assistant Surgeon Ryan had informed him that the soldier had to

23. The Hope Inn and Stade Mill, Hythe, *c.*1880. The premises began life as the canteen for the Waggon Train before it became a licensed inn in 1827.

pay the cost of 5*s* 'as they were used on his person when not in hospital'. White assisted the soldier 'in another manner'.

Closer attention was now paid to the economics of running the canal. The master-general suggested that it should be managed not by 'effective sappers' who had been sent to Hythe by 'mistake' but 'old discharged soldiers' who would be very glad to be sent to Hythe Barracks and receive 6*d* a day plus their pensions; the inspector-general replied that it was better to select efficient good old soldiers than discharged pensioners, who would find the work arduous and would be required in greater numbers.[2] The master-general temporized — 'In another six months we shall be better able to determine as to any change that may be advisable either to promote efficiency or economy'.

Major Thompson at once set to work to reorganise the canal. It was a unique occupation for an army officer and as different as had been his earlier service with the Prussian Army. The property of which he now found himself the master, covered 615 acres, of which 213 were water; the length of the fences alone was 50 miles and there were 88 adjoining landowners ready to complain of any nuisance. Although revenue exceeded the cost of maintenance by £200 p.a., no provision had been made for the cost of troops. The canal had to be made to pay its way and the first thing to do was to examine it in detail.

24. The RSC Commandant's House Hythe, 1971.
In 1809 a house and garden formerly belonging to the Board of Ordnance was purchased for the Commandant of the Royal Staff Corps who was also the Director of the Royal Military Canal. Lt. Col (later Major-General) John Brown took up residence in June 1809 and lived here until his death in 1816. W. H. Ireland in his history of Kent (c.1830) remarked that the commandant's house above the barracks was 'remarkably pleasant and commodious'.

When the Royal Staff Corps was disbanded in 1837, the building temporarily housed the resident Royal Engineer. It became the residence of the Inspector-General of Musketry in 1853.

The inspector-general recommended that Thompson should be allowed two horses but the master-general commented, 'I cannot from what I saw during my visit, think that two horses are necessary. Whatever may be the regulation as to travelling expenses it can hardly be considered as applicable to this case when the whole of the officer's duties are within the short space of 26 miles, and when he has the canal boat when he may require it for the inspection of the work in any part'. Some of the perks disappeared. It was pointed out that the soldiers of the Staff Corps had to work a good deal in mud and water and had in the past, been granted an issue of spirits when the commanding officer thought it necessary, but this view was not accepted by the inspector-general of fortifications.

Thompson's investigations revealed that the buildings at Hythe housed great quantities of old stores, tools, carts, harnesses, equipment and armaments dating back to the Peninsular War. In March 1838 Folkestone

FREEHOLD
PROPERTY

AT

HYTHE.

TO BE SOLD,

BY ORDER OF

THE HONORABLE BOARD OF ORDNANCE,

A FIELD

To the North of the Road from Hythe to Romney adjoining and to the East of Penny-Pot House called the *Old Beach Field* : containing

5^{A.} 0^{R.} 33^{P.} more or less.

For further Particulars apply to Mr. KELLY, or at the Office of the R. M. Canal.

TENDERS to be sent under cover to the

Secretary to the Board of Ordnance,
Ordnance Office.

London,

ON OR BEFORE THE 14th OF DECEMBER, 1839.

R. M. CANAL OFFICE,
Hythe, 23d November, 1839.

WILLIAM TIFFEN, PRINTER, LIBRARY, HYTHE.

hoys conveyed some of these stores to the Tower of London; others were sold and some condemned as being old and unserviceable. The plantations, which contained 12,500 elms, 1,180 ash trees, 214 sycamores and 5,200 quicks were either let or put up for sale. A new source of revenue was obtained from impounding cattle found wandering on canal property.

The ten remaining horses working on the canal and their five keepers were scrutinised by the new commanding officer. Could their expense of £300 p.a. be justified — did they earn their keep he asked. Thompson reported in October that all the horses employed on the canal were very old, two were broken-winded, one was blind and one had shrivelled legs. Four were sold by auction and their two soldier-keepers ordered to Chatham.

The Ordnance found they had inherited a host of problems; not least was to ascertain exactly what belonged to them. An example of the laxity into which the accounting system had fallen was revealed by Swan's comments in July 1838 when he advised the Board that Thomas Boys Jnr, who had rented the old soldiers' barracks of the Waggon Train from January 1834 for £5 p.a., had not paid his rent for nine months. 'I cannot find any adequate reason for his having thus fallen behind and see little prospect of his soon paying the arrears more punctual in future, as his occupation is that of a labourer, and he has a wife and five growing children. I take the liberty of stating as the result of experience that I do not think there is much advantage in letting such small tenements to persons without property.' The inspector-general of fortifications proposed to demolish the property — but this revealed that the former officer's quarters were now occupied as a residence for the toll collector and the barrack master was using a shed as a coal store.

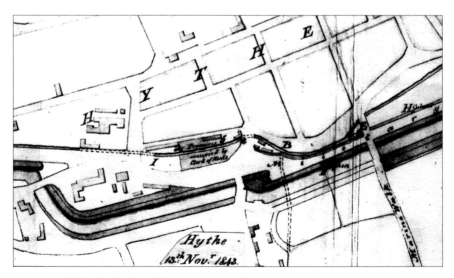

Location of the Clerk of Works premises, Hythe 1843.

A case arose in 1845 when Stephen Ward — a tenant at will — applied to the board for permission to purchase a patch of land at Iden and add a room to his cottage. He had apparently, without any legal authority, rather enterprisingly established a public house on a piece of land on the left bank of the Rother during the building of the canal about 1806. Later he had lost an arm in the 'service of his country (without receiving a pension)' and the board generously allowed him to lease the land on which he had built his hut for 21 years at £1 p.a.

John Hignett, the Ordnance solicitor, advised the board in November 1840 that 'this property had been much neglected regarding legal rights and liabilities' but that he hoped that with the assistance of a disinterested law agent on the spot and the RMC officers, the property might be secured for the future. Major Thompson and Richard Kelly were praised for their 'activity, zeal and intelligence' of which it was impossible to speak too highly.

The right to close parts of the military road to the public was contested. In 1839 James Watt of Marwood Farm was asked to refrain from using the road by Eldergate as his waggons were damaging the surface; he replied that he had a right of access. In 1840 an employee of Mr Figg of Brent Farm between Eldergate and Jiggers Green insisted on driving his loaded waggon along the military road — Mr Figg claimed it was a public road and that he had used it for many years. Such claims were contested by the Board but the disputes were drawn out and sometimes inconclusive. The drawbridge over the Sea Brook at Shorncliffe was removed in April 1840 and the unfinished defence work blocking part of the Sandgate to Hythe road and the cause of frequent accidents to carriages and riders was removed in 1841.

After the master-general had considered further reports from Major Thompson and the inspector-general of fortifications on the future maintenance of the canal, it was agreed that the employment of sappers should be superseded by pensioners from the Ordnance Corps at very reduced wages, and that only eight of the station houses needed to be manned. The master-general wrote on the papers put before him 'The suggestion of the inspector-general of fortifications is itself the one I proposed. I therefore concur'. Accordingly, in December 1840, the detachment of Royal Sappers & Miners was further reduced to 32 and in May 1841 to 7.

Captain Patten wrote a rather plaintive note from Hythe on 27 April 1841, saying,

> I hope I may be excused if I mention notwithstanding the refusal which has been given that I do now see how it is possible to carry on the

FREEHOLD
PROPERTY
ROYAL MILITARY CANAL.

TO BE SOLD,

BY ORDER OF THE
Honorable Board of Ordnance.

A MEADOW, in the Parish of *NEWINGTON*,
To the North of the Military Road between *Eldergate* and *Jiggers Green Bridge*,
Containing 4A. 1R. 4P. more or less,
And lately let to Mr. WATTS, for £9 : 10 : 0 per Annum.

ALSO,

An ARABLE FIELD, *in the Parish of ALDINGTON*,
To the North of the Military Road a little East of the Bridge at *Eldergate*,
Containing 1A. 1R. 8P. more or less,
And lately let to Mr. POSS, for £3 : 3 : 0 per Annum.

Further Particulars may be learnt at the Office of the Royal Military Canal, at Hythe.

Tenders to be sent under Cover to the
Secretary to the Honorable Board of Ordnance,
Ordnance Office,
London,
On or before the first day of September, 1840.

Royal Military Canal Office,
Hythe, 3ᵈ. of July, 1840.

T. SHREWSBURY PRINTER, HYTHE.

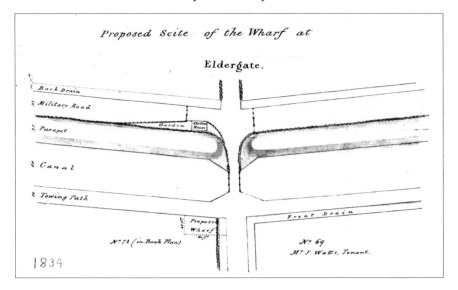

Proposed Scite of the Wharf at

Eldergate.

1834

duty here which will now embrace the engineer, barrack and coastguard services between Folkestone and Dungeness, as well as the canal, without an office.

The stations along the canal were now manned as follows:

Station	Responsibility (Miles)	Distance	Station keeper
1. Shorncliffe	Shorncliffe Sluice to Hythe	2	Bowers
2. Hythe	Hythe to Eldergate	4	? Ralph Eddlestone
3. Jiggers Green	Eldergate to Bilsington	4	Cornelius Scanlan
4. Ham Street	Bilsington to Kenardington	4½.	McCauley
5. Appledore	Kenardington to Stone	4½.	John Hunt
6. Iden	Royal Military Lock	–	Sgt Wilcockson (collector)
7. Iden	Stone to No.1 toll gate (Rye)	5¾	John Axom
8. Winchelsea	No. 2 toll gate (Rye) to Cliff End	5	Davies

Pensioners were also sent to occupy the martello towers and were paid 6*d* a day.

It was also found that the six horses on the canal could not be fully employed and that it would be cheaper to carry out all maintenance work by contract. In the summer of 1842 Corporal Turner, the NCO in charge, together with three grooms and two sappers, were discharged. The withdrawal of the barge horses gave rise to a soldier's moan since now that the weekly traffic returns could no longer be brought back to Hythe by horse on Saturday nights the station keepers had to do this on Sundays, and were thus deprived of the opportunity of attending divine worship. At the end of October the last soldier departed leaving the canal in the hands of Mr Kelly and the pensioners.

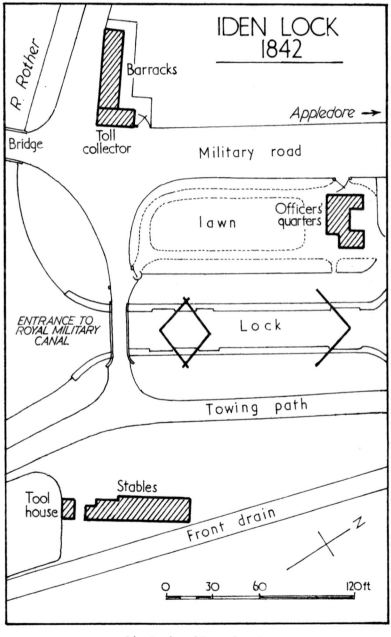

Iden Lock and Barracks, 1842.

From 1 November the storekeeper also became the toll collector at Hythe and took over the quarters formerly occupied by the sergeant. The brushings of the banks, the reeds and weeds were the prerequisites of the men at the stations. Thompson now had them collected and sold. The seven station houses no longer occupied were let by tender.* However economy minded they might be, the board was considerate in its treatment of those who were made redundant or retired. On relinquishing his job as station-keeper at Iden, John Axom was granted £2 to return to his home at Sheffield.

The Board of Ordnance was prepared to reconsider the operation of passage boats on the canal — suspended since 1833 — provided that they did no damage to the banks. Major Thompson wrote to the inspector-general of fortifications on 3 July 1839 to say that he had that morning gone on an experimental trip on Mr G. Pilcher's new iron passage boat with which it was intended to ply daily from Shorncliffe to Iden lock and back. 'The boat', wrote Thompson, 'draws very little water, caused no wave and appears well adapted for the purpose intended'. The service appears to have been successful for in March 1841 the board allowed John Friend of Newington to take passengers in his boat as a temporary measure and there is mention by Kelly in 1844 of two light passage boats, which although licensed, had not made any trips that year. This suggests that the service was operating up to this date but as the railway from London and Ashford reached Folkestone in 1843 and no precise reference is made to these boats in later reports it is probable that they were withdrawn that year; could the old launch sold in 1847 for £1 10s have been one of these? However; some sort of passenger-carrying may have continued until the opening of Appledore station and the Rye to Ashford line in 1851. In August 1849 John Hogben was permitted a rowing boat on the canal 'upon the terms you have suggested with regard to the alterations of terms in the event of the boat being used as a regular passage boat' and in June 1850 Mr Driscoll of Hythe was authorised to run a packet boat from Ham Street bridge to Shorncliffe for the conveyance of passengers. The third edition of Murray's *Hand-Book of Kent and Sussex* (1868) mentions that 'for some years a packet-boat ran on the canal, which suggests that the last service was not so many years before.

A contemporary description of a canal scene described by Nimmo could be similarly applied to the packet boat from Hythe arriving at Ham Street, Appledore or Iden.[3]

---

* Stone station house was accidentally burnt down on 22 July 1843 and was not rebuilt. The ruins were removed in 1850.

When they drew near the station-house, Jack in huge delight spied at some distance beyond, and coming towards it, the long white passage-boat, and the black caps and scarlet jackets of the outriders. At the station-house the boat stopped to allow passengers to get out, and to take in others . . . The station-house, situated on the bank of the canal, was a small white inn, which, if one might judge from its somewhat dilapidated appearance, did not drive a roaring trade. Behind were one or two out-houses, and on the same line with itself was a large shed in which luggage for the passage-boat was stored. The whole place was sleepy enough usually, and only when the boat appeared did it wake up to some semblance of life. Half a dozen intending passengers came out of the inn with their parcels and stood upon the little wharf. Up trotted Smiler and Paddy from Cork (horses employed on the canal) with their riders, who seemed to look down haughtily, as befitting their dignity. The drag-rope was immediately unloosened, and the long boat with its white awning came alongside the wooden wharf with a bump. Parcels were tossed in, parcels were tossed out; passengers stepped in carefully and disappeared under the awning; passengers emerged from the awning and stepped out carefully upon the wharf.

In an attempt to increase traffic on the navigation, the toll rates were reduced in November 1840. The desired effect was partially mitigated, however, by requiring all barges trading on the canal to pay an annual licence fee of £1, which effectively discouraged many of the barges which traded regularly on the Rother Navigation from using the canal occasionally — these had numbered 22 in 1839 and now fell to 15 in 1840 and 14 in 1841.

Kelly was also the canal's accountant during the 1840s and 1850s. Every quarter he submitted a report to the chief clerk at the surveyor-general's office in Hythe — a procedure introduced to check the effect of the reduced toll rates. These commentaries on the canal's traffic were presumably much appreciated (or rarely studied), for although Kelly regularly queried whether his reports were really required, five, seven and even ten years after the toll rates had been reduced, he was not asked to change their presentation. At all events they made rather sad reading for although the tonnage carried generally increased, receipts fell by over 25 per cent.

In October 1842 Kelly reported that there had been a very considerable increase in the carriage of coals, timber and miscellaneous articles from Rye to Bilsington and Bonnington from where they were taken by cart to Ashford, for the use of the South Eastern Railway. The coal for the railway's locomotives had more than doubled the canal's normal traffic.

This, however, ceased as soon as the railway had advanced to Folkestone for in October 1843 it was stated that the traffic in coals by the canal had fallen to its old level.

> I am sorry to see a general decrease in all other articles except manure. This is attributable in the first instance to many of the bargemen, who have been engaged for the harvest this year; there being a great want of hands in this part of Kent and Sussex. In the second instance that two of the three barges that usually take in their lading at Hythe, have been for some weeks under repair at Rye while the men went to harvest work. Thirdly, all traffic from the westward through the lock was closed in the month of August last, in consequence of the commissioners of the Kent and Sussex Rother Levels having given public notice that the water was to be drawn out of the river Rother in order to have certain repairs done to the banks, bridges, etc. The advantage was therefore taken of this circumstance by the Engineering Department here to fix a new pair of lock gates.

In April 1844 Kelly was pleased to report 'a considerable increase in the tonnage carried in hop poles, for which there has been greater demand this year than for many years past, in fact nearer double the quantity'. In July, however, he sounded a more depressing note —

> In the coal trade there is a considerable diminution, and I am informed that the South Eastern Railway has established depots at various stations on the line where coals are sold to the inhabitants of the neighbouring towns and villages, cheaper than when formally conveyed by the canal or land carriage, which although most beneficial to the public, has injured the traffic in coal by the canal very materially.

And in the late summer toll receipts were further reduced because traffic between Rye and Iden lock was interrupted for four weeks by water in the river Rother being drained for the purpose of repairing the banks.

During the winter of 1844-45 the canal was frozen over for 45 days, and an indirect consequence was increased cargoes of beach and broken stone being carried in the summer for the repair of roads. In October Kelly reported that

> the vicinity of the South Eastern Railway has injured the revenue very considerably and it is to be feared that the projected line from Rye to Hythe will injure it still more, particularly the carriage of groceries and salt which are the chief miscellaneous articles brought from Rye to Hythe.

V. R.

FREEHOLD PROPERTY
AT HYTHE.

TO BE SOLD,

BY ORDER OF THE HON. BOARD OF ORDNANCE,

A

DWELLING
HOUSE,

ith Stable and Offices, Garden, and Field, comprising altogether
0 A. 2 R. 8 P. of Land, more or less,

N THE TOWN OF HYTHE,

d now occupied by Mr. RATLIFF, Clerk of Works, Royal Engineer
Department.

The Field is eligibly situated for Building upon.

rther particulars may be had at the Royal Engineer Offices,
Hythe and Dover.

Tenders to be sent under Cover, addressed to the
Secretary to the Honorable Board of Ordnance,
Ordnance Office,
London,
On or before the 12th. day of February, 1844.

In 1846 he was still bemoaning the lower toll rates —

> It is much to be regretted that the reduction in the rates ever took place and there is every reason to believe that the tonnage would have been the same had no reduction taken place. In 1840 commenced the ill-judged measure (as it has proved) of exacting payment of £1 per annum for each licence.

A fee of £1 was also demanded for regauging each barge should the indices be found incorrect after it had been repaired, and also should the barge be one year out of the canal; consequently some of the barges withdrawn in 1840 had never since entered the canal but 'are employed on the rivers Rother and Brede, between Winchelsea, Rye and the interior'. However, there was a mild spring and in July Kelly reported that —

> The trade in hop poles this season is unprecedented, there having been already double the quantity conveyed than in the whole of any former year. The increase in the conveyance of chalk, lime and manure is also very considerable but owing to this being the summer quarter, the carriage of beach for the repair of roads has decreased.

In December the canal was frozen over for 25 days.

The building of the Ashford to Hastings Railway in 1847 brought a considerable increase in the tonnage of coal, timber and building materials, especially to where the railway crossed the canal at Warehorne to which place and Ham Street adjoining they were conveyed. As the railway did not open until four years later, traffic receipts were not affected until 1851, although the London-Ashford line began to attract an increasing proportion of the timber and hop pole trade.

In 1847 the tolls on the navigation (£453) exceeded those of 1840 (£452) for the first time since the toll reductions. This was due to the increase in tonnage of coal and timber and the total absence of frost. The traffic in hop poles again exceeded 10 per cent of the canal's total traffic.

Hardly a year went by without traffic being interrupted for a month or more. Some years it was the harsh winter which froze the canal over for weeks at a time; in others it was the need to carry out major repairs. Sometimes it was a combination of both, as had happened in 1844. In the summer of 1848 the construction of a syphon culvert under the canal near Bilsington to take the surplus water from the back drain into the front drain to relieve the land on the north side of the canal in time of floods, necessitated building two dams which obstructed navigation for five weeks. In the following summer repairs to the banks of the Rother Navigation caused a similar stoppage.

25. The London & South-Eastern swing railway bridge over the Rother navigation at Rye, from The *Illustrated London News*, 15 February 1851. The two windmills stand on Playden Heights overlooking the Military Road where a toll gate was established. The bridge was replaced by a double track fixed span bridge in 1903.

In January 1850 Kelly reported that because of the building of the new railway the barge owners were not replacing the old barges as they became worn out, and unserviceable; consequently there were none now to come on to the canal even were the licence charges abolished, and a return to the former toll rates would have simply driven the few remaining barges off the canal altogether.

During the summer, however, there was a further considerable increase in the carriage of hop poles and a small increase in coal and miscellaneous articles. Nevertheless in the autumn the barge masters were complaining greatly of the stagnation in trade and their consequent want of employment. For some weeks the bargemen around Hythe and the eastern portion of the canal had employed themselves in harvest work and the barges were laid up for a time. Only ten barge licences were taken out during the year, the least number on the canal since it was opened to the public. 'The effects of the completion of the South Eastern Railway in the carriage of merchandise and particularly coals for the supply of the villages in the neighbourhood of the canal, is also felt in a progressive diminution in the revenue in the last few years.'

In 1851 the drop in the traffic of farm produce was 'mainly attributable to the facilities afforded by the South Eastern Railway to the agricultural interests in the neighbourhood of the canal'. There was, however, an increase in tonnage of beach for the repair of parish roads.

Toll receipts averaged rather over £300 p.a. during the decade 1841 – 1850 while the cargoes carried were in the region of 13,000 tons. Three-fifths of this total consisted of beach for the repair of the turnpike and occasional roads crossing Romney Marsh. Coal represented one-fifth; hop poles one-tenth. The table below, showing the annual cargoes carried indicates the pattern of traffic.

	1842	1845	1847	1850
Beach	7,996	8,808½	6,827	5,327
Coal	3,955	2,167	2,737	2,098
Hop Poles	794	863	1,789	1,260
Timber	486	435	2,343	41
Agricultural Produce	212	291	111½	165
Chalk, lime & manure	173½	422	440½	270
Groceries & miscellaneous	1,285	1,328½	1,518	1,355
Total (tons)	14,901½	14,315	15,766	10,516

Some 325 acres continued to be let for sheep grazing. Half of this area consisted of the parapet and the remainder the military road and tow-path. Every three years it was put up to tender to the highest bidder. In 1839 it was let for £481 and in 1842 for £453 — the drop being accounted for by the fact that parts of the military road had ceased to be let because the sheep lay on the road and caused accidents. The conditions laid down by the Board of Ordnance stipulated that the land could only be grazed by sheep, and should heavier beasts arrive on the scene, then it was to be clearly understood that they would be impounded. The ground had also to be weeded, the nettles cut and thistles spudded at least three times a year on or before 5 May, 5 July and 24 September. The reeds, flax and rushes along the edge of the canal were excluded from this agreement but the government labourers, who cut them, were forbidden to encroach unnecessarily upon the adjoining land.

An unexpected problem arose in 1840 when Hythe Corporation challenged the army's right to impound sheep trespassing on canal property at West Hythe. The Town Clerk, Edward Sedgwick, claimed that the 'damage they do is nothing and the right was established of impounding such stock, after a lapse of 30 years, seems somewhat extraordinary'. Major Thomson responded by pointing out that sheep were not only a great nuisance to travellers, but they did much mischief to the quick fences and young trees. Fines had in fact been levied on five occasions since the

Ordnance Department had taken over and the right to impound had been upheld by their legal office. As might be expected this correspondence did nothing to improve the relationship between Hythe Corporation and the canal authority.

Over the years the military authorities had acquired land and materials which were no longer required. At fairly regular intervals sales by tender of land and property took place. In 1839 the sales took place of the site of Read's battery on the Brede at Winchelsea, a five-acre beach field disused since 1823 for £125 and the waggon train barracks; in 1840 a four-acre

ROYAL MILITARY CANAL.

TO BE LET BY TENDER, for THREE YEARS from the 11th Day of October, 1845,

FOR SHEEP-GRAZING ONLY;—THE PARAPET and WORKS,

LOT	DESCRIPTION OF LOT.	CONTENTS more or less.				At present let for		
		Parapet, &c.	Military Road, &c.	Towing Path.	Totals.	£	s.	d.
		A. R. P.	A. R. P.	A. R. P.	A. R. P.			
1	Parapet and Military Road from Cliff End to Winchelsea with Reeds opposite the same lot, (three crops) at per annum	10 2 10	14 1 31		25 0 1	73	0	0
2	Towing Path from Cliff End to Winchelsea Sluice { open / inclosed			2 0 7 / 9 0 37	11 1 4	10	0	0
3	Parapet from Read's Battery to Toll-Gate No. 2	17 0 3			17 0 3	40	5	0
4	Parapet from Scot's Float to within 200 feet of the Rother Bridge	5 2 29			5 2 29	8	10	6
5	Parapet and Towing Path (including Patch 0A. 3R. 9P.) from the Lock to Stone	8 2 15		5 1 5	13 3 20	17	5	0
6	Parapet and Towing Path between Stone and Appledore Bridge	13 0 22		8 2 32	22 0 4	27	15	0
7	Parapet, Military Road, and Towing Path, between Appledore and Kennardington,—including Osier Bed near Appledore	12 2 9	10 2 15	9 2 2	32 2 26	40	0	0
8	Parapet, Military Road, and Towing Path between Kennardington and Warehorne	5 3 29	4 3 6	3 1 17	14 0 12	20	7	6
9	Parapet, Military Road, and Towing Path between Warehorne and Hamstreet	5 1 6	3 3 26	2 2 10	11 3 2	15	2	6
10	Parapet, Military Road, and Towing Path between Hamstreet and Ruckinge	9 3 3	7 1 26	3 2 0	20 2 29	28	12	6
11	Parapet, Military Road, and Towing Path between Ruckinge and Bilsington	7 0 0	4 1 12	2 1 0	13 2 12	18	0	0
12	Parapet, Military Road, and Towing Path between Bilsington and Bonnington	6 1 0	4 3 14	2 1 2	13 1 16	21	12	0
13	Parapet, Military Road and Towing Path between Bonnington and Jigger's Green	6 0 0	4 1 6	2 0 20	12 1 26	22	10	0
14	Parapet and Roads between Jigger's Green and Eldergate Bridges	12 2 0	9 0 31	4 2 0	26 0 31	23	0	0
15	Parapet and Roads between Eldergate and West Hythe	9 2 25	6 3 21	3 1 10	19 3 16	26	0	0
16	Parapet and Roads between West Hythe and Government Wharf, Hythe	11 0 27	7 2 18	5 0 0	23 3 5	31	10	0
17	Parapet between the two Romney Road Bridges at Hythe, with the field opposite on the South side of the Canal, now inclosed with a stone wall, and including the site of the late Waggon Train Barracks, and two paddocks	1 3 29		2 3 0	4 2 29	9	0	0
18	Parapet and Towing Path from the Bridge on the Romney Road opposite the Duke's Head to Twiss Bridge	3 2 30		2 2 24	6 1 14	3	0	0
19	All the Canal Land between Twiss Bridge and Shorncliff Bridge and Sluice	7 3 24	16 1 38	7 0 23	31 2 5	15	0	0
20	Patch North side of Canal between Stone and Appledore				0 0 25	0	12	0
21	Two triangular Patches South side of Canal between West Hythe and Hythe				0 0 16	0	6	0
22	Patch North-west corner of Ordnance Field adjoining the old Barrack Road to Saltwood Heights				0 2 10	1	15	0

Hythe, 1st September, 1845.   **the Secretary to the Honorable Board of Ordnance, Ordnance Office, London.**

meadow between Eldergate and Jiggers Green bridge and another small field adjacent to the military road in Aldington; in 1844 the house occupied by Mr Ratcliff, the clerk of works at Hythe. The Royal Military Canal office at Hythe became known as the Royal Engineer Office after 1844. The site of the old Waggon Train barracks was levelled in 1853.

With the departure of the last troops in 1842 the barracks at Hythe remained unoccupied except for the occasion when a detachment of the 29th Foot were sheltered there after being shipwrecked at Dymchurch Wall in May 1842 and its use by various regiments furnishing guards for Shorncliffe. Then in June 1853 the School of Musketry was established at Hythe to provide troops with instruction on the new Enfield rifle. The barracks were used to accommodate the staff and those attending courses and the commandant's house was occupied by the inspector-general of musketry.

In August 1853 George Pain, barge master of Cheriton Mills, was authorised to land cargoes of coal on the rough ground opposite Shorncliffe battery and deposit them on the canal wharf on payment of the normal wharfage charge of 1d a ton per week. It was also used by W. Marshall of Hythe who gave up using Bonnington Coal Wharf in October 1855.

A tight budget and a general run down of the canal's facilities was becoming increasingly evident. In April 1854 the inspection boat was beyond serviceable repair and 17 months later it was again reported as 'quite decayed and inspection of the canal thus rendered likely to be given up altogether'. However, nothing was apparently done as in October 1860, the boat now 'nearly unserviceable', was still kept in the boat house.

Martello Towers at the School of Musketry, 1855.

26. The remains of the Redoubt at Shorncliffe, 1990.

Although the canal was now managed by pensioners they had to be fit. Robert Davis's appointment as collector at Hythe was not approved by the Board of Ordnance on account of his defective sight; instead they offered the position to Pensioner William Routledge of the Royal Artillery, even though it entailed posting him from Enniskillen to Hythe for which he was paid £5 'in aid of his travelling expenses'. Routledge received 6d a day as collector from 6 January 1855 and also 1s 7d a day for assisting Kelly with the issue of stores. The eight station keepers were now paid 7s a week. In 1860 the Board would not permit a one legged man to take over at Ham Street.

From time to time the government reconsidered the value of the canal as a work of defence and whether it should continue to be maintained. In 1846 the Duke of Wellington, who had by then retired from political office but was still at the age of 77, Commander-in-Chief and Lord Warden of the Cinque Ports, reported on this particular point. His knowledge of the canal dated back over 40 years to the summer of 1805 when he had just returned from India with the rank of Major-General. During the month of November when he was appointed to the staff of the Kent District he had had the opportunity to see the work in progress and had the opportunity on several occasions of meeting Pitt, who had told his brother, Lord Wellesley, that 'he had never met with any officer with whom it was so satisfactory'to converse';[4] and there is little doubt that the two men had discussed the great defence work then in progress. He took command of

27. Aerial views of the canal looking towards Hythe from Shorncliffe.

a brigade at Hastings in February 1806 and on 1 April he was elected a Member of Parliament for Rye. His views on canals may also have been initially influenced by Pitt for while Chief Secretary of Ireland in 1807 he recommended increased expenditure on canals to improve agriculture and provide employment. Later between 1828 and 1830 when Wellington was First Lord of the Treasury and one of the commissioners of the canal, he had attended meetings and having also been Lord Warden for the past 17 years was familiar with the locality.

The Duke of Wellington had long felt that Britain's military and naval strength had, since the peace following Waterloo, been reduced in a degree incompatible with her safety. The application of steam to maritime operations had rendered Britain assailable on all parts of the coast. While residing at Walmer Castle, like Pitt before him, he had taken the opportunity to make careful examination of the fortifications of the Kentish coast. Assuming Romney Marsh would be in possession of the enemy, wrote the Duke, on the subject of the canal,

> The position is good, but would probably require a larger army to defend it against the attack of a large army than could be allotted for that service, if an enemy's army of sufficient strength could be collected in the marsh to attack the position.

But with its flanks secured, as proposed, it appears impossible to force it in front, as the north-east bank of the canal is so formed as to afford the means of opening a flanking fire of artillery at points at short distances from each other.

The road of communication along the canal, from right to left, is excellent, very broad, and convenient for the march of troops: There are excellent roads leading to the canal from the rear; the country behind the canal is high, and commands a view of the whole marsh in front; in short there cannot exist anywhere a more commanding position.[5]

Lord Raglan, when Master-General of the Ordnance, and before he became Commander-in-Chief of the Expeditionary Army to the Crimea, also reported in 1853 that in his opinion the canal presented a considerable obstacle to an enemy, and should not be abandoned, unless the expenses rose to a degree altogether disproportionate to its object; and that, even then, the department would not be justified in making a free gift of it. At this period there still appeared a slight excess of income over expenditure, upon a return of the preceding three years, and the board accordingly refused to entertain the proposition.

Several attempts were made, at various times, to purchase or take over control of the Royal Military Canal from the government. In January 1844, the Provisional Committee of the Hastings, Rye & Tenterden Railway Company had made application to the Board of Ordnance to be allowed to purchase the canal. The Treasury, on being referred to, stated that they saw no objection to the sale;[6] and the Ordnance Solicitor proposed to effect it by simply inserting a clause in the Company's Bill for that purpose. The Bill, however, did not pass Parliament.

In 1848, a formal application was made conjointly by the Lords of Romney Marsh and the commissioners of all the adjacent levels, to undertake the entire control and management of the canal, and relieve the Board of Ordnance from all liabilities. Mr Clarke, the Ordnance solicitor on being referred to, stated that he saw no legal object to the transfer in question, but that it would be necessary for the commissioners to obtain the authority of the legislature for the purchase, and, at the same time, to repeal the whole or part of the Act of 1807.

General Fanshawe, in a letter of 6 September 1848, recommended that the Board should give the canal to the commissioners unconditionally and Mr Clarke, in a subsequent letter, adopted the same view, but proposed to annex a condition, that the Lords of the Levels should keep the Dymchurch redoubt in repair. The Board of Ordnance, however, on finding that there was some excess of income over expenditure, replied to the commissioners that they could not part with the canal without adequate compensation and the negotiation fell to the ground.

28. Lympne Castle and Church, 1829.
The castle overlooking the Royal Military Canal and Romney Marsh was in ruins until the turn of the twentieth century. Below the Castle half way down the hill towards the canal lie the ruins of the Roman fortress, Studfall Castle.

In 1853 the same proposition was renewed by the same parties. The Ordnance solicitor, in a formal statement dated 11 July 1853, repeated his former opinion that there was no legal objection to the transfer, but Sir John Burgoyne, the inspector-general of fortifications to whom the application was referred, put it to the consideration of the board, whether

> the Ordnance should thus give away, without remuneration, what must be of considerable value; not as a canal, because its value, if to be maintained, may perhaps be shown to be little, or perhaps worse; but if it is to be abandoned as such, and probably filled up, as seems to be the desire of the Romney Marsh Commissioners, it is to be presumed that a great deal of it might be disposed of throughout its great extent very advantageously, and there can be no reason why the government should not obtain at least that return for its great outlay.

The outbreak of the Crimean War brought a flurry of activity to the area. The need to establish camps for the assembly and training of troops before their dispatch overseas had prompted the War Office to establish a permanent military camp at Aldershot in April 1854 only a few days after war had been declared against Russia.[7] The School of Musketry under the direction of Major-General Hay was also permanently established at Hythe on the land

29. Studfall Castle, 1829.
Studfall Castle was once a Roman fortress on the Saxon shore until a landslide carried
it away in the time of Henry V. Martello Towers align the foreshore.

between the barracks and the sea. The camp formed at Shorncliffe during
the Peninsular War was also made permanent and in 1855 Queen Victoria
received the Foreign Legion on the heights above Sandgate.

In May 1855 the powers of the Board of Ordnance were vested in the
Secretary of State for War* and the Commander-in-Chief took over from
the Master-General the supreme command of the Royal Engineers and the
Royal Artillery as well as the Royal Military Canal. However, the CRO at
Dover remained director of the canal.

---

* The office of the Secretary at War was merged in that of Secretary of State for War
in February 1855.

30. The remains of an ancient chapel close to the banks of the canal at West Hythe 1829, with Lympne Castle visible on the heights above. Ford Hueffer writing in 1900 described how the church of our Lady of West Hythe had been turned to "agricultural purposes and as a byre undergoes an honourable eclipse". Today it stands a ruined shell, its exterior clad in ivy.

chapter 9

The Secretary of State for War Assumes Responsibility (1855–1872)

The Wrottesley Report (1857)—Traffic in the 1860s—Act of Parliament for sale of the canal (1867)—Seabrook Harbour Company—the Lords Bailiff and Jurats of Romney Marsh—Henry Stringer—Act of Parliament for disposal of canal (1872).

Now that the Royal Military Canal had become once more the responsibility of the Secretary of State for War, Lord Panmure, the waterway's future had again to be reconsidered. In August 1856 a Mr Smith proposed, on behalf of some clients, to purchase the canal, and all rights and lands connected with it, but the war minister, in a minute dated 18 August 1856 decided that the canal should not be relinquished, unless new circumstances had arisen since the last decision upon the subject in 1853. A memorandum by the inspector-general of fortifications on defences for Great Britain in November 1856, however, ignored mentioning the canal although it stated that 'the dispersed towers and batteries of old date might be left standing and armed on a chance of being of service against small desultory efforts'.

Then early in 1857 Captain the Hon George Wrottesley of the Royal Engineers was asked to look into the whole question and in March he produced a detailed report reviewing the canal's history and commenting on its position as a work of defence, as an impediment to smuggling, as a navigation and what should be done with it in the future.[1]

In addition to the great extent of the position, mentioned by the Duke of Wellington, Wrottesley referred to other objections to its value as a defence work which had been made at various times. One particular criticism was that it was equally assailable along its entire front, a condition which violated the first principle of defence, viz, that of reducing the points of attack to as few as possible. It had, besides, the disadvantage of being convex towards the defenders; a serious defect, where the line to defend was long, as the defenders acted upon the circumference of the circle, while the assailants operated upon the radii. Thus, if an enemy were collected in force at Old Romney he would be within five or six miles of every portion of the canal, the defenders of which would be operating over a line or more than treble that distance.

These defects had become all the more serious in consequence of the great increase in the value of the marsh lands over the past 20 years; farmhouses, hamlets, and enclosures, had risen up as more land was brought under cultivation, 'and would in a great measure, mask the operations of an enemy in front of the position'.

Having regard also to the 'difficulties of any concentrated retreat from the position when forced and of providing a sufficient armament in a time of pressure, for its numerous flanks', Wrottesley considered that the canal now possessed little value whether viewed as a military position or a defensive work. However, considered

> merely in the light of an obstacle, it deserves attention; it cuts off the whole of the Romney Levels from the interior of the country, retains the means of filling the ditches, and if there were time, of inundating the greater part of the marshes, by the operation of its sluices on the Shorncliffe flank; and, as it may fairly be expected, if all the bridges were broken up, to retain an enemy some few hours longer in the intricacies of the marsh country, it may be presumed that the knowledge of the existence of such an obstacle would deter an enemy, on the calculation of chances, from landing anywhere between Sandgate and Rye.

The custom-house authorities stated that the canal was not 'at the present time' of any value to their department as an impediment to smuggling. Wrottesley advanced the view that the navigation had never appeared to have been of much value and concluded his report with a masterly summing-up:

> Undertaken at a period of panic and great public excitement, it would be unfair to criticise too closely any of the works raised to defend the country against the threatened invasion in the early part of this century; but viewing the project dispassionately, at this distance of time, it must be allowed to have been a very improvident one for the country. A canal is dug in a most unfavourable soil, at the foot of a range of hills, with an outlet on the open beach, and a large portion of it constructed on the bed of the old Hythe Haven, the filling up of which from natural causes

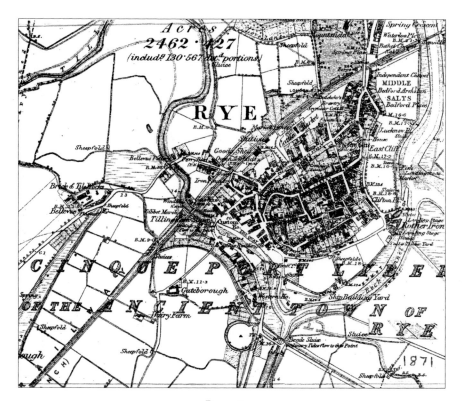

Rye, 1871.

might have perhaps suggested, to less sanguine projectors, a similar fate for the canal.

Twice damaged by heavy storm, which entailed additional works, the canal cannot have cost much less, from first to last, than £200,000 — a sum which would have been sufficient for permanent works of defence, of greater efficacy for the object in view. But the cost of the canal is of minor importance to the liabilities assumed by the Government, when they executed this project. Constructed at the foot of a range of hills, the drainage of which is intercepted and diverted from its natural course, it is evident that the Government rendered itself responsible for maintaining a proper outlet for the drainage of the whole upland district, and thus placed itself in a position from which it appears almost impossible to retreat, except by the surrender of the whole property to some public body — a condition of things, which appears to be thoroughly well understood by the commissioners of the adjacent levels, who have hitherto refused to give the Government any consideration whatever for the property, upon the plea that taking upon themselves the liabilities of the undertaking is a fair set off against any value that the property may possess.

But between the policy of the original undertaking, and the policy of abandoning it when constructed, there is a wide distinction. It does not appear, even including three years of heavy expenditure upon the canal, during which the fencing has been entirely renewed, and the works placed in a good state of repair, that the expense to the country annually, exceeds upon an average of 12 years, £440, or about the same sum which is required to keep in repair a barrack for a regiment of infantry. It would appear then that the period has not yet arrived when the expenses

COMPARATIVE STATEMENT of the

Income of the Royal Military Canal,

from the year 1846 to 1855.

	1846.			1847.			1848.			1849.			1850.		
	l.	*s.*	*d.*	*l.*	*s.*	*d.*	*l.*	*s.*	*d.*	*l.*	*s.*	*d.*	*l.*	*s.*	*d.*
Canal Rates	360	15	9	452	16	2	345	7	2	229	8	11	275	12	4
Turnpike Tolls	446	0	0	446	0	0	446	0	0	400	0	0	366	0	0
Rents of Land	482	10	0	483	4	0	488	11	0	467	14	0	458	19	4½
Ditto of Buildings	69	9	0	63	1	6	65	3	0	62	2	4	58	3	6
Annual Acknowledgments	6	19	0	5	3	0	6	5	6	6	2	6	5	4	6
Fishery of the Canal	....			....			....			15	0	0	16	5	0
Tickets to ride on Towing Path	4	4	0	3	17	0	4	4	0	4	18	0	4	18	0
Barge Licenses, &c.	17	0	0	19	0	0	15	0	0	12	7	0	10	0	0
Trespass of Cattle	0	13	0	0	1	0	0	8	0	0	3	0	0	1	0
Wharfage	0	18	0	1	1	6	0	14	7	1	3	11	0	10	6
Sale of Land	....			....			†5	10	5	....			....		
Ditto of Old Stores	....			1	2	0	7	16	10	....			7	10	7
Ditto of Reeds, Litter, &c.	3	19	0	7	8	6	3	3	6	3	0	6	3	3	0
Ditto of Sand, Mud, &c.	11	3	0	2	17	6	....			8	2	3	6	14	4
Medical Stoppages	0	14	0	0	14	0	0	14	0	0	14	0	0	14	0
£	1,404	4	9	1,486	6	2	1,388	18	0	1,210	16	5	1,213	16	1½

	1851			1852.			1853.			1854.			1855.		
	l.	*s.*	*d.*	*l.*	*s.*	*d.*	*l.*	*s.*	*d.*	*l.*	*s.*	*d.*	*l.*	*s.*	*d.*
Canal Rates	279	13	2	246	2	2	243	10	7	250	1	10	248	15	1
Turnpike Tolls	366	0	0	366	0	0	335	0	0	335	0	0	335	0	0
Rents of Land	458	11	7	459	5	4	433	1	11½	*424	1	11½	427	2	0
Ditto of Buildings	58	19	9	59	1	0	58	4	3	*42	9	3	23	19	0
Annual Acknowledgments	7	5	0	7	6	0	7	4	0	6	10	0	5	17	0
Fishery of the Canal	12	15	0	7	10	0	7	14	0½	6	6	4½	7	15	0
Tickets to ride on Towing Path	2	16	0	3	17	0	4	4	0	4	4	0	3	10	0
Barge Licenses, &c.	12	10	0	12	0	0	14	10	0	15	0	0	15	0	0
Trespass of Cattle	....			....			0	2	0	....			....		
Wharfage	0	13	9	0	15	1	0	6	10	5	12	3	0	5	2
Sale of Land	....			....			....			....			....		
Ditto of Old Stores	....			2	1	6	16	13	3	....			....		
Ditto of Reeds, Litter, &c.	2	18	0	2	7	0	2	12	0	2	16	0	2	14	0
Ditto of Sand, Mud, &c.	2	12	7	7	3	7	7	4	0	....			....		
Medical Stoppages	0	14	0	0	14	0	0	14	0	0	14	0	0	13	0
£	1,205	8	10	1,174	2	8	1,131	0	11	1,092	15	8	1,071	10	3

C. B. EWART, *Major, Resident Royal Engineer.*

R. V. KELLY, *Accountant, &c., R. M. Canal.*

Hythe, January 1857.

can be said to be altogether disproportionate to the objects served by the work; but upon a consideration of the prospects of the canal, and the awkward liabilities of the government under the Canal Act, it would not appear advisable to forego any occasion which may arise, of disposing advantageously of the property in question.

In the event of the Government intending to give up the canal, and the commissioners of the levels requiring it for the purpose of converting it into an arterial drain, as in 1853, the best plan that the Government could adopt would be to offer them the canal and towing path as a free gift, and to sell the tolls and station houses, and to dispose, in lots, of all the ground on the north side of the canal, which is now under pasturage. This is the best bargain which the Government could make, but could only be obtained by taking advantage of any necessity which may arise for additional drainage in the adjacent districts — The surrender of the canal to some public body, under more or less favourable conditions, would appear to be the only mode in which the Government can relieve itself of its liabilities; for the other method, adverted to by Sir John Burgoyne, in 1853, of fitting up the canal, and selling the whole property in lots, presents many difficulties; not the least of which would be the opposition which would be experienced from the Lords of Romney Marshes, to any attempt to throw the drainage of the upland country upon the district under their jurisdiction.

Whatever decision is arrived at with regard to the canal, I would recommend that a survey be made of the elm trees planted along it, with a view to their being cut down and sold. Most of them are upwards of 50 years old; they will never be worth more than they are at present — The situation is not congenial to them, their roots being saturated with the water, and in many places exposed from the wearing away of the banks — Should it be determined to retain the canal, alders and such trees as flourish in acqueous sites might be substituted for them; but those descriptions should be selected which can be cut periodically, for the purpose of disposing of them as hop poles, a commodity in considerable demand in the neighbourhood.

In the event of the canal being retained, it appears to me also worthy of consideration, whether a larger sum might not be obtained from the canal rates, by farming them, as is done in the case of the other tolls. It is a question also whether the rates per ton at present levied, should not be reconsidered; and in the event of the canal rates being farmed, for which the Act gives power, whether Government should interfere at all in settling the amount to be imposed, or whether they should not leave the rate per ton for each description of merchandise to be settled by the parties who farm the rates.

The first edition of Murray's *Hand-Book for Travellers in Kent and Sussex* (1858) ominously mentions that 'all the purposes for which this canal was designed are now obtained far more effectually by the railway from Ashford to Hastings.' It also went on to mention that the Preventive Service now used some of the military stations. There was also a project to turn part of the canal bed into a railway to link Hythe with London by a line through the Weald.[2] The station houses continued to be occupied by pensioners of the Ordnance Department who acted as 'walksmen' and exercised a 'kind of supervision of the traffic'.

The amount of traffic on the canal during the 1860s averaged 10,000 tons while the annual revenue was about £1,200 compared with expenditure of £1,600 on salaries and repairs. A small economy was effected in 1865 when the clerk of works ceased to be employed exclusively on the canal and the Royal Engineers' office at Hythe was removed to Shorncliffe. The same year the War Office succeeded in persuading the Hastings Highway Board to maintain the military road from Appledore to Iden lock for £215 p.a. for 3 years; in 1868 this agreement was renewed at the increased rate of £300 p.a. but as the two turnpike tolls were let for £320 p.a., a small surplus resulted. In August 1867 Parliament authorised the secretary of state for war to sell or lease the canal and its collateral works.

In October 1867 Henry Stringer, the clerk to the Lords and Bailiff of Romney Marsh, wrote to the War Department requesting to know on what terms the canal might be bought or leased. In February 1868 the Lords were taken by surprise when an advertisement in the *Kentish Gazette* gave formal notice that the War Department were about to sell the canal, and military road to the Seabrook Harbour & Dock Co.; apparently the company wanted the waterway for scouring purposes connected with the building of a dock. However, James Elliott, the expenditor, pointed out that if used for such a purpose it was highly probable that the risk of the banks overflowing would be vastly increased and as the scouring must be had by letting in salt water from the sea, loss and damage would also be vastly increased resulting in constant complaints and litigation. Stringer at once wrote to the War Department advising them that the 'Seabrook Dock Co.' was, to say the least, somewhat undeveloped and asking for a stay of execution which the War Office refused. However, if the Seabrook Co. did not take up their option in the given time, the Lords were invited to take the transfer of the canal at the price agreed with Seabrook, i.e. for the sum originally paid by the Crown for the land, which was given by Colonel Wrottesley as £55,450 19s 3d. The Seabrook scheme failed and the War Office prepared a statement of the income and expenditure of the Royal Military Canal from all sources from 1856 onwards, which was circulated for the private information of the Committee of the Lords

Bailiff and Jurats of Romney Marsh appointed on 12 December 1868 to consider whether to purchase the canal or not.

The carrying figures of around 10,000 tons remained surprisingly high for a waterway serving only a few scattered agricultural communities. Tolls for the 12 years 1856 – 67 had averaged around £250 p.a. with a peak of £322 in 1862 and a trough of £196 in 1864. The turnpike tolls averaged £350 p.a. and rents of land over £500 p.a. Miscellaneous items like fishing, tickets to ride on the tow-path, barge licences, wharfage, trespass of cattle; sale of trees blown down and medical stoppages brought the total revenue to around £1,200 p.a.; Against this had to be set the salaries of £400 p.a. for the clerk of works 8 station keepers and the toll collector, and some £1,200 for the cost of repairs — leaving an annual deficit of £400 or so. The War Office also pointed out that no charge was made against expenditure for the time consumed in correspondence at Hythe, Dover or London.

The accounts were closely studied by Elliott and Stringer, and they, in March 1869, considered that this sum was a fair assessment of the average loss of the War Office by their management of the canal and it now only remained for their committee to estimate what would be the result if the canal were in the hands of the Level. Excluding canal tolls and station keepers' salaries from any computation, they estimated that the income derived solely from the turnpikes and rents of land and buildings and expenditure only on to new works and repair, would show a surplus of £150 p.a.

For several years negotiations with the Commissioners of the Lower and Upper Levels dragged on and came to naught. The main difficulty was any agreement over price. In September 1870 Col Jervois wrote to Mr Hugesson

> Financial objections have been raised to the transfer of the canal for other than a valuable consideration without a special Act of Parliament, and it has been suggested that arrangements shall be made by which a lease shall be granted of the portion required for drainage purposes. The matter is consequently necessarily delayed.

On 20 December 1870 a special meeting of the Lords of the Level decided to press the War Department to obtain a further Act to empower them to cede the canal so that there would be no delay in their contemplated drainage improvements. The War Office refused until an agreement in detail had been approved by them. At length after observations on this proposed agreement had been made by the War Department's solicitor, it was signed in June 1872 and the Government agreed to give the canal away if necessary to 'any person or body willing to take the same'. The fourth Royal Military Canal Act was passed on 10 August.

chapter 10

Pleasure Boating

Requests for permission to use pleasure boats on the Royal Military Canal (1841)—introduction of licence fee (1846)—first Hythe Venetian Fête (1860)—boating and fishing in the 1870s—Bonthron's voyage to Sandgate.

Throughout its history the Royal Military Canal has provided people with the means of enjoying a wide range of recreational activities and there is little doubt that from very early on in the waterway's history the officers stationed at Hythe used the canal for sculling and for taking their wives and families for a row on Sundays. However, once the threat of invasion was over the local inhabitants were also permitted to enjoy its facilities for boating since the 1807 Act allowed licensed pleasure boats to use the canal; failure to obtain a licence meant a fine of up to £5 and not less than £1.

The first recorded excursions by private individuals date from April 1841. It was then that the Board of Ordnance agreed that the Rev J. D. Lamb of Iden should be allowed to pass up the canal to Hythe and back in a small boat and in October that year they also approved as 'a special case' the application of Ensign Douglas of the 71st Light Infantry to paddle a small birch canoe on the canal. In 1842 Thomas Gybbon Moneypenny of Rolvenden wrote to the Board saying that he had a 'little pleasure boat' which he was 'in the habit of sailing on the River Rother', and that as he had some relations living at Hythe, 'it would be an accommodation to me if you would grant me your permission to sail along the canal at such times as I may wish to do so'. J. Twisdden Hodges of Sandgate also requested permission to keep 'a galley with four oars and a wherry with a pair of sculls' on the waterway. Both requests were passed by the Resident Officer at Hythe and the Accountant to the Commanding Officer of the Royal Engineers at Dover, who obtained the Board of Ordnance's consent provided that no impediment was put in the way of barges trafficking on the canal.

In April 1846 Mr Pocock was allowed to keep a small boat on the canal between Winchelsea and Cliff End and in July Theodore Walsh wrote to the Board telling them that 'Having been accustomed to rowing while in London and being a resident of Folkestone, I am desirous of having a London wager boat on the canal between Sandgate and Hythe for the purpose of recreation and exercise', and undertook to take the strictest care that their kindness should in no way be abused. The Board asked the Commanding Officer of the Royal Engineers at Dover for his recommendation and Lt-Col Tylden replied that if the indulgence was granted without payment 'it will undoubtedly bring many applicants for similar favours on like terms and cause serious inconvenience'. The Board, therefore, this time agreed that permission should only be granted on payment of the annual barge licence fee of £1. In 1847 Thomas Denne of Hythe was allowed to use a Thames skiff for occasional recreation on similar terms.

At no time has the urge to scull along its reaches or fish its waters appeared to have declined although complaints were made about the amount of weed from time to time. The Folkestone Amateur Rowing Club were granted permission for a trip in their regatta-built galley in 1853. In 1860 the first Hythe Venetian Fête was held. In those early days it was a novel feature of Hythe Cricket Week. One night of the week the festivities were transferred to the Canal. Rowing skiffs — Indian canoes and punts were hired for the occasion, from the licensee of the boating rights, and were decorated and festooned with strings of fairy lights. Strains of music from a banjo or guitar, from Hythe's own gondolas for the occasion, wafted across the calm waters.

During the 1870s Henry Stringer, the clerk to the Lords Bailiff and Jurats of Romney Marsh received a stream of letters asking for permission to use the canal. On 30 March 1870 Richard and Thomas Tabra wrote 'me and my brother have come on a visit to Sandgate from London and we have a great desire to have some fishing in the canal. If you could grant us permission you would greatly oblige'. A memorandum from Mrs Sandwith presented her compliments to Henry Stringer, Esq, and she

> would be extremely obliged for permission for her sons to fish during the next 6 weeks. Mrs Sandwith's sons have always been allowed to fish and until recently their uncle commanded the camp at Shorncliffe and permission was obtained from him. Mrs Sandwith hopes Mr Stringer will grant the permission as it is a great amusement.

31. Iden lock, *c*.1930.
The trees on the Royal Military Canal were mostly Huntingdon Elms planted *c*.1820
by Edward Relf, a small farmer & gardener of Appledore who died in 1863 aged 101.
Dutch elm disease caused many trees to be felled in the 1980s.

32. Barge and pleasure boat by Iden Bridge, *c*.1925 .
Mr Ward's house at left. The entrance to the Royal Military Canal is at right.

William Norris, a station keeper, asked if he could have a licence for a small boat to float on the canal. An application from the Folkestone Rowing Club in April 1874 to us '2 wager galleys for two days for a pleasure trip from Hythe to Rye and back' stated that this had been an annual trip for 4 or 5 years 'and that permission had been previously given by Col. Wrottesley and Col. Nicholson, to "us the young tradesmen of Folkestone"'. The applicant pointed out, however, that 'as the trip depends on the weather being fine the trip may have to be postponed 'til another time'. The following year William Dunk, the honorary secretary again hoped to be allowed to use two racing galleys for a pleasure trip on the canal from Seabrook to Rye and back on the 5 and 6 May or in the event of bad weather within a week of that date, 'hoping the permit you so kindly gave us last year, and the military authorities the previous 6 years, will be again accorded'. Caister & Son of Dymchurch also 'proposed having a picnic' in July and requested permission to put a boat on the canal between Hythe and Lympne.

Never was pleasure boating so popular as in the 1880s when the ornamental gardens, established by the Hythe Corporation along the canal had matured, and troops attending the six-week courses at the School of Musketry had time for 'boating and bathing and cricket in the pretty little ground by the Ladies' Walk. Lympne is a very popular resort for water parties; it is about an hour's row up the military canal'.[1] In 1896 the Lords of the Level put up a notice at West Hythe Dam (erected in 1883) warning people that they could only use the west end of the canal if they obtained a licence.

Although the latter half of the nineteenth century saw a number of oarsmen's guides to the waterways of Britain, the remoteness of the Royal Military Canal either discouraged would-be adventurers because of its distance from the nearest inland navigation or caused it to remain unknown. The canal was not shown on Bradshaw's map of *Canal's, Navigable Rivers and Railways* (1832), nor was it included in Prothero & Clark's guide to the *Rivers and Canals of Great Britain and Ireland*, published in 1896. The Board of Trade, active at this period in securing information, as well as compliance to regulations governing the carrying of gunpowder, also ignored its existence in their published returns of 1888 and 1898. However, not many years after the turn of the century,* that great lover of waterway exploration, P. Bonthron, did spend his Whitsun vacation

---

* Iden lock was in use in both 1902 and 1909. No commercial traffic is recorded as having passed during the years between but there seems no reason why it should not have been available for use as the lock-keeper lived by the lock. Miss Anne Roper, the Honorary Archivist of Hythe, has also advised me that Grayvenor was licensed to let rowing boats from about 1908 until 1914. A date for the voyage between 1910 and 1914, therefore, seems the more probable.

navigating the 'Grand Military Canal' and recorded the story of his trip in
My Holidays on Inland Waterways, published in 1916. Not surprisingly,
he commented that 'strangely enough in all our many experiences of canal
travelling we had never heard before of this waterway, nor had we seen
it mentioned in the numerous guidebooks on English Canals. However,
we were amply repaid for exploring these parts'. After spending the night
at Rye, they motored to Iden where 'a double-sculling skiff had been sent
on from Hythe for the trip'. Iden lock was 'not now in use', and the canal
was dammed up not far from Hythe, which necessitated a portage, but
the channel was in excellent order and they were able to sail nearly half
the distance. Thereafter they towed the boat for some of the way from
a good grassy tow-path and then sculled the remainder to Sandgate. A
striking feature of the canal was the fine belt of trees long the north bank
— chiefly ash and elm trees and standing possibly 60 or 70 ft high. From
the beginning to the end of the route there are no towns, and only one or
two straggling villages, and during all the journey we did not meet more
than a score of people, so that civilization is at a discount in these parts.
We only came across a few skiffs and canoes, and a couple of small motor
boats, all privately owned on the canal. At Hythe, however, boating is very
popular, and the boatman, W. Gravener [sic], from whom we had our skiff
had some 90 craft of all descriptions for letting out purposes.

'We found the Grand Military Canal a fine waterway, and no pleasanter
trip could be undertaken, particularly from a sculling point of view, and it
seems strange to credit the fact that the journey is very seldom made'.

chapter 11

Aftermath (1872–1990)

Agreement to transfer the Iden—Shorncliffe section of the Royal Military Canal to the Lords, Bailiff and Jurats of Romney Marsh (1872)—lease granted (1873)—sale of the western section of the canal from Winchelsea to Cliff End (1874)—Hythe Improvements Act 1874—second lease (1877)—dwindling commercial traffic—last barge to Appledore (1909)—Hythe in 1900—the Royal Military Road in 1917—sailing barges on the Rother—changes in ownership of the Royal Military Canal—the Hythe Venetian Fête—the canal's use as a line of defence during the Second World War—present-day uses—demolition of Hythe barracks—the Hythe Marina Bill (1990)

Although the fourth Royal Military Canal Act empowered the secretary of state for war to grant the canal to any person or body willing to take the same, and an agreement to transfer the canal between Iden and Shorncliffe to the Lords, Bailiff and Jurats of Romney Marsh was reached in June 1872, the difficulties which arose in negotiating a lease were complex to say the least.

In December 1872 Elliott is writing to Stringer of 'the great advantage the canal will be to the Level if we can get possession of it. I hope you will do all you can to get possession'. The lease was held up by the War Office requiring the history of the constitution of this body of which they doubted the entity, and about which Stringer said that it was a 'very difficult matter' and one of which he declined the responsibility.[1] The expenditor wrote back helpfully to Stringer saying:

> I remember that in the great contest with the Level a Mr Bevan, who acted with and for your father producing and reading an Old Charter

that he had found in some of the old depositories — the Charter of Henry of Bathania 1252; do you know if Mr Bevan is still alive? If so would he help in any way the matter in dispute with the War Department? It is the oldest charter in existence and on which the Level is still acting, and shews clearly that the constitution was composed of Lords, Bailiff and Jurats.

At last on 5 June 1873 the War Department agreed to lease the canal to the Lords of the Level for 999 years at an annual rent of 1s. No sooner was this done than the Hythe Corporation petitioned for a Bill to authorise their purchase of the portion of the canal passing through the borough and for powers 'to convert the same into ornamental waters or to fill up the whole'.

A petition was lodged against this Bill by the Lords of the Level but was later withdrawn and at the end of June Hythe got their Act. Among the powers the borough acquired was the right to make a new channel from the canal, at the parish boundary in West Hythe to the sea, and to make byelaws against bathing without permission and for the control of fishing and pleasure boating.

The remainder of the waterway was disposed of as best as possible. In 1874 the western portion between Winchelsea and Cliff End was sold to four private owners and the rights of way along the tow-path and military road extinguished. In June 1874 it was decided to repair the bridges now in a bad state. Henry Stringer, as clerk to the body controlling the canal, now found himself assailed by a host of correspondents, seeking a variety of concessions. Some sought permission to row, to fish, to carry a gun, to ride along the tow-path, to rent some ground or other; others to complain. Mr Green of Seabrook wrote on 18 August 1874:

Col Nicholson allowed my man to exercise my mare on the side when I was from home; of course there was no racing or jumping, but I find the present man at the gate objects to my man using the towpath as he has no permit — he suggested to my man that I should add his name to the end of mine on the permit — I presume the fellow has no objection to my forging my name, doubtless accepting a decent remuneration for winking at the said forgery.

A Mr Crowe of Folkestone wrote

having knowledge that the Romney Marsh have purchased the Hythe canal from the government I take the liberty of writing to ask permission to ride along the side of it; of course on the understanding that I do no

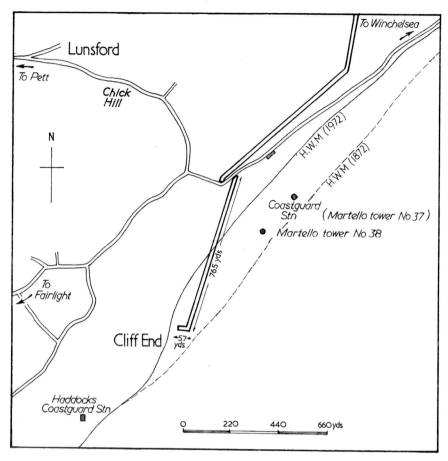

Cliff End 1872-1972.

harm in doing so. I am told it is from you that this permission is to be asked which must be my excuse for troubling you.

James Jarvis wrote in September 1875

I see by the notices that next Friday you receive tenders for the hire of towing paths. If J. Russell Esq. is anywhere near the mark I hope you will let him have it. He lives close to the canal, consequently he can prevent anyone driving along the t.path. So many people will do that if they can, that they may miss the hills between Ruckinge and Bilsington, but since Russell is at the towing path they are obliged to go the upper road.

On 25 September 1874 Nathan Bates, who rented the towpath from Appledore to Iden, complained about a man cutting reeds on land above the water mark. 'When the man was questioned he swore.' Hardly the action one hopes of station-keeper Norris at Appledore who had written 'I take it as a great favour if you will kindly permit me to cut a few bundles of reeds' and had been granted this licence only a week or so before. James Southee was also complaining in 1875 about the barge horses running at large on the tow-path.

A more serious matter was a letter in December 1874 requesting to know what was to be done during the winter when the water was run off. A case of diphtheria in the mayor's family could only be attributed by 'the medical man' to the effect of the malaria arising from the canal. 'The ditch should be covered in so that the mud banks are not left exposed'. The mayor, however, was anxious that nothing should be done 'to cause the slightest irritation between public bodies, as responsibility lay as much with the Lords of the Level as with the authorities'. However, he was quick to point out that it could not be attributed to the sewage which ran towards Seabrook.

The War Department was finally relieved of responsibility for the canal when in May 1877 the Lords of the Level of Romney Marsh agreed to lease the waterway from Iden to West Hythe for 999 years at a rental of 1s a year. At the same time the Corporation of Hythe took a similar lease at £48 p.a. of the section from West Hythe to Shorncliffe. Movable stop gates, 16 ft 6 in wide were erected in 1877 across the canal close to the old beach wharf at Hythe on the understanding that navigation would not be impeded. In 1883 the borough obtained the agreement of the Lords of the Romney Marsh Level to construct West Hythe Dam in the interests of land drainage. On this evidence it would appear that barges had ceased to go to Hythe after 1883 and may have ceased to do so some years earlier.

Few details are known about the barge traffic on the canal between 1868 and 1886. In 1871 Colonel Wrottesley estimated the tolls at around £300 p.a. which seems rather high; certainly this traffic must have steeply declined in the 1870s judging by the accounts of the state of the navigation. In November 1875 Hoad Brothers of Rye, ship-owners, coal, coke, soda and salt merchants, wrote to Stringer explaining that they had not licensed their two barges that year as in the previous year there was very little water and asking if the canal was now navigable to Appledore. Correspondence in 1882 reveals the state into which the canal had fallen. 'Fishing in the last year was a failure. I have not earned one shilling since last February,' wrote William Watson in December, 'in consequence of the canal being laid nearly dry. All the summer there was not enough water to fish with a net,' and 'I have not received anything from the canal for two years and expect to catch a few eels out of the mud.' There is no record of barge traffic above Iden lock. Certainly from 1886 onwards the only toll charged was 2*d* a ton on all traffic passing through Iden lock. In most years this seldom exceeded three or four barge loads of shingle.

33. Station house, Iden, 1971.
The initials RSC and the year 1824 are cut above the front door.

34. Entrance to Iden lock from the Rother Navigation, 1971.

35. Iden Barracks and toll house, 1971.

```
No.

          ROYAL  MILITARY  CANAL.

               BARGE LICENSE.

            NEW HALL, DYMCHURCH, _____ 18

     A License or Authority for a Barge called the_____
   marked R. M. C., No._____ of _____ Tons burthen, belonging to
   _____ of _____
   _____to pass upon the said Canal without unnecessary
   interruption, until the _____ day of_____, 18__ , unless revoked in
   the meantime, and upon payment of all Tonnage Dues and Toll upon the Cargo
   thereof._____ For the Lords, Bailiff, and Jurats of Romney Marsh.

   £ _____          _____Clerk.

   N.B.—This License is revocable by the Lords, Bailiff, and Jurats, at any time, and is subject to any Bye-Laws and Regulations which may be,
   from time to time, made by them with reference to Barges, and to any stoppage by reason of the reduction of the depth of the water in the
   Canal, which it may be considered necessary to make for the purpose of the drainage of the Level or any Works connected therewith.
   And the holder of this License will be held liable for any infringement of such Bye-Laws and Regulations, and of any Act or Acts of
   Parliament now existing, or which may hereafter be passed with reference to the Royal Military Canal.
```

1893, 1897 and 1898 were exceptional only in that the total annual tolls rose from shillings to over £3 as *Charlotte, Dolphin, Nellie, Mistletoe, Mullet, Otter, Rother, Tyne, Tees, Wear, Victory, Viking, Victoria, Vulcan* and *Vulture* carried some 500 or 600 tons of rock and granite on the canal to an unknown destination — but probably Stone or Appledore; there was also one load of Cherbourg stone in 1893. The majority of these craft belonged to Vidler & Sons of Rye but in September 1898 their barges ceased to use the Royal Military Canal.

Spencer Catt became lock-keeper at Iden in 1890 and continued to live at the station house there until his death. In March 1902 the *Primrose* and *Myrtle*, now owned by J. Baldock, ceased to carry beach. For the next 7 years Mr Catt apparently collected no tolls — rather a hardship since he was allowed to retain 25 per cent before passing the balance to Richard Jones the clerk of the Commissioners of Romney Marsh Level. And then, just when it might have been presumed that no commercial carrying barge would again pass through Iden lock, Mr J. Terry's sailing barge, *Vulture*, nosed gently through the gates on 15 December 1909 with 27 tons of shingle on board and paid the last recorded toll of 4s 6d.

R. M. CANAL LOCK.

Dec 15th 1909

Received of *Mr J. Terry* of the Barge *Vulture*

the sum of £ — : 4 : 6 being the amount of Tolls

for 27 Tons of *Shingle* @ 2d per Ton.

Signature of Toll Collector, *J b clt*

Toll receipt on last barge to pass Iden lock, 1909.

A local historian writing about Hythe at the turn of the century[2] mentioned that 'on the other side of the narrow street of the town one meets with the canal, its banks bordered by avenues of lofty trees, pleasant enough on a sunny day'; and that at the School of Musketry

> one may see a singular assortment of uniforms for the place is used for the instruction of picked men from various regiments. The School is ugly as only military buildings know how to be but it is agreeably hidden by trees. It is pathetic to see on the green space on the opposite side of the canal stalwart men conning books of instruction like to many unfortunate school boys examining one another or stretched on the grass with the ominous little treatises in hand. Such work must add another to the horrors of warlike men in peace times, to the horrors of war itself.
>
> A little further to the west one may hear and see the principles of the books put in practice. [After complaining about the continual clatter of small arm and maxim fire, the writer continues] as if to afford compensation, the canal between Hythe and West Hythe, which is also War Department property, is extremely beautiful. West Hythe is an almost non-existent hamlet. It contains a primitive hostelry, a number of large signs announcing the procurability of refreshments and a few very small cottages. The old church has been turned to agricultural purposes, and as a cow-byre, undergoes an honourable eclipse. There are a number of such sacred edifices along the slopes of the hill. A little farther to the west, indeed, there is a parish church — that of Fawkenhurst — that has entirely disappeared. The vicar holds a service once every two years preaching from the cart-tail, to a large congregation who range themselves on forms.
>
> The sea, as a rule, is sleepy and washes the foot of the wall with a lazy murmur. But once a year — more often in some years — it wakes up and

Right: 36. The Kent/Sussex county boundary stone erected in 1806.

Below: 37. Second World War Pill box near Jiggers Green Bridge. One of the many concrete pill boxes built along the canal parapet as part of the 1940 antiinvasion defences. This view taken near Jiggers Green Bridge.

38. Station house No. 5 at Jiggers Green 1971. The house had been let in 1935 to J. Simpson at £5 0d p.a. By 1990 two additional windows and a second chimney pot had been added to the building.

39. Site of Station house No. 8 at Ruckinge.
A comparison of the plan drawn in 1845 of Ruckinge showing the location of station house No. 8 (see p. 219) with the present day view of the site shows little alteration to the road alignment.

makes a plaything of the wall, tears great masses out of it, and carries them off to unknown depths. This is more particularly the case at the juncture of Seabrook and Sandgate. Here, perhaps because of its situation in the bottom of the bay, the sea invariably works its winter will. I do not remember ever to have passed through the place without seeing works of some sort in progress. In the winter the sea is engaged in making gaps; throughout the rest of the year the local authorities in repairing them.

A. G. Bradley, writing in 1917 described the varying condition of the military road from Appledore to Iden.[3]

Its quality varies from year to year — I was going to say from day to day. It is not much used, but being on a dead flat and gravelly (to put it mildly), not muddy, people on wheels of any kind are often inclined to venture it if they have not done so for a long time and forgotten its deceptive appearance. I have cycled it several times in the last dozen years and always regretted it but once, when they must have been doing something to it. It was constructed from Appledore to Winchelsea as a link in the chain of military communications in the Napoleonic war. But I only allude here to the Appledore section, which does well enough now for heavy lorries or even cars, but for a cycle of any kind is to be avoided. A hundred yards away it looks at any point an excellent road. The result is that you are always imagining that smooth water is visible just ahead and expecting in a few seconds to be out of the grinding, slithery, loose gravel and be happy, and so mile after mile continue labouring, with ever blasted hopes, till you emerge on to a decent surface near Rye, and are then confronted by a toll gate! I cannot imagine who pays toll there except people who don't know the country, or the road or the many alternatives of entering Rye, from that direction by fine roads on the upland above or on the Marsh beneath. There are not many old toll gates left in England, and this is the most humorous one I know.

However, Bradley admitted it was a 'most engaging path with the big trees giving character and even beauty of a tranquil kind to the solitary and deserted old canal'. The road remained in much the state described until shortly after the end of the Second World War. Nor was it until 1926 that the Corporation of Rye succeeded in purchasing Battery House and Gun Garden from the War Office and that the County Council take over the military road from Winchester to Rye.[4]

In the First World War many of the Rye barge crews joined the RNR where they did useful work on the canals of Belgium. The work aboard the barges could not be called hazardous, yet there were accidents enough

40. Ruckinge church from the canal bank.
The church has two splendid Norman doorways, massive stonework in the walls and much good woodwork. The small church has a celebrated porch made from an oak 600 years ago.

to cause concern. One man slipped on a frosty deck, hung on a rope for a few moments, slipped and was washed out to sea before his mates could do anything to save him. Another man slipped whilst unlocking the cabin. Because no one else was there he was drowned and his body was found next day in the river. Two others lost their lives in the Rye lifeboat disaster of 15 November 1928.

Pleasure boats from Rye continued to use the Royal Military Canal until the lock-gates fell into disrepair about 1910; since that date the only boating activity has been by those who have hired skiffs from the several boating points by Marine bridge in Hythe. On the Rother, however, sailing barges continued to ply up to Newenden and Maytham Wharf until the 1930s. Sheila Kaye-Smith remembered the 'lighters with red sails that tacked along it, carrying coal to the inland villages from Rye'.[5] In 1933 land drainage needs were given priority over navigation above Scots Float.

In 1933 the Secretary of State for War sold the freehold of the canal from West Hythe to Jiggers Green bridge to Sir Philip Sassoon. In September 1935 eight miles of the north bank of the canal between Jiggers Green and Appledore was, by order of the War Department, offered for auction at Ashford. Included in the sale was the canal, towing path and back drain as well as six station houses, all with tenants except No. 7 which was vacant. Station house No. 6 at Bonnington was not included in the sale. The property was bought as a whole by Mr R. Price who transferred it to Miss Dorothy Johnstone in July 1936 who in turn donated it to the National Trust, the current owners.

The Environment Agency has a long term lease on the section from Cliff End to West Hythe, whereas that from the dam to Seabrook Outfall is designated a Scheduled Ancient Monument which is managed nowadays by Shepway District Council for amenity purposes. The section from Winchelsea to Cliff End remains in private ownership.

The Hythe Venetian Fête continued to be held from time to time. In 1928 it was organised by the Hythe Chamber of Commerce. G. P. Walter of Hythe describes the scene as follows:

Parades of decorated tableaux, depicting historical, cultural or humorous themes, according to their classes, were imaginatively presented. These were built over the licensee's own rowing boats and punts; the more enterprising lashing two together, or making their own rafts. A Venetian beauty queen, on her own float, was selected, who presided for the day. As dusk fell the tableaux presented a fresh picture under their own illuminations. Hundreds of fairy lights were lit across the bridges

41. Pleasure Boating at Hythe, 1919.

BY ORDER OF THE WAR DEPARTMENT. 119/Eastern/1344.

G.   R.

THE
ROYAL MILITARY CANAL

GIGGERS GREEN TO APPLEDORE, KENT.

TO BE OFFERED FOR SALE BY PUBLIC AUCTION AT

3 o'clock in the Afternoon,

ON

Tuesday, September 17th, 1935,

AT

SARACEN'S HEAD HOTEL, ASHFORD, KENT.

F. W. BUTLER, F.A.I.,

Estate Offices, HYTHE, Kent.

Telephone: Hythe 6608.

W. S. PAINE & CO., HYTHE. 'PHONE 6243

and amongst the trees. Search lights, by a local territorial unit, added a dramatic effect to the lighting; though, for some more unfortunately placed, this was a blinding experience. An aerobatic display of bombing with bags of flour, by K. K. Brown from a light aircraft, to a moving target, added a non-Venetian, though thrilling spectacle. Water sports were indulged in, which produced entertainment for the spectators as well as for the participants. The night's festivities ended with a firework display.

In 1935 a pageant of the Cinque Ports was enacted on the canal for the first time. Boats from the Hythe fishing fleet were brought to the canal from the seashore and transformed into replicas of each of the Cinque Ports' insignia. The Mayor of each Cinque Port, with the Ancient Towns, processed in their tableaux; who were received by the Lord Warden of the Cinque Ports — the Marquis of Reading. Since when it has been customary for the neighbouring mayors of the Cinque Ports to be guests at the fête. The release of 100 pigeons, followed by a fanfare of trumpets, signalled the opening of the event. Decorative electric lighting at dusk made the canal a romantic setting.

In 1936 the Committee formed itself into a charitable society, with the object of not only producing entertainment for its own people and visitors alike, and donating any surpluses to local causes which it had done in the past, but with the precise object of supporting the Old People's Welfare Committee in producing homes for Hythe's old people. Financial worries ever bedevilled the fête committee since the uncertainties of weather have always made the size of income problematical for a single one evening show which could not be postponed. The fête was held annually until 1939 when the war intervened.

During the Second World War the canal once again reverted to its role as a second line of defence. In the summer of 1940 the threat of invasion caused the sheep to be removed from the Marsh, part of Pett Level to be flooded and the main road bridges to be mined, the occupation and minor road bridges and peculiarly the ruined lock gates at Iden, destroyed.[6] Pill boxes were built on the sites of some of the old station houses and the vigilant Home Guard may well have seen the ghosts of the sentries of the Royal Staff Corps as they watched for another invader.

In 1946 the Venetian Fête was revived. One of the major difficulties, after the war years, was to find suitable craft on which to stage the tableaux. After a lot of trouble, some 36 collapsible landing pontoons were acquired from a naval disposal unit in Surrey and brought to Hythe. Though their expectation of life was limited, these provided competitors with a larger platform on which to construct their displays and the tableaux, from that time, became more ambitious and the standard of the Hythe Venetian Fête more sophisticated. Subsequently, these pontoons were replaced by a fleet of the committee's own floats, made locally for the purpose. An overall theme for each year's fête gave a lead to competitors on which to place their ideas. Colour changing fluorescent lighting was introduced to add further beauty to the setting. Portable generators, producing neon lighting, were used by some enterprising competitors; then came water fireworks.

Success followed success and the crowds who have supported the fête grew to estimated attendances of between 25,000 and 30,000 people. The annual task of planning the fête and soliciting support from so many of the same people, year after year, became so onerous that in 1954 it was decided to hold the event every other year. Fêtes have been opened by leading national personalities. They have been much photographed and reported nationally. They are now regularly televised and Hythe has become renowned for its Venetian Fête.

The canal from Iden to Appledore and beyond was completely choked with reeds in the 1950s so that the channel was of no benefit to anglers nor did it serve as a proper drainage channel. The Kent River Catchment Board repaired the lock gates and completely cleared the old canal bed from Iden to West Hythe in the early 1960s, built a dam at Appledore

42. Venetian fête at Hythe, 1970.

and diverted the Knock Channel into the canal.* The waterway has now regained much of its former fine appearance and its present state would certainly have met with General Brown's approval!

Hythe barracks continued to be used by the Small Arms School (formerly the School of Musketry) until 1969 when it was transferred to Warminster. Left empty Hythe Borough Council acquired the site in 1971 and decided to sell the land to the South Eastern Electricity Board for £58,000. A local valuer determined that the buildings were in so ruinous a condition that they were worth nothing. However the Hythe Civic Society and other local organisations protested at the proposed vandalism of this historic structure. The local and national Press took sides, because if the council were forced to buy back the site, rate payers might have to foot the bill. George Allan, a determined Cambridge undergraduate, drew the Department of the Environment's attention to its failure to list the buildings as being of historic importance. An oversight apparently and listed consent was quickly attained. Jeffery Davies, the architect, produced a booklet showing how this group of buildings might be usefully developed to provide housing, a museum and community centre. A public inquiry was held at Hythe Town Hall in February 1974 but to no avail. The ministry inspector considered that the buildings were not of sufficient historical or architectural value to justify overturning planning consent. And so, in spite of Allan's valiant efforts on behalf of posterity, the last Georgian army barracks in Kent were demolished in the same year as those at Canterbury. Not many years passed before Seeboard decided to move from Hythe and the new offices were redesigned to suit the new occupiers. The commandant's house where John Brown lived, has survived however. Bought by Shepway District Council, the building was tastefully converted into flats in 1976 and its exterior appearance has little changed.

In 1990 the Secretary of State granted outline planning permission for a harbour, marina and leisure facilities at the eastern end of the canal, and on the adjacent land which had been formerly used as a refuse tip and car park. This proposal gave rise to a great deal of support as well as objection. The loss of the 1,100 yards of canal would have been mitigated by the developers intending to provide access from the marina into the canal to Hythe and the provision of a heritage centre to increase public awareness of the waterway's historic importance. However, concern was expressed as to the possible damage to the existing revetted stone wall of the redoubt leading to the main Sandgate road.

A public enquiry was held in Folkestone in the closing months of 1987

---

*The Kent River Authority took over the obligations of the River Board in 1965. Nowadays (2010) they are the responsibility of the Environment Agency.

Kentish Express, July 5th 1974

Death sentence on old buildings

GEORGIAN   Now the Department of   Hythe Civic ...

School of Infantry: 'No time to comment'

which the council had sold the site to Seeboard.

"At no time was the public in a position to comment," he said.

The Mayor of Hythe, Councillor Chris Capon, said: "I feel as president of the society that before the decision was taken to support the listing of the school, a special meeting of the society should have been called.

"It has concerned me dur-

Seeboard fights back

By Ron Green and Nick Manson

SEEBOARD has started the long fight-back over its plan to redevelop the Small Arms School site at Hythe. At best it can escape with a few months' delay to its plans.

At worst it will have to start searching for a new site for the offices, workshops and depot it needs to build — and find a way to dispose of the

asked for its advice and is certain to back Seeboard.

But that decision will have to be confirmed by the De-

Kent County Council will then make a decision.

Seeboard site: A warning

8/3/73

RATEPAYERS might have to foot the bill if Hythe Town Council is forced to buy back the Smalls Arms School site from Seeboard. This was the shock warning issued at the town council meeting on Monday by Councillor Philip Bond.

An error of omission

THE listing of the School of Infantry at Hythe as buildings of special architectural or historic interest could not be avoided, the Department of the Environment has stated in a letter to local M.P., Mr. Albert Costain.

MP IN HYTHE SITE ROW

A STORM broke at Hythe this week over the shock preservation order put on the Small Arms School buildings. Anger has mounted because the order blocks a vital new industrial development for the town — and because it was made without any prior consultation with the town council.

Folkestone Herald, 29th

Building doomed

SEEBOARD WINS FIGHT FOR HQ

PROTECTED Small Arms School buildi Hythe ... to be demolished after all. - led by Hythe Civic Soc litary buildings, ended in eek with a statement and, Secretary of State I

with a ministry inspect al and historical value not sufficient to justif the face of Seeboar an.

Traders' Yes to Seeboard proposals

SEEBOARD is unlikely to find another site for its south Kent district headquarters if its plan to build on the Small Arms School site at Hythe falls through. Instead, it will continue to use its present inadequate facilities at Folkestone, Dover and Ashford.

Small Arms School's future?

CAN it be true what we hear about Hythe? That this aged and famous Pet loft, who has grown in its glorious and beautiful

Threatened barracks

SIR, — The ...

Twenty-four attempts to save the RSC barracks from demolition, 1974.

Left: Ramblers Association protest leaflet at not being allowed access to the towpath.

Right: Hythe Venetian fête poster, 2009.

after which the Hythe Marina Bill was brought to the House of Commons where it had its first reading in January 1990. After the second reading it was referred to a Select Committee chaired by John Cummings, the Labour member for Easington. David Clelland (Lab Tyne Bridge), Ian Bruce (Con Dorset South) and Sir Trevor Skeet (Con Bedford) completed the panel.

The committee hearing began on 7 June and continued for five weeks until 18 July. A dozen or more witnesses were examined in the attempt to prove or contest the allegations contained in the Preamble to the Bill. Concerns were raised by the opponents of the Bill as to how the development would impact upon local housing and its effect on the development of Hythe. Other matters raised were the possible impairment of land drainage, the likelihood of increased local flooding and the effect upon traffic conditions. Furthermore it was feared the canal, which was now listed as a scheduled monument, would be detrimentally affected.

At length, on 18 July Mr Cummins reported to the House that the Preamble to the Bill had not been proved to its satisfaction and he had been directed to report the Bill without amendment. Amen.

Epilogue

Across the English Channel an imposing marble pillar was begun in 1804 to celebrate the invasion which never took place. Murray's *Hand-Book for Travellers in France* in 1848 mentioned that 'A conspicuous memorial of this projected but unaccomplished invasion exists at the distance of nearly a mile from Boulogne in the Colonne Napoleon, which surmounts the heights traversed by the road to Calais. It was begun by the Grand Army assembled for the invasion of England, as a monument to their leader and Emperor. The first stone was laid by Marshal Soult, but its construction was discontinued after the departure of the troops, and with the withdrawal of the subscriptions which they contributed out of their pay.' Construction was resumed under Louis XVIII to commemorate the restoration of the Bourbons but following the July revolution the monument (164 ft high) was re-dedicated to Napoleon I in 1841, and surmounted by a bronze statue by Bosio of the Emperor in his coronation robes. It was destroyed in 1944. A medal to commemorate the intended conquest was also struck by the French Mint bearing the words 'Frappé à Londres'. Further along the coast another marble monument commemorated the distribution of the order of the legion of honour by Bonaparte to his troops during one of his visits to the camp. In 1877 Murray stated that 'the hills for miles round Boulogne are still crowned with decaying redoubts, constructed on the same occasion; but these are fast disappearing, the Government having sold them on condition of their being levelled'.

In England the defences built to resist the intended invasion of Kent and Sussex by Napoleon remain much more in evidence. The appearance of the Royal Military Canal forms an attractive border to Romney Marsh; a few more bridges span its length and the wooden joists and decking

43. Soldiers approaching Winchelsea, 1817 drawn by J. M. W. Turner and etched by W. B. Cooke. The Brede Navigation is at right.

44. Soldiers marching into Winchelsea, 1830
The canal played a useful role in conveying troops between Rye and Hythe. During the period 1809-1814, over 12,500 soldiers were carried by barge.

45. Sailing barge on the Brede Navigation which formed part of the Royal Military Canal between Rye and Winchelsea *c*.1900.

of the original structures have been replaced by steel and concrete, but the enfiladed channel and tree-lined parapet have hardly changed since the days of the Royal Staff Corps. The military road remains part thoroughfare, part pasture where a fork soon strikes beach beneath the turf. The barracks at Hythe and the canal director's house only ceased to be occupied by the army in 1969.

The ultimate fate of the martello towers between Folkestone and Cliff End has varied. The line of towers numbered 1 to 9 began on the cliffs to the east of Folkestone overlooking East Wear Bay and continued to the end of Romney Marsh where the Dungeness promontory projects into the English Channel.

Towers numbered 10 to 12 were the first of the long line in front of Hythe. These were demolished during the late nineteenth century when the promenade was built. No. 11 stood near Saltwood Gardens and No. 12 at the south end of Stade Street.

Tower No. 13 which stood at the western end of West Parade in Hythe was sold by the War Department in 1906 and become a private dwelling until it was requisitioned at the outbreak of the Second World War in 1939 and became an Observation post for the coast artillery. In 1960 it was bought by Ronald Ward, the designer of the new lighthouse at Dungeness. Six towers (14 to 19) stood in the midst of the flat land where the Hythe

46. This view of the Pett Level in John Everett Millais' painting of the Blind Girl, 1855, shows the line of the canal below Winchelsea. (Courtesy of Birmingham Museum and Art Gallery).

School of Musketry was formed during the Crimean War. Three of these were partially destroyed by the sea before the Second World War. Towers 20 and 21 collapsed and disappeared some hundred years ago.

The last group of towers in Kent were Nos 22 to 27 which were built to guard the outfall of the Romney Marsh sluices. Brigadier Twiss explained that they were built to defend Dymchurch Wall from an enemy landing and to ensure the opening of the sluices when the order was given to flood the marsh. No. 24 was restored in 1966 by the Ministry of Public Buildings and Works.

A total of forty-seven towers were built in Sussex. They started at Rye where three protected the harbour mouth, the harbour and the sluices of the Royal Military Canal and the rivers Brede and Tillingham. Twiss considered the expanse of marsh between the harbour and Pert Level could be easily flooded so towers were considered unnecessary. Then followed a line of eight towers numbers 31 to 38 at 600 yard intervals along the beach in front of Pett Level and the extension of the canal from Winchelsea to Cliff End. The end of the canal was cut into the cliff face but the sea had eroded this by 1900. The Royal Engineers blew up No. 37 in June 1864 and numbers 35 and 38 in April 1872 (see map 14). No towers were built between Cliff End and Hastings.

During the Second World War, the War Department used some as observation posts with machine guns mounted on their flat roofs. A few have now been converted into private houses, other lie incongruously on promenades and among caravan sites. The Environment Agency provides a list of those that have been classed as Ancient Monuments. The historical significance of those that have survived cannot be disputed. Although of limited architectural appeal their stark simplicity and weathered walls create points of great visual interest.

47. The canal and parapet viewed from the tow-path in Pett Level, 2009.

48. Strand Quay, Rye.

49. The site of the terminus at Cliff End, 1971

No trace of the short western section of the canal originally built by the Board of Ordnance existed at Cliff End in 1971, as this photograph shows. The concrete pill box of 1940 is already lost to the advancing beach, as happened to the eight Martello towers which were built directly on the shingle. The nearest tower to this point would have been No. 38 whose ruined brickwork was deemed unsafe and was one of those blown up by the Royal Engineers in April 1872.

50. Sandgate, 1855.

Notes

CHAPTER I (PAGES 16–27)

1. Lt-Gen Sir Henry Bunbury, *Narratives of Some Passages in the Great War with France 1799–1810*, 1854.
2. Arthur Bryant, *Years of Victory*, 1944, p. 68.
3. Sir J. W. Fortescue, *History of the British Army*, 1923, vol. XI, pp. 43–5.
4. Public Record Office, WO, 30/76, pp. 106–203. A fuller account of the substance of this and other correspondence will be found in S. P. G. Ward's, *Defence Works in Britain (1803–1805)*.
5. MSS, Lt-Col John Brown to the Commander-in-Chief, the Duke of York, 3 October 1804 (WO 30 178).
6. MS, Lord Chatham to Lord Hobart, dated 9 February 1804 (WO 1/783, pp. (277–83).
7. Thomas Amyot, *Speeches in Parliament of the Rt Hon William Windham*, 1812, vol. II, p. 139–40.
8. MS, Lt-Col Beckwith to Lt-Col Littlehales, Dublin, 5 January 1804 (HO 100/120, p. 47–51).
9. MS, Commander-in-Chief to Lord Hobart, Horse Guards, 31 March 1804 (WO 1/627, pp. 432–3).
10. Quoted in Ford M. Hueffer's, *The Cinque Ports*, 1900, p. 197.
11. P. A. L. Vine, *London's Lost Route to Basingstoke*, 1968, p. 68, 1994 p. 54.
12. Beatrice Brownrigg, *The Life and Letters of Sir John Moore*, 1923, pp. 145–6.
13. MS, Admiral Lord Keith to the Duke of York, 21 October 1803 (WO, 30/75).
14. Charles Duke Yonge, *The Life and Administration of Robert Banks, second Earl of Liverpool*, 1868, vol. I, p. 164.
15. Quoted in S. Baring-Gould, *Life of Napoleon Bonaparte*, 1897, pp. 314–16.
16. *Kentish Gazette*, 11 September 1804.
17. MS, Commander-in-Chief, to Lord Camden, 4 June 1804.
18. Master-General's private secretary to Lt-Col Robert Morse, 7 July 1804 (WO 55/778).
19. MS, Col William Twiss to Lt-Col Robert Morse, Dover, 23 September 1804 (WO 55/778).
20. General Sir David Dundas' Report on Brig-Gen Twiss's system of fortifying the coast of Kent and Sussex by martello towers, 18 October 1804.

CHAPTER 2 (PAGES 28–42)

1. Report Lt-Col John Brown to Sir David Dundas, Rye, 19 September 1804 (WO 629/1).
2. MS, John Brown to George Brown, Tobago, 14 September 1780 (National Library of Scotland).
3. *Ibid*, 20 April 1781.
4. MS, Brown to J. Willoughby Gordon, Bantry, 9 May 1797
5. Sketch Book in National Library of Scotland (MS 2863).
6. PRO, WO, 1/630, p. 465, 26 March 1803.
7. S. P. G. Ward, *Defence Works in Britain (1803–1805)*, p. 24.
8. PRO, WO, 30/75, September 1804.
9. Minutes of the First Meeting of the Commissioners for the Royal Military Canal, 15 September 1807, p. 17.
10. *Kentish Gazette*, 26 and 30 October 1804. The names of some of the proprietors attending the meeting are listed in that of 26 October.
11. John Rennie, Report on the Best Mode of Clearing the Works of the Proposed Canal between Shorncliffe and the River Rother from Water, while they are under Execution, 29 October 1804.
12. John Rennie, Report on the Mode of Supplying the Shorncliffe Canal with Water and of the Works Necessary for that purpose, 31 October 1804.
13. Diary of Maj-Gen Brown. National Library of Scotland, 21 October 1804 (MS 3269).

CHAPTER 3 (PAGES 43–65)

1. Beatrice Brownrigg, *The Life and Letters of Sir John Moore*, 1923, pp. 147–8
2. One local paper however reported that 'much difference of opinion has arisen as to the utility of this canal, as a defensive military work, but this much is certain, that it opens an easy communication with that part of the country (the Weald of Kent) which from the badness of its roads, and consequent difficult of getting its produce (consisting of timber) to market, has been cut off from intercourse with the rest of the county.' (Quoted by Carola Oman, Sir John Moore, 1953 p. 229.)
3. *Kentish Gazette*, 2 November 1804.
4. *Ibid*, 2 November 1804.
5. MS, William Pitt to Lt-Col John Brown, Downing Kent, 20 November 1804 (error for Downing Street?).
6. John Rennie, Report on the State of Works executing between Shorncliffe and the River Rother, 12 March 1805.
7. *Ibid*.
8. Minutes of a meeting held at the Horse Guards, 6 June 1805, printed in the 'Eleventh Report of the Commissioners of Military Enquiry', 1810, p. 114
9. Smiles, S., *Lives of the Engineers*, 1861, vol. II, p. 283.
10. Jean Lindsay, *The Canals of Scotland*, 1968, pp. 143–4.
11. PRO, WO, 1/630, p. 453.
12. Oral evidence, Lt-Gen Robert Brownrigg to the Commissioners of Military Enquiry, 28 April 1809.
13. MS, Lt-Col Brown to Quartermaster-General, Hythe, 14 July 1805.
14. J. Holland Rose, *Dumouriez and the Defence of England against Napoleon*, p. 375.
15. MS, Lt-Col Brown to Quartermaster-General, Hythe, 14 July 1805, PRO, WO, 1/630, PP. 393–5.
16. MS, Commander-in-Chief to Lord Castlereagh, 15 July 1805, PRO, WO, 1/630, p. 389.

17. Hon. George Pellew, *The Life and Correspondence of the Rt Hon Henry Addington, First Viscount Sidmouth*, 1847, vol. II, p. 396.

18. MS, Major Todd to Lt-Col Freeth, 24 February 1834 [RMC Ledger, Hythe Museum].

19. Wheeler & Bradley, *Napoleon and the Invasion of England*, 1908, vol. II, p. 240.

CHAPTER 4 (PAGES 66–82)

1. Quoted from ledger in East Sussex Record Office, D733, p. 48b.
2. 'Eleventh Report of the Commissioners of Military Enquiry', 1810, p. 118.
3. Report of Director of Works for 1822 dated 1 July 1823, included in 'Minutes of Nineteenth' Meeting of the Commissioners', 30 July 1823.
4. 'Eleventh Report of the Commissioners of Military Enquiry', 1810, Appendix E, p. 122.
5. C. F. de Méneval, *Memoirs to serve for the History of Napoleon I*, 1894, vol. I, p. 366.

CHAPTER 5 (PAGES 83–94)

1. Quartermaster-General's Report for 1809 dated 22 March 1810, included in Minutes of Fifth Meeting of the Commissioners, 18 April 1810.
2. John Rennie, Report to John Rickman, Esq, on the Drainage of Certain Lands near the Royal Military Canal, 12 November 1810 (Institution of Civil Engineers).
3. Lt-Col F. S. Garwood, *Royal Engineers Journal*, vol. LVII, 1943, pp. 81–96, 247–60.
4. 'Eleventh Report of the Commissioners of Military Enquiry, 1810, p. 31.
5. See Lt-Col C. H. Masse, *The Predecessors of the Royal Army Service Corps*, 1948, for further details.
6. Minutes of Eighth Meeting of the Commissioners, RMC, 10 July 1812.
7. *Ibid*, Tenth Meeting, 4 July 1814.
8. W. H. Ireland, *A New and Complete History of the County of Kent*, 1829, vol. II, p. 288.
9. Major Hancock, *Royal Engineers Journal*, vol. LXXXVIII page 209.
10. *Gentlemen's Magazine and Historical Chronicle*, 1816, vol. 86, part I, p. 375.
11. MS, George Brown to George Robertson of Edinburgh, 8 April 1816.

CHAPTER 6 (PAGES 95–103)

1. Alexander Sutherland, Reports with Estimates, Plans and Sections of the Proposed Canal through the Weald of Kent, etc., 1802, pp. 27–8.
2. *Ibid*, p. 8.
3. The report of John Rennie concerning the practicability and expense of making a navigable canal through the Weald of Kent to join the rivers Medway, Stour and Rother, 1809.
4. MS, John Rennie to the Committee of Management of the Weald of Kent Canal, London, 7 August 1810 (Institution of Civil Engineers).
5. MS, John Rickman to John Rennie, 22 February 1811.
6. John Rennie, Report on the proper place of junction of the Weald of Kent Canal with the Royal Military Canal, 27 February 1811.
7. See P. A. L. Vine, *London's Lost Route to the Sea*, 1965, and Charles Hadfield, *The Canals of South & East England*, 1969, for an account of this line of navigation.

CHAPTER 7 (PAGES 104–133)

1. Minutes of the Fourteenth Meeting of the Commissioners of the RMC, 8 June 1818. Three RSC companies had returned to Hythe in November 1818 when the Army of Occupation had been disbanded.
2. Extract from Royal Staff Corps Regimental Orders dated 2 January 1819.
3. Minutes of the Fourteenth Meeting of the Commissioners of the RMC, 8 June 1818.
4. *Ibid*, Fifteenth Meeting of the Commissioners of the RMC, 14 July 1819.
5. Report of the Director of Works, 1 June 1819 included in Minutes of the Fifteenth Meeting of the Commissioners of the RMC, 14 July 1819.
6. Minutes of the Twentieth Meeting of the Commissioners of the RMC, 13 July 1824.
7. William Cobbett, *Rural Rides*, September 1823.
8. W. H. Ireland, *A New and Complete History of the County of Kent*, vol. II, 1829, p. 226-7.
9. In September 1813 a Mr Bradford agreed with the Commissioner for the Affairs of Barracks that he could rent the small canteen at Hythe for £15 for one year and for an additional £510, the right to sell 'provisions, liquors and other articles normally sold by sutlers.

   Bradford agreed not to allow any beer or liquors to be removed from the canteen except by officers. In due course he was licensed by the justices of the peace and the excise officers to retail ale and spirits as were publicans. The question then arose as to whether Bradford should be charged rates based on the £15 rent or on £393 being the reduced proportion of the aggregate sum of £525.

   After various court sittings the case came to be heard in the High Court on 10 June 1815. The hearing, reported as 'The King against Bradford', was heard before Lord Ellenborough, (Edward Law 1750-1818) the Lord Chief Justice who was better known in his younger days as leading counsel in the Warren Hastings trial. Various authorities were quoted by barristers in favour of both rates but it seemed to the three eminent judges that 'the defendant was rateable not only in respect of the £15 reserved nominally as the rent, but also in respect of the further sum. Per Curiam. Rate confirmed.
10. Report of the Director of Works, Hythe, 10 August 1837.
11. W. S. Miller, *The School of Musketry at Hythe*, 1892, pp. 13-14.
12. Report of the Director of Works for 1833 dated 15 July 1834.
13. Minutes of the Twenty-Sixth Meeting of the Commissioners of the RMC, 22 December 1830.
14. MS, Major Todd to Lt-Col Freeth, 24 February 1834 (Royal Military Canal Record Book, Hythe Museum).
15. Minutes of Twenty-First Meeting of the Commissioners of the RMC, 13 July 1825.
16. Report, Captain White, RSC, to the Quartermaster-General, Hythe, 8 July 1832 [WO, 43/50/36154].
17. MS, Major Todd to Lt-Col Freeth, 24 February 1834.
18. PRO, WO, 43/50.

CHAPTER 8 (PAGES 134–160)

1. MS, Memorandum of the Master-General of the Ordnance, 7 December 1837, approved by the Board of Ordnance, 13 December 1837.
2. S. Matson, Brigade-Major Royal Sappers & Miners to Inspector-General of

Fortifications, Woolwich, 21 July 1838.
3. William P. Nimmo, *A Book about Travelling Past and Present*, 1880.
4. Dr C. L. Meryon, *Memoirs of Lady Hester Stanhope*, 1845, vol. II, p. 292.
5. Duke of Wellington, Report upon the Defence of the Coast of Kent, 1846.
6. MS, 8 March 1844 (PRO, T.101).
7. P. A. L. Vine, *London's Lost Route to Basingstoke*, 1968, p. 123.

CHAPTER 9 (PAGES 161–167)

1. Captain G. Wrottesley, RE, Report on the Royal Military Canal, Hythe, 24 March 1851.
2. John Murray, *Hand-Book for Travellers in Kent and Sussex*, Third Edition, 1868, p. 40. The fifth edition (1892) continued to refer to the 'small houses' mostly occupied by pensioners of the Ordnance Department.
3. *Kentish Gazette*, 4 February 1868.

CHAPTER 10 (PAGES 168–172)

1. W. S. Miller, *School of Musketry at Hythe*, 1892.

CHAPTER 11 (PAGES 173–191)

1. MS, H. Stringer. to E. H. Knatchbull-Hugesson, MP, March 1873.
2. F. M. Hueffer, *The Cinque Ports*, 1900.
3. A. G. Bradley, *An Old Gate of England*, 1918, pp. 65-6.
4. L. A. Vidler. *A New History of Rye*, 1934, p. 150.
5. Sheila Kaye-Smith, *Weald of Kent and Sussex*, 1953, p. 16.
6. Peter Fleming, *Invasion 1940*, p. 234.

APPENDIX A

Bibliography

(1) ACTS OF PARLIAMENT

1721   An Act for the better preservation of the harbour of Rye, in the County of Sussex.

1723   An Act for completing the repairs of the harbour of Dover, in the County of Kent, and for restoring the Harbour of Rye, in the County of Sussex, to its ancient goodness.

1761   An Act to impower the Commissioners and Trustees (named and appointed by and in pursuance of an Act of Parliament made in the Tenth Year of the reign of His Late Majesty King George the First, for making more effectual an Act made in the Ninth Year of His Majesty's reign, intituled An Act for compleating the Repairs of the Harbour of Dover, in the County of Kent and for restoring the Harbour of Rye in the County of Sussex, to its ancient goodness, so far as the same relates to the Harbour of Rye to let the sea and tides into a new cut or channel, made in pursuance of the said Act of the Tenth Year of His said Late Majesty's reign, as far as a wall called Winchelsea Wall.

1761   An Act for continuing One Moiety of the Duties granted by an Act of the Eleventh and Twelfth Year of King William the Third, for the Repair of Dover Harbour, and which have been by several other Acts, convened till the twelfth day of May, one thousand seven hundred and sixty five; and for applying the same to completing and keeping in repair the harbour of Rye, in the County of Sussex, and for more effectually completing and keeping in repair the said Harbour.

1797   An Act for discontinuing the New Harbour of Rye, in the County of Sussex and for repealing several Acts relating thereto, and for providing for the discharge of a debt accrued on account thereof; and for the making reparation for certain losses; and for the improvement of the Old Harbour of Rye.

1801   An Act for more effectually improving and maintaining the old harbour of Rye in the County of Sussex.

1807   An Act for maintaining and preserving a Military Canal and Road, made from Shorncliffe in the County of Kent, to Cliff End in the County of Sussex; and for regulating the taking of rates and tolls thereon. (Royal Military Canal Act.)

1812   An Act for making and Maintaining a Navigable Canal from the River Medway, near Bradbridges in the parish of East Peckham in the County of Kent, to extend to and unite with the Royal Military Canal in the Parish of Appledore in the said county; and also certain Navigable Branches and Railways from the said intended Canal. (Weald of Kent Canal Act.)

1826   An Act for more effectually draining and preserving certain Marsh Lands or Low Grounds in the Parishes of Sandhurst, Newenden, Rolvenden, Tenterden, Wittersham, Ebony, Woodchurch, Appledore, and Stone, in the County of Kent; and Ticehurst, Salehurst, Bodiam, Ewhurst, Northiam, Beckly, Peasmarsh, Iden, and Playden, in the County of Sussex. (Rother Levels Act.)

1830   An Act to amend an Act passed in the forty first Year of His Late Majesty King George the Third, intituled An Act for more effectually improving and maintaining the Old Harbour of Rye in the County of Sussex; and to appoint new Commissioners; and to enable the Commissioners to raise additional Funds on the Tolls, by way of Mortgate or otherwise. (Rye Harbour Act.)

1830   An Act to amend an Act of His Late Majesty, King George the Fourth, for more effectually draining and preserving certain Marsh Lands or Low Grounds in the Parishes of Sandhurst, Newenden, Rolvenden, Tenterden, Wittersham, Ebony, Woodchurch, Appledore, and Stone in the County of Kent; and Ticehurst, Salehurst, Bodiam, Ewhurst, Northiam, Beckly, Peasmarsh, Iden, and Playden, in the County of Sussex. (Rother Levels Act.)

1833   An Act to alter and amend the powers of Several Acts passed relating to the harbour of Rye in the County of Sussex and for granting further powers for improving and completing the said harbour and the navigation thereof. (Rye Harbour Act.)

1837   An Act for transferring and vesting the Royal Military Canal, Roads, Towing Paths, and the Ramparts and other Works belonging thereto, and all Estates and Property taken and occupied for the same, in the Counties of Kent and Sussex, and also the Rates and Tolls arising therefrom, in the principal Officers of His Majesty's Ordnance. (Royal Military Canal Act.)

1867   An Act to authorize a Sale or Lease of the Royal Military Canal and its collateral Works; and for other Purposes. (Royal Military Canal Act.)

1872   An Act to amend the Royal Military Canal Act, 1867.

1874   An Act to extend the borough of Hythe in the County of Kent; and to enable the mayor, aldermen, and burgesses thereof to construct new Waterworks, Streets, and Sewers, and to make further provisions for the drainage and improvement of the borough and for other purposes. (Hythe Improvement and Waterworks Act.)

1880   An Act for the improvement of the drainage of the Upper and Wittersham Levels, otherwise Kent and Sussex Rother Levels. (Rother Levels Act.)

1990   Hythe, Kent, Marina Bill.

(II) BOOKS OF REFERENCE

1724   Daniel Defoe, *A Tour thro' the whole Island of Great Britain.*
1810   'The Eleventh Report of the Commissioners of Military Enquiry' — Departments of the Adjutant-General and Quartermaster-General.
1823   W. Tiffen, *Sandgate, Hythe and Folkestone Guide.*
1826   William Cobbett, *Rural Rides.*
1828–30   W. H. Ireland, *A New and Complete History of the County of Kent.*
1831   Joseph Priestley, *Historical Account of the Navigable Rivers, Canals and Railways of Great Britain.*
1843   John Murray's *Hand-book for Travellers in France.*
1847   William Holloway, *The History and Antiquities of the Ancient Town and Port of Rye.*
1849   William Holloway, *The History of Romney Marsh from its earliest formation in 1837.*
1853   Sir Harry Verney, *The Journals and Correspondence of General Sir Harry Calvert.*
1854   Lt-General Sir Henry Bunbury, *Narratives of Some Passages in the Great War with France 1799–1810.*
1857   T. W. J. Connolly, *History of the Royal Sappers & Miners.*
1877   John Murray's *Hand-book for Travellers in France.*
1886   Hasted's *History of Kent*, edited by H. H. Drake.
1892   W. S. Miller, *The School of Musketry at Hythe.*
1894   C. F. de Méneval, *Memoirs to serve for the History of Napoleon.*
1897   S. Baring-Gould, *The Life of Napoleon Bonaparte.*
1899–1927   Hon J. W. Fortescue, *A History of the British Army.*
1900   F. M. Hueffer, *The Cinque Ports.*
1904   Maj-General Sir J. F. Maurice, *The Diary of Sir John Moore.*
1907   Walter Jerrold, *Highways and Byways in Kent.*
1908   Cecil Sebag-Montefiore, *A History of the Volunteer Forces.*
1908   H. F. B. Wheeler and A. M. Broadley, *Napoleon and the Invasion of England.*
1909   J. Holland Rose, and A. M. Broadley, *Dumouriez and the Defence of England against Napoleon.*
1914   Duchess of Cleveland, *Life and Letters of Lady Hester Stanhope.*
1916   P. Bonthron, *My Holidays on Inland Waterways.*
1918   Arthur G. Broadley, *An Old Gate of England.*
1921   Arthur G. Broadley, *England's Outpost.*
1921   Donald Maxwell, *Unknown Kent.*
1927   The Marquess Curzon of Kedleston, *The Personal History of Walmer Castle and its Lords Warden.*
1934   Leopold A. Vidler, *A New History of Rye.*

1936   C. F. Dendy Marshall, *History of the Southern Railway*.
1944   Arthur Bryant, *Years of Victory*.
1948   Lt-Col C. H. Massé, M.C., *The Predecessors of the Royal Army Staff Corps*.
1951   George G. Carter, *Forgotten Ports of England*.
1953   Sheila Kay-Smith, *Weald of Kent and Sussex*.
1953   Carola Oman, *Sir John Moore*.
1954   L. A. Vidler, *The Story of the Rye Volunteers*.
1957   Peter Fleming, *Operation Sealion — The project Invasion of England in 1940*.
1969   Charles Hadfield, *The Canals of South and South East England*.
1972   P. A. L. Vine, *The Royal Military Canal* (first edition).
1972   Sheila Sutcliffe, *Martello Towers*.
1973   Richard Glover, *Britain at Bay — Defence against Bonaparte 1803-14*.
1978   John Collard, *A Maritime History of Rye* (second edition 1985).
1982   Duncan Forbes, *Hythe Haven*.
1990   John Winnifrith, *The Royal Military Canal Guide*.
1990   Michael Glover, *Invasion Scare 1940*.
1991   H. J. Compton and A. Carr-Gomm, *The Military on English Waterways 1798-1844*.
1995   G. Hutchinson, *The Royal Military Canal — A Brief History*.

(III) JOURNALS

The following articles are of interest:

'Historic Water-Colours' (The West India Committee Circular, 20 October 1927).
'Defence Works in Britain (1803–1805)', S. P. G. Ward (*Journal of the Society of Army Historical Research*, vol. XXVIII, Spring 1949).
'Pageant of Old Venice Lived Again at the Cinque Ports' (*Tatler*, 10 September 1952).
'The Royal Military Canal', Professor Richard Glover (*Army Quarterly*, October 1953).
'The Story of the Royal Military Canal', Lt-Col C. H. Lemmon (*Rye Museum Association News Letter*, February-May 1963).
'England's Napoleonic Heritage', S. Sutcliffe (*Country Life*, 18 September 1969).

APPENDIX B

TABLE OF DISTANCES ON THE ROYAL MILITARY CANAL, ROTHER AND BREDE NAVIGATIONS, 1810

Navigation	Station house	Place	Distance		Distance from Shorncliffe	
			m	f	m	f
Royal Military	1	From Shorncliffe to:				
Canal		Twiss Bridge	1	2½	1	2½
(22 miles)		*Marine (or Ladies') Bridge	0	1	1	5
	2	Town Bridge and Wharf Hythe	0	1	1	6
		*Romney Road (or Duke's Head) Bridge I	0	1½	1	7½
		Romney Road Bridge II, Toll House and Barrack Wharf	0	2½	2	2
	3	West Hythe Bridge	1	7½	4	1½
	4	Eldergate Bridge	1	4½	5	6
	5	Jiggers Green Bridge	1	7	7	5
	6	Bonnington Bridge	0	7	8	4
	7	Bilsington Bridge	1	0	9	4
	8	Ruckinge Bridge	0	7	10	3
	9	Hamstreet Bridge and Barracks	1	4	11	7
	10	Warehome Bridge	0	6	12	5
	11	Kenardington Bridge	1	0	13	5
	12	Appledore Bridge	2	1	15	6
	13	Stone Bridge	2	0	17	6
	14	Royal Military (Iden) Lock, Toll House and Barracks Junction Rother Navigation	1	3	19	1
Rother Navigation		Boonshill Bridge	0	3	19	4
		Scots Float Sluice (lock)	0	6	20	2
		Junction River Tillingham	1	7	22	1
River Tillingham		Brede Lock & Martello Tower no 30	0	4	22	5
Brede Navigation	15	Strand Bridge, Winchelsea	2	2	24	7
Royal Military Canal		Cliff End	3	1	28	0

* Bridges built in 1813.

Two toll houses were erected on the military road between Iden and Rye (1825) and Rye and Winchelsea (1826).

Navigation	Place	Distance		Distance from Shorncliffe	
		m	f	m	f
Rother Navigation (17½ miles)	From Bodiam Bridge to:				
	Newenden Bridge & Wharf	4	1	4	1
	New Bam	1	6	5	7
	Junction Hexden Channel	1	0	6	7
	Junction Potman's Heath Channel	0	4	7	3
	Blackwall Bridge	0	7	8	2
	New Bridge	2	1	10	3
	Stonebridge (Iden Bridge) } Junction Royal Military Canal}	1	5	12	0
	Scots Float Sluice (lock)	1	1	13	1
	Junction River Tillingham	1	6½	14	7½
	Rye Harbour	1	3	16	2½
	Rye Harbour Mouth	1	1½	17	4
Hexden Channel (¼ mile)	From Maytham Wharf to:				
	Junction River Rother	0	2		
Reading Sewer and Potman's Heath Channel (3 miles)	From Small Hythe Bridge to:				
	Potman's Heath Wharf	2	0		
	Junction River Rother	0	7		
River Tillingham (2 miles)	From Marley Farm to:				
	Strand Quay, Rye	1	4		
	Junction Brede Navigation	0	1		
	Junction River Rother	0	4		
Brede Navigation (8 miles)	From Brede Bridge to:				
	Langford's Bridge Wharf	2	3	2	3
	Ferry Bridge Wharf	3	0½	5	3½
	Strand Bridge, Winchelsea	0	3½	5	7
	Brede Lock & Martello } Tower no 30 } Junction River Tillingham }	2	2	8	1

APPENDIX C

THE COMMISSIONERS OF THE ROYAL MILITARY CANAL (1807–1836)

The dates refer only to the period during which the Commissioners attended meetings and not to the period of their tenure of office.

The Speaker of the House of Commons
1807–16	Charles Abbot
1817–33	Charles Sutton
1833–4	Sir Charles Sutton
1836	James Abercromby

The Lord High Treasurer of Great Britain and the First Lord Commissioner of the Treasury
1809–12	Spencer Perceval
1812–26	Earl of Liverpool
1827	George Canning
1828–9	Duke of Wellington

The Chancellor of the Exchequer
1807–12	Spencer Perceval
1812–22	Nicholas Vansittart
1823–6	Frederick Robinson
1827	George Canning
1828	Henry Goulburn

The Principal Secretaries of State
1807	Lord Hawkesbury (later Earl of Liverpool)
1808–9	Viscount Castlereagh
1808	George Canning
1810	Earl of Liverpool
1811	Richard Ryder
1812–21	Viscount Sidmouth (Home)
1812–26	Earl Bathurst (Colonies)
1822–6	Robert Peel (Home)
1827	Viscount Goderich (Colonies)
1827	Marquess of Lansdowne (Home)
1828	Sir George Murray (Colonies)

The Commander-in-Chief of HM Forces
1807–8   HRH The Duke of York
1800–10   General Sir David Dundas
1811–26   HRH The Duke of York
1829–36   General Lord Hill

The Lord Warden of the Cinque Ports
1807–26   Lord Hawkesbury (later Earl of Liverpool)
1829   Duke of Wellington

The Secretary at War
1807–9   Lt-Gen Sir James Pulteney
1811–27   Viscount Palmerston
1828   Sir Henry Hardinge
1832   Sir John Hobhouse
1834   Edward Ellice
1836   Viscount Howick

The Master-General of the Ordnance
1811–18   Earl of Mulgrave
1832   Lt-Gen Sir James Kempt

The Quartermaster-General of HM Forces
1807–8   Maj-Gen Robert Brownrigg
1809–11   Lt-Gen Robert Brownrigg
1813–25   Maj-Gen Sir J. Willoughby Gordon
1826–36   Lt-Gen Sir J. Willoughby Gordon

APPENDIX D (1808–1909)

OFFICERS AND SERVANTS OF THE ROYAL MILITARY CANAL

Consultant Engineer
1804–5 John Rennie

Director of the Royal Military Canal
1805–8	*Lt-Col John Brown
1808–13	*Col John Brown
1813–16	*Maj-Gen John Brown
1816–19	*Col Sir Benjamin D'Urban
1820–5	*Col Sir Richard Jackson
1825–36	*Maj-Gen Sir Richard Jackson
1836–7	Lt-Col James Freeth
1837–8	†Col Sir Andrew Leith Hay
1838–41	‡Lt-Col E. Fanshawe
1841–2	‡Lt-Col F. Ringler Thompson
1842–5	‡Lt-Col K. H. Rice Jones
1845–50	‡Lt-Col W. B. Tylden
1850–2	‡Lt-Col T. Blanskard
1853	‡Lt-Col C. D. Streatfield
1869	‡Lt-Col T. B. Collinson

Secretary to the Commissioners
1807–17	John Rickman
1817–19	Edward Phillips
1819–28	Francis Dighton
1828–37	John O'Neil

Commanding Officer of the Royal Staff Corps at Hythe
1808–15	Lt-Col William Nicolay
1815–17	Captain William Dumaresq
1817–19	Col John Pine Coffin
1819–20	Lt-Col William Marlay
1820–4	Col William Nicolay
1824–30	Lt-Col Charles Murray
1830–7	Captain Edward P. White
1837–8	Maj Edward P. White

Resident Royal Engineer (Hythe)
1838–41	Maj F. Ringler Thompson
1841–3	Captain E. B. Patten
1843–4	Captain Williams

1845–8	Captain A. Gordon
1849–51	Captain C. F. Skyring
1853	Captain James Freeth
1855–7	Maj C. B. Ewart

Accountant

1805–38	Alexander Swan
1838–65	Richard S. Kelly

Barrackmaster (Hythe)

1810–38	Alexander Swan
1838–65	Richard S. Kelly

Toll collectors / lock-keepers

Iden

1823–1838	Sgt William Barnes (RSC)
1838–18??	Sgt Herbert Wilcockson (RSC)
1890–1909	Spencer Catt

Hythe

1823–1838	Sgt James Baker (RSC)

* Commandant of the Royal Staff Corps
† Clerk to the Board of Ordnance
‡ Commanding, Royal Engineers, Dover

APPENDIX E

ROYAL MILITARY CANAL TRAFFIC RECEIPTS (1808–1909)

Year	Canal Tolls	Commersial Tonnage	Turnpike Tools	Rents £	Total (incl. misc.) Revenue £
1808	40	300	-		
1809	130t	1,000*	-		
1810	542	15,000*	87		
1811	421	10,000*	163	172	770
1812	576	15,000*	194	213	1,041
1813	426	10,000*	294	189	987
1814	377	7,500*	305	165	907
1815	305	5,500*	316	197	839
1816	292	5,000*	316	253	881
1817	359	7,000*	299	263	980
1818	316	7,000*	367	306	1,045
1819	458	10,500*	378	356	1,223
1820	536	13,000*	352	315	1,229
1821	383	9,000*	364	313	1,135
1822	359	7,500*	371	285	1,149
1823	377	8,000*	371	218	1,048
1824	412	9,000*	378	322	1,240
1825	412	9,000*	373	316	1,190
1826	332	6,500*	366	389	1,161
1827	264	5,000*	369	263	984
1828	298	5,500*	392	408	1,254
1829	333	6,500*	353	262	1,025
1830	263	5,000*	375	337	1,058
1831	343	7,000*	371	269	1,104
1832	396	7,000*	371	296	1,198
1833	453	9,000*	371	306	1,312
1834	472	10.000*	433	353	1,463
1835	496	11,000*	433	350	1,501
1836	508	12,000*	433	?	1,530

Year	Barges Licensed	*Canal Tolls*	Commercial Tonnage	Turnpike Tolls	Rents £	Total (incl. misc.) Revenue £
1837†	21	411	9,000*			
1838	21					
1839	22					
1840	15‡	452				
1841	14	294	7,500*			
1842	16	425	14,901½		460*	
1843	17	281	11,211½	375	460*	
1844	19	295	13,429	375	460*	
1845	18	333	14,315	375	460*	
1846	16	361	14,765	446		1,404
1847	17	453	15,766	446		1,486
1848	15	345	14,701	446		1,389
1849	12	229	10,612	400		1,211
1850	10	276	10,516	366		1,214
1851	12	280	11,500*	366		1,205
1852	?	246	10,000*	366		1,174
1853	?	244	10,000*	335		1,131
1854	?	250	10,000*	335		1,093
1855	?	249	10,000*	335		1,072
1856	15	292	12,500*	352	514	1,200
1857	15	286	12,500*	352	529	1,274
1858	14	225	9,500*	346	512	1,374
1859	14	213	9,500*	355	523	1,134
1860	14	277	11,500*	355	545	1,236
1861	12	263	11,000*	355	544	1,208
1862	17	322	13,500*	363	587	1,294
1863	16	242	10,000*	363	635	1,284
1864	15	196	8,500*	363	625	1,227
1865	14	221	9,500*	295	585	1,142
1866	15	242	10,000*	307	912	1,517
1867	18	260	11,000*	320	562	1,176
1868– 1885	Not known					

Year	Canal Tolls £	Tonnage
1886	5*	600
1887	1	158
1888	1	127
1889	<1	24
1890	<1	105
1891	<1	26
1892	<1	46
1893	4	471
1894	<1	89
1895	2	299
1896	<1	100
1897	4	515¼
1898	6	670¾
1899	1	136
1900	<1	80
1901	<1	54
1902	<1	54
1903	-	-
1904	-	-
1905	-	-
1906	-	-
1907	-	-
1908	-	-
1909	<1	27

* estimated
† 9 months to 30 September
‡ Charge for licence introduced
< less than

APPENDIX F

DIRECTIVE ON ACTION TO BE TAKEN ON THE ENEMY ATTEMPTING TO LAND – 1803

Should the regiment be drawn up on a beach to oppose the landing of the enemy, it will probably be ordered to reserve its fire, as the horizontal fire of musketry against men well covered in boats must be very ineffectual. In such cases it is only cannon which can play on the enemy with effect. The battalion, therefore, will reserve its fire till the boats take the ground, when each officer commanding a platoon will pour in his fire on the boat opposite to him, at the instant the enemy expose themselves, by rising up in the boat in order to leap on shore — a well-directed fire against men so huddled together must be destructive, and the battalion will instantly give them the bayonet, before they have time to form and recover from their confusion. It is hardly possible that any troops can withstand this mode of attack; whereas, if met only by a distant fire from the heights, they will suffer little — will infallibly land and form, and press on with all the spirit and advantage which usually attend the assailants. This as precisely the error which the French committed when opposing the landing of our troops in Egypt.

Should the boats of the enemy be fitted with guns in their bows, the battalion will endeavour to shelter itself behind sand-hills, walls, or broken ground, while the enemy pull for the shore; and it will not be advanced to the beach till the boats are nearly aground, when, of course, the enemy cannot give above one discharge of their guns, which becoming useless the moment they attempt to land, then the regiment will attack them as already directed.

Adhering to these hints, steadily obeying orders, restraining their impetuosity, and fighting with the cool, determined courage of their native minds, instead of imitating the intoxicated and blind fury of their enemy; and above all calling on the God of Battles to aid them in the preservation of those blessings which He has conferred upon them, this regiment may hope to render essential service, and to merit a large share of that glory which shall be acquired by all the forces of their country in repelling the threatened invasion.

Extract of Order issued by Lt-Colonel Hope, commanding officer, 1st Regiment of Royal Edinburgh Volunteers, Edinburgh. 8 October 1803. Quoted by Wheeler & Broadley, *Napoleon and the Invasion of England*, 1908, p. 345.

APPENDIX G

BARGES LICENSED TO TRAFFIC ON THE ROYAL MILITARY CANAL IN 1837

Number & Name		Registered Tonnage	Owner	From
3	Bee	27	John Higgins	Ruckinge
27	Dove	32	John Vidler	Rye
28	Pigeon	33	John Blackman	Appledore
22	Providence	25	John Blackman	Appledore
32	Ann	33	Samuel Mills	Bonnington
11	Una	32	James Relfe	Rye
33	Sarah	30	Thomas Ayerst	Newenden
23	Linnet	30	James Relfe	Rye
12	Princess	31	Charles Pilcher	Rye
15	Eliza	32	Charles Pilcher	Rye
17	Hempsted	26	Charles Pilcher	Rye
26	Fanny	38	Charles Pilcher	Rye
29	Charles	30	Charles Pilcher	Rye
7	Fox	22	Smith, Hicks & Co	Rye
13	Nile	23	Smith, Hicks & Co	Rye
16	Tyne	28	Smith, Hicks & Co	Rye
19	Wear	30	Smith, Hicks & Co	Rye
34	Hunter	32	Smith, Hicks & Co	Rye
30	XL	32	Eldridge, Hessel & Co	Rye
2	Ox	23	Richard Stickler	Bilsington
Luggage Boat			George Paine	Cheriton Mills
Luggage Boat			G Pilcher	Shorncliffe

APPENDIX H

STATION HOUSES

The location of the original fifteen station houses is show below. Completed in 1809, each station house had a slate roof, earth floor and was constructed of brick noggin. Most were capable of accommodating one nco and eight men. Candles and coal provided light and heat. After 1820 all were rebuilt in stone and in 1837 plank floors were introduced and privies provided 'where required most'. In 1841 pensioners replaced soldiers as keepers of 8 stations (see p. 144) and paid a nominal rent in return for their services. No. 13 was burnt down in 1843 and not rebuilt. In 1935 seven houses were still occupied by tenants. Some buildings were demolished before the Second World War, othere were rebuilt. Only the station house at Iden remains little changed.

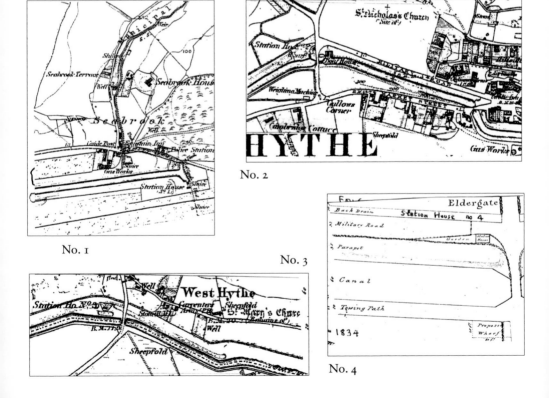

No. 1

No. 2

No. 3

No. 4

No. 5

No. 6

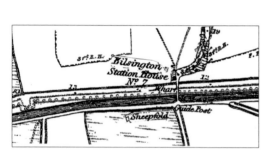

No. 7

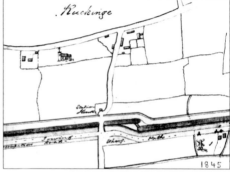

No. 8

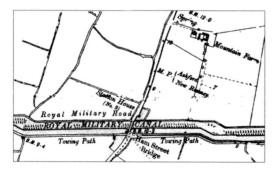

No. 9

No. 10

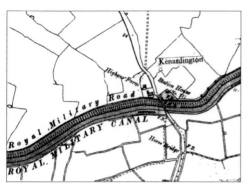

No. 11

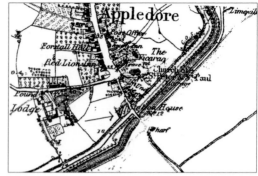

No. 12

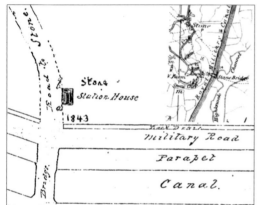

No. 13

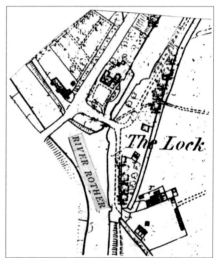

No. 14

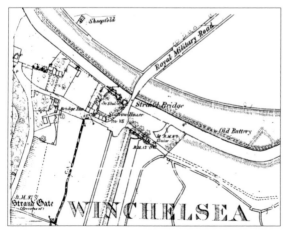

No. 15

Index